Milton among Spaniards

THE EARLY MODERN EXCHANGE

Series Editors
Gary Ferguson, University of Virginia;
Meredith K. Ray, University of Delaware

Series Editorial Board
Frederick A. de Armas, University of Chicago; Valeria Finucci, Duke University; Barbara Fuchs, UCLA; Nicholas Hammond, University of Cambridge; Kathleen P. Long, Cornell University; Elissa B. Weaver, Emerita, University of Chicago

Titles in the Series
Milton among Spaniards, Angelica Duran

The Dark Thread: From Tragical Histories to Gothic Tales, edited by John D. Lyons

Women Warriors in Early Modern Spain: A Tribute to Bárbara Mujica, edited by Susan L. Fischer and Frederick A. de Armas

Advertising the Self in Renaissance France: Lemaire, Marot, and Rabelais, Scott Francis

Retelling the Siege of Jerusalem in Early Modern England, Vanita Neelakanta

The Enemy in Italian Renaissance Epic: Images of Hostility from Dante to Tasso, Andrea Moudarres

Involuntary Confessions of the Flesh in Early Modern France, Nora Martin Peterson

Milton among Spaniards

Angelica Duran

UNIVERSITY OF DELAWARE PRESS
Newark
Distributed by the University of Virginia Press

University of Delaware Press
© 2020 by Angelica Duran
All rights reserved
Printed in the United States of America on acid-free paper

First published 2020

978-1-64453-171-6 (cloth)
978-1-64453-172-3 (paper)
978-1-64453-173-0 (e-book)

9 8 7 6 5 4 3 2 1

Library of Congress Cataloging-in-Publication Data is available for this title.

Cover art: Opening collage of *Lorca en color* (1969) by Gregorio Prieto. (Fundación Gregorio Prieto; image by Kristin Leaman, courtesy of Indiana University Libraries)

Milton among Spaniards

Angelica Duran

UNIVERSITY OF DELAWARE PRESS
Newark
Distributed by the University of Virginia Press

University of Delaware Press
© 2020 by Angelica Duran
All rights reserved
Printed in the United States of America on acid-free paper

First published 2020

978-1-64453-171-6 (cloth)
978-1-64453-172-3 (paper)
978-1-64453-173-0 (e-book)

9 8 7 6 5 4 3 2 1

Library of Congress Cataloging-in-Publication Data is available for this title.

Cover art: Opening collage of *Lorca en color* (1969) by Gregorio Prieto. (Fundación Gregorio Prieto; image by Kristin Leaman, courtesy of Indiana University Libraries)

To Sean O'Connor

Todas cosas bajo / Del cielo eres tú para mí, todos lugares tú
(*Paradise Lost* 12.617–18)

Contents

List of Figures ix
Acknowledgments xi

Introduction 1

1. Heretic Milton, "Of the Devil's Party" per the Spanish Catholic Inquisition 17

2. "As May Express Them Best": Spanish Translations of *Paradise Lost* 46

3. "To the Well-Trod Stage Anon": Milton on the Spanish and International Stage 84

4. "By Shading Pencil Drawn": Spanish Illustrations of *Paradise Lost* 110

Epilogue: Juan Milton, el Inglés 149

Appendix A. Class I and II Entries of English Authors in Volume I of the Spanish Catholic Inquisition's 1707 Marín Index 163
Appendix B. First Editions of Full Spanish Translations of *Paradise Lost*, Listed Chronologically 167
Appendix C. The Doré Illustrations in *Paradise Lost* (1866 and c. 1880–1885) and *El Paraíso perdido* (1873 Rosell and 1883 Escóiquiz) 169
Notes 173
Bibliography 205
Index 223

Figures

1. Gregorio Prieto's "Sketch 3, Adam's Back, Eve's Profile," in *Milton | El Paraíso perdido* (1972).   11
2. Milton entries in the Spanish Catholic Inquisition's 1707 Marín Index, 1790 Rubín Index, and 1844 Palacios Index.   18
3. John Baptiste de Medina's illustration of book 5 in the 1688 Tonson *Paradise Lost*.   117
4. Detail of the table scene in John Baptiste de Medina's illustration of book 5 in the 1688 Tonson *Paradise Lost*.   118
5. Plate 20, *PL* 5.12, 13, by Gustave Doré in the 1873 Rosell *El Paraíso perdido*, and in the 1883 Escóiquiz *El Paraíso perdido*.   120
6. Book covers of the 1873 Rosell *El Paraíso perdido* and 1883 Escóiquiz *El Paraíso perdido*.   124
7. Cover and title page of *Milton | El Paraíso perdido* (1972).   126
8. Gregorio Prieto's "Sketch 7, Adam Grasping a Tree," in *Milton | El Paraíso perdido* (1972).   132
9. Gregorio Prieto's "Sketch 15, Adam and Eve Entwined," in *Milton | El Paraíso perdido* (1972).   136
10. Opening collage of *Lorca en color* (1969) by Gregory Prieto.   140
11. Gregorio Prieto's "Sketch 10, Adam Walking and Lying Down," in *Milton | El Paraíso perdido* (1972).   142
12. Gregorio Prieto's "Sketch 4, Eve's Upper Torso and Head," and adjoining text in *Milton | El Paraíso perdido* (1972).   144
13. Gregorio Prieto's "Norma de pecho" and adjoining text in *Lorca en color* (1969).   145
14. Portrait of John Milton by Gregorio Prieto in *Milton y Gregorio Prieto* (1974) and by an unknown artist, c. 1629.   152

Acknowledgments

In this book I hope to share the exhilaration I have experienced in researching and writing it, the only apt response to the rich works that constitute the Miltonic strand of the complex, vital, and long-standing conversations of two of the westernmost countries of Europe, England and Spain. My home institution of Purdue University provided invaluable support for this project, including a Library Scholars Grant that funded my summer-long tour of Spanish libraries and cultural institutions (summer 2005), College of Liberal Arts Dean's Research Incentive Grants (2003, 2005, 2007), research leaves (spring 2007, autumn 2013–spring 2014, spring 2016, autumn 2016–spring 2017), and a Center for Humanistic Studies fellowship (autumn 2007) that released me from teaching duties; the encouragement from the administrative staff and faculty of the Comparative Literature and Religious Studies Programs; the flexibility that the English Department afforded me in teaching undergraduate and graduate courses that gave me forums for developing many of the ideas herein; and the Purdue University Libraries for its extraordinary and personalized service. I thank my Purdue colleagues Howard Mancing and Elena Benedicto for welcoming me to their Spains.

I was touched throughout the creation of this book by the generosity of librarians and scholars throughout the U.S., Europe, and Mexico. The Newberry Library's Audrey Lumsden-Kouvel Fellowship (summer 2008) was invaluable to me in the middle stages of the research for this project, as was the University of Texas at Austin Harry T. Ransom Center Fellowship (winter 2016) and Fulbright-García Robles Grant (fall 2016–spring 2017) during the final stages. From beginning to end I received advice about and copies of noncirculating rare works from the librarians and curators at the Dalí Museum in St. Petersburg, Harvard University, National Library of Spain in Madrid, Newberry Library, Northwestern University, Scottish National Portrait Gallery, Stanford University, University of California at San Diego, University of North Carolina–Chapel Hill, and members of the Milton Society of America. I thank the audiences at the Modern Language Association of America conventions (2005, 2007, 2011, 2013, 2015), Conferences on John Milton (2005, 2007, 2009, 2015), International Milton Symposiums (2005, 2008, 2015), Newberry Milton Seminar (2007), Midwest MLA Conference (2007), Renaissance Society of America Conference (2008), International Milton Conference (2008), and Reception Studies Society Conference (2009) for their incisive comments on material for this book that I presented. Earlier versions and portions of this book have appeared as journal articles and book chapters, which I acknowledge in the notes. I am grateful to the Herraderos de Federico García Lorca for permissions to publish Lorca's "Adán" and "Dos Normas" in Spanish, as well as to the institutions that provided the illustrations, as noted in the captions.

For their support in the form of letters of recommendations for research grants and finessing of my arguments and interpretations, I thank Edward Jones, Laura Knoppers, Mario Murgia, and Elizabeth Sauer. I am especially grateful to David Gies and Jonathan Culler for their willingness to provide a (then) stranger with the aid of their expertise; Robert Fallon, John Leonard, and John Shawcross for reviewing early versions of these chapters; and Nicholas von Maltzahn for reviewing the final draft of chapter 1, Wendy Furman-Adams the final draft of chapter 4, and Elizabeth Sauer the epilogue. I thank John Rumrich and Jacqueline Borchert for practical help in the final stretch, and all encouragement before that. I am indebted to the members of the University of Delaware Press: Director Julia Oestreich for her professionalism and guiding spirit, the anonymous reviewers for their generous and smart comments, and Tim Roberts and the editorial staff for attending to the details of format and legibility.

For their interest, enthusiasm, and intelligence at dinner-table conversations about our daily labors, I thank my children, Jacqueline and Paul. I bear full (and sad) responsibility for the faults of this book. For its strengths, I credit my most beloved husband, Sean O'Connor, to whom this book is dedicated. For making wondrous adventures out of otherwise wearying research trips in Spain, Latin America, and the U.S., demanding that I attend to the humane elements of my study and its audiences, and providing me with the rare experience of the ideal relations of individuals recorded in this study, I am ever grateful.

Y como siempre, se termina con Adiós.

Milton among Spaniards

Introduction

> Blessed the time, and blessed the centuries, called by the ancients the Golden Age—and not because, then, the gold which we in our age of iron so value came to men's hands without effort, but because those who walked the earth in that time knew nothing of those two words, *thine* and *mine*.
> —Miguel de Cervantes Saavedra, *Don Quixote*, translated by Burton Raffel (emphases mine)

As John Phillips would have it, John Milton's presence among Spaniards began by 1605—three years before Milton's birth in 1608.[1] Milton's nephew and one-time student Phillips inserts an anachronistic reference to his uncle's masterwork, *Paradise Lost* (1667), in his 1687 English translation of Miguel de Cervantes Saavedra's *Don Quixote* (1605), where the character Don Diego de Miranda describes his disappointment in his son's preference for the study of literature over the more profitable study of law or divinity:

> He spends whole days in his *Criticisms*, whether *Homer* said well or ill, in repeating Ton'd Apomeibomenos so often?—whether such an Epigram in *Martial* ought not to be expung'd for its Obscenity—whether *Virgil* had he liv'd, could ha' better'd his *Eneads*—He is a great admirer of *Horace, Juvenal* and *Persius*—but as for the Modern Poets, he allows

very few to be worth a Straw; among the rest, he has a particular Peek against *Du Bartas*; and *Paradise lost*, which he says has neither Rhime nor Reason.²

In his translation, Phillips often forsakes denotative accuracy for tonal accuracy. In this case, the anachronism effectively translates Cervantes's trademark understated and wide-reaching humor. Savvy readers would enjoy detecting the anachronism; others would find humor in the characterization of Don Miranda's son as a buffoon for perceiving of foreign, religious epics as senseless, Guillaume de Saluste Du Bartas's French work, no less than Milton's English one; others would gain a sense of satisfaction from detecting the slightly deeper allusion of "neither Rhime nor Reason" to the first invocation of *Paradise Lost*, which states its pursuit of "Things unattempted yet in prose or rhyme" (PL 1.16).³

I begin this study with the brief, sly insertion from Phillips's 619-page translation because it is representative of many of the chief characteristics of Milton among Spaniards: isolated, oftentimes unexpected, pithily meaningful, and always complex, with extensions to religiopolitical censorial institutions, national and international relations, and a web of literary traditions and reader receptions. Don Miranda's list of a burgeoning Western literary canon forefronts the national elements that adhere in world literature, with Milton among the most recent inductees. There is also the attendant matter of translation as a component of world literature. Multilingual training in Milton's own education and in his curriculum for his small, elite home school of the 1640s provided his one-time pupil Phillips with the linguistic foundation that contributed to his translation of *Don Quixote* and by extension the popularization of a literary epitome of Spanish culture in England.⁴ Phillips's English translation implicitly advocates for the value of a Spanish work to English readers, contradicting the early modern English anti-Hispanism so often advertised, as does the fact that his is not the first English translation of *Don Quixote*; indeed, the first translation of *Don Quixote* "into any language was" into English, Thomas Shelton's, in 1612.⁵

Complicating the matter of the deeply imbricated relationship of literary greatness at the heart of Don Miranda's paternal complaint and his son's national prejudices against neighboring France and England is the project of national distinction and self-definition. The Spanish gentleman's logic is that certain literary works, or perhaps all foreign ones, distract individuals from doing their jobs to fortify their own nations.⁶ In turn, Englishman Phillips's implication is that the disdained *Paradise Lost* is in fact valuable for forward-looking England and would be for its backward-looking neighbor to the south if its powers-that-be had the good sense to know it.

Don Miranda's reference to the possibility of the work of Ibero-Roman Martial being "expung'd for its Obscenity" also alludes lightly but powerfully to a Spanish institution that so deeply affected Spain's literary self-definition as well as its definition by others: the Spanish Catholic Inquisition. Phillips's translation maintains Cervantes's carefully veiled but recognized refusal to yield to the Spanish Catholic Inquisition's authority: Cervantes's novel includes references and allusions to many works listed in the Spanish Catholic Inquisition's series of proscribed texts and authors, the *Index librorum prohibitorum*. Secure in English liberty, Phillips and his English readers would have yet another occasion to laugh at Spaniards. That laughter would be bittersweet for some, since the *Index* effectively kept from most Spanish readers such English texts as the *Utopia* (1516) by Thomas More, whom the Roman Catholic Church canonized in 1935; *A Defence of Poesy* (1595) by Philip Sidney, the namesake and godson of King Philip II of Spain; and all works circulating under Milton's name, starting in 1707. It is indeed the Spanish Catholic Inquisition's series of indexes and Milton's permutations on it that are the chief matters of chapter 1. Today's readers will recognize that the fictional dangers of reading romances on Don Quixote's psyche and of "Criticisms" on the job prospects of the younger Miranda are satiric doubles for the real threat of possessing censored books of any genre in any authoritarian country.[7] Comic elements diffuse the fears of state power that accompanied the rise of nationhood that Europe was experiencing at the time of Phillips's translation, no less than of Cervantes's novel and Milton's epic.[8]

The passage also concisely refers to the two literatures, Latin and French, which most regularly crop up in the Spanish reception of Milton and other major English authors. Martial (c. 40–104 CE, Hispania) highlights the tension of national identity and cosmopolitanism. In Milton's day, when classical texts were translated in mass into various European vernaculars, and even today, Martial's Ibero-Roman identity is sometimes highlighted and sometimes erased, in England, Spain, and elsewhere.[9] Du Bartas's presence registers the Anglo-Hispanic dialogue as part of an international conversation and France's status as one of the most highly influential vernacular mediators in the Western cultural tradition.[10] As chapter 2 records, for example, the translator of the first full Spanish version of *Paradise Lost* expressly states that he based some of his translational practices on those of the French translator Jacques Delille, and as chapter 4 discusses, it is the set of fifty illustrations by France's Gustave Doré that graces the first two fully illustrated editions of *El Paraíso perdido*.

I also begin with the epigraph from *Don Quixote* for reasons important to the broader nature and aims of this study. *Milton among Spaniards* recognizes the multiple ways in which "thine" and "mine" exist for all readers with all texts, due to historical, spatial, and linguistic proximity and distance, as has been amply and helpfully discussed in terms of Milton's near-contemporaries William Shakespeare and Cervantes. Howard Felperin notes the diachronic paradox of Shakespeare, at once our contemporary, "not of his or ours but 'for all time,'" even though his language alone can "scarcely be" called contemporary.[11] Ronald Paulson addresses the related synchronic paradox in relation to Cervantes's work outside of its homeland, original language, and time period: "In [eighteenth-century] England *Don Quixote* was read, interpreted, and utilized in a way it was not and could not have been in its native Spain or (where it was also immensely popular) in France."[12] Paulson's recognition of the variety of reader receptions based on national or cultural affiliations in relation to Cervantes accords with Miguel de Unamuno's lament regarding the unique national reading and interpretive habits of his Spanish compatriots, according to Eric Griffin: "Spain remains one of the nations where the book [*Don Quixote*] is least read: moreover, it is without a doubt the country where it is worst read. . . . I go so far as to believe that *Don Quixote* gains in translation, and that if it has been understood better outside of Spain, it is in good part because a preoccupation with the language has not veiled its beauty in foreign lands."[13]

Shakespeare and Cervantes have long occupied the position of "mine" and "thine" to varying degrees at various times in England and Spain. Paulson's claim, that by "1700 at least *Don Quixote* was an immensely popular work in England," cannot be said about *Paradise Lost* or any of Milton's other works in Spain at any time.[14] Certainly the low presence and prestige of the English language and its literature in general in seventeenth-century Europe contributed to Milton's low and slow reception in Spain early on.[15] Rubén Benítez and John George Robertson agree that Spanish reception was markedly lower than French, German, Italian, and Swedish reception. Benítez marks the rise in the familiarity of *Paradise Lost* by readers "fuera de Inglaterra y Alemania" (outside of England and Germany) as starting in 1712, when Joseph Addison began to publish his series of notes on Milton in *The Spectator* and Robertson the rise of Milton's fame more generally as starting in 1727–28 due to Voltaire's essays. Benítez also observes, however, that Milton's "lectores españoles del siglo XVIII" (Spanish readers from the eighteenth century) remained an elite group of "intelectuales, eclesiásticos, letrados hombres de leyes, en fin, personas ilustrados" (intellectuals, ecclesiastics, lettered men of law, in sum, Enlightened persons).[16] Robertson agrees, stating, "It cannot be said that the interest of Spain in Milton during the eighteenth century was more than an indifferent curiosity."[17] Finally, Luis Pegenaute notes that the Spanish translations of "algunos fragmentos de su obra principal . . . por las primeras plumas del país" (several fragments of his [Milton's] most famous piece . . . by the chief pens of the country) circulated in the eighteenth century among Spanish intellectuals and adds that Milton's presence "no puede en modo alguno denominarse influencia si la comparamos, por ejemplo, con la que ejercieron otros poetas ingleses como Pope, Young y Thomson durante el período prerromántico o Byron y Scott más tarde" (can in no way be called influence, if we compare it, for instance, with that of other English poets such as Pope, Young, and Thomson during the pre-Romantic period, or later on, Byron and Scott).[18]

I state clearly here at the outset that I did not uncover a generalized Spanish Miltoniphilia or a strong Miltonic influence among Spaniards that contradicts these determinations for the eighteenth century or subsequently. What I did find, however, was a series of powerful engagements within and outside of the traditional domains of literature.

"Transactions betwixt the English and Spaniards"

Milton among Spaniards is the first book-length exploration of the Hispanic afterlife of the titular author of the Age of Milton, spanning the seventeenth to the twenty-first century.[19] Drawing on religious discourse, literature, history, dramatic theory, and art history, I spotlight the Miltonic-Hispanic dialogue within the otherwise unwieldy Anglo-Hispanic conversation. This study attends to the sometimes volatile but also at times irenic responses that Milton (1608–1674) elicited from Spanish clerics, writers, statesmen, and artists.

The title *Milton among Spaniards* echoes the titles of signal monographs that have positioned Milton among groups that at initial glance might seem far from companionate, from Leo Miller's *John Milton among the Polygamophiles* (1974) to Stephen Fallon's *Milton among the Philosophers* (1991, 2007) and Richard DuRocher's *Milton among the Romans* (2001). Also foundational are the multi-author collections that have explored Milton's influence and reception in specific locales, such as Mario DiCesare's *Milton in Italy* (1991), Christophe Tournu's *Milton in France* (2008), Catherine Martin's *Milton's*

Italy (2016), and Islam Issa's *Milton in the Arab-Muslim World* (2016). Even more extensive and of most benefit to this study is *Milton in Translation* (2017), which I coedited with Islam Issa and Jonathan R. Olson and which sheds light on translations of Milton's works in twenty-three languages from across the globe.

While *Milton in Translation* contains two chapters on Milton's Spanish translations—those that emerged from Continental Spain and from Latin America—only one other book-length study to date has begun to redress the stark assessment two decades ago by the Miltonist John Shawcross that "little has been written about Milton and Iberia," echoed by the historian of Spanish literature David T. Gies, that too "little is done to connect the British and Spanish literary worlds."[20] In *Presencia de Milton en la literatura española, 1750–1850* (Milton's Presence in Spanish Literature; 2010), Benítez provides well-contextualized close readings of the literary "trazos" (traces) of Milton's presence produced by a Spanish coterie within the limited time frame of 1750–1850, per the volume's title. What results is a convincing sense of the impassioned interest and Miltonic presence embedded in the select literary works from the group and era he discusses—none of them major works, all of them fascinating—in contrast to the "indifferent curiosity" that Robertson attributes to eighteenth-century Spanish readers more generally.[21]

Milton among Spaniards extends the incisive studies of Anglo-Hispanic literary relations during the coeval Elizabethan Age and Siglo de Oro into its afterglow of the Age of Milton in the seventeenth century and beyond. Lois Parkinson Zamora notes the "rarity of comparative studies of seventeenth- and eighteenth-century English and Spanish literary cultures" and conjectures that it "may be incidental to the nonalignment of their systems of periodization" and that "periodic denominators are powerful; they accrue weight over time as they are defined, developed, and applied, and thus they come to organize knowledge in their areas."[22] This study has benefited from the methodological paths and information of short and long studies focused on the preceding Elizabethan Age and Siglo de Oro, from the many dedicated to Shakespeare, such as *Shakespeare en España* (1918), *Representaciones Shakespearianas en España* (1936), *Shakespeare in Spain* (1949), and *España en Shakespeare* (1991), to works with broader purviews, such as Richard Helgerson's *Forms of Nationhood: The Elizabethan Writings of England* (1992), which details the literary developments and nation formation in and between England and Spain, the two "leading nation-states of Europe in the early modern period," and Eric J. Griffin's *English Renaissance Drama and the Specter of Spain: Ethnopoetics and Empire* (2009), which so expertly discusses the "profound ambivalence" of alterity and affinity in major English literary works.[23] Most germane to this study in Griffin's demonstration of the role of the specter of Spain in the dramatic works of Thomas Kyd, Christopher Marlowe, and Shakespeare is the Janus-faced nature of nationalism and transculturalism.[24] As Griffin notes, "Rampant Hispanophobia notwithstanding, Renaissance England simultaneously inclined towards Hispanophilia. Residual notions of Anglo-Spanish complementarity—the inheritance of several centuries' worth of prior cultural exchange and interaction—could not easily be overturned."[25] We should, then, not be surprised that Spanish Miltoniphilia and Spanish Miltoniphobia are "involv'd and interwoven."[26]

Comparative and transnational critical approaches like Griffin's are requisite to bridge early modern English and Spanish studies, especially Milton studies. Just over a century ago, in his *American Literature in Spain* (1916), John de Lancey Ferguson pointed to Milton studies to clarify the deficiency in Anglo-Hispanic critical exchange: "So omnilegent and omniscient a scholar as Professor [George] Saintsbury mentions, in his bibliography of Milton in *The Cambridge History of English Literature* (1907–16), translations of *Paradise Lost* into French, German, Italian, Latin and Hebrew, but seems unaware of the fact that there existed, at the time he wrote, no less than four different Spanish versions of the epic."[27] Ferguson's own work acknowledges and reflects the very deficiency in Anglo-Hispanic critical exchange that he discusses. He refers to only four of the eight full Spanish translations of *Paradise Lost* at the time, and he errs with the dates of those translations, which he lists as 1814, 1872, 1883, and 1883 (see Appendix B).[28] These years imply first publication dates, but Juan Escóiquiz's translation—listed third—was first published in 1812. It was only in 1883, with the addition of the Gustave Doré illustrations, that the Escóiquiz translation gained attention outside of Spain.[29]

The historian Christopher Braider locates one source of the dearth of Anglo-Hispanic critical comparative studies in Western practices in literary training of the late twentieth and early twenty-first centuries "dating from the immediate postwar generation of the 1950s and 60s": "The widespread interest in the novel, in literary modernism, and in existentialist philosophy tended to identify comparative literature with the Iron Triangle of nineteenth- and twentieth-century English, French, and German. . . . Subsequent developments reinforced the narrow linguistic and historical scope of mainstream comparatism."[30] This state of affairs is changing in the twenty-first century, which has witnessed a rise of Hispanophone readers and speakers in general and also within arenas of higher education.[31] Correlatively, a comparative literature inflected with globalization has fostered a reassessment of the international and transnational. This combination has fostered an urgency about studying the literary relations between England (at the head of the Triangle) and Spain (south of it), to which this study is one response.[32]

Milton's presence among Spaniards is, fortunately, sufficiently isolated at this historical moment to sustain a unique kind of analysis, unlike that of his near-contemporaries Cervantes and Shakespeare. Certainly the genres with which Milton is associated—ode, sonnet, masque, pastoral, polemical prose, tragedy, and especially epic—are more varied than the genres with which Cervantes and Shakespeare are primarily associated. Further, Milton's writings, early biographies, and documentary remains give a deep enough sense of a unified personality associated with a specific age and time.[33] Thus the single-author focus of this study is especially helpful in sketching out the personal, textual, and historical elements of processes that can otherwise seem impersonal or unwieldy. There is, moreover, the vibrant nature of the figure and works of this specific author. In *Is Milton Better than Shakespeare?* (2008), Nigel Smith argues convincingly that at the beginning of the twenty-first century "there are certain ways in which Milton is more salient and important than Shakespeare because he is the poet who places liberty at the center of his vision."[34] It is indeed in arenas of contested liberty—religious, linguistic, and artistic—where we find Milton among Spaniards.

Ours and Others

This exploration of Milton among Spaniards foregrounds affiliation and alterity, or Ours and Others, as the texts under review so clearly demand.[35] The plural nature of Ours and Others prompts vigilance about the ways in which various features of Spanish representations of Milton maintain and accrue, so that we witness not a singular Our or singular Other but rather plural Ours and Others, not a Spanish Milton but rather Spanish Miltons. The concentric categories of Ours and Others range from authors' relationships with precursors, as Harold Bloom's *Anxiety of Influence: A Theory of Poetry* (1973) has aided us in understanding; to artistic representations of the triangular plane of a subject's imitation of a model Other to create a new object, as René Girard has detailed (serendipitously with *Don Quixote* as one example); to the irreducible plurality of language that Ferdinand de Saussure asked us to puzzle through with him. While the experience of affiliation as transcendence or heteronomy can be a strong component of the experience of alterity, as Emmanuel Levinas and others have exposed, it is often bypassed or minimized in "Criticisms," to invoke Don Diego de Miranda's term. It cannot be in this one, however, because over and over in the textual and artistic sites where Milton emerges among Spaniards, the plurality and possessiveness signaled by the genitive plural pronoun Ours, that which belongs to us, correlates with the Levinasian terms of authenticity and authorship—that is, the *ourness*—of works, authors, publishers, and readers. Literature in translation moves us perforce further and further away from an insular *mine* because of the plural mechanisms of the production, transportation, and reception of nonnative mobile literatures.[36]

These important perspectives inform this study's exploration of four major forms of reception: censorship, translation, dramatic representation, and visual art. Emphasizing the various degrees of affiliation and alterity in these forms of Spanish reception of Milton is grounded in my sensitivity to the texts themselves, reacting to rather than rejecting Roland Greene's articulation of "an almost superstitious obeisance to the category of the national."[37] I heed Eric Griffin's autobiographical caution: "Like a number of scholars who came into the profession in [the wake of the New Historicist movement of the 1980s and 1990s], I began to sense that as much as some New Historicist criticism spoke of crossing borders and as committed as many of its practitioners were to unmasking the apparatuses of ideology, New Historicist critical methodologies—like those of the older historicisms they claimed to be interrogating and displacing—often failed to envision a time when the boundaries between nations were substantially different from what they were in modernity."[38]

It is precisely this sensitivity and caution that precipitated, for example, my observation of the intentional modifications by the translator and Catholic cleric Juan Escóiquiz in his translation of *Paradise Lost* as based on discrete linguistic, literary-cultural, and religious foundations rather than only religious ones, and the artist Gregorio Prieto's illustrations as chiefly modernist, with modernism's investments in an increasingly borderless world.[39] Escóiquiz's, Prieto's, and other Spaniards' struggles with their own perceptions of Spain and their beliefs about perceptions of Spain by other Western groups defined by language and nation also affirmed my retention and use of the national—be it Spanish, English, French, or in key places U.S.—as a category too useful to be abandoned.

Such categories often overlap, certainly with Spanish and English receptions of Milton. For example, Milton's fame in his homeland as its great epic poet emerged only after English critics and readers could think of him as something other than a divorcer and king killer because of his public advocacy of divorce and his government post with the regicidal Cromwellian government. As Roy Flannagan notes, in the mid-eighteenth century, "[Samuel] Johnson seems to take Milton the regicide personally, as if Milton were still threatening the existence of the British monarchy."[40] Milton's fame underwent a similar if less pronounced *volta* in Spain. His Spanish reception was formalized as infamy in the early eighteenth century through his placement on the Spanish Catholic Inquisition's *Index librorum prohibitorum*. But over time Milton was converted to a Spanish Ours: linguistically in the nineteenth century with the first Spanish translation of *Paradise Lost* of 1812, which explicitly presents a Catholic version of the epic, as discussed in chapter 2, and representationally in the Spanish play *Milton: Cuadro dramático en un acto y en verso* (Milton: A Dramatic Scene in One Act and in Verse; 1879), which constructs a Spanish Milton by having him alone, among all the characters, speak in the quintessentially Spanish verse form of the *décima*, as detailed in chapter 3.

Synthesizing Our and Other responses enables us, if we are willing, to incorporate them actively into our and others' literary experiences and interpretations. Indeed, such synthesis and expansion are the bread and butter of literary scholarship. The value of human plurality that underpins humanity's great (mono-, inter-, and intra-) cultural achievements is often overlooked, perpetuating glaring absences in "Criticisms." In *Puritan Conquistadors: Iberianizing the Atlantic, 1550–1700* (2006), Jorge Cañizares-Esguerra demonstrates that Hispanic and Latino historiographies have been subordinated to or erased from "Western Civilization" in Anglophone criticisms of various fields. (A particularly germane exception that he cites is J. Martin Evans's *Milton's Imperial Epic*.) So, for example, Spain and its former American territories are either excluded from the technologically savvy and powerful narrative of the Northwest paradigm or included only "to describe the underbelly of modernity."[41] In Anglophone literary "Criticisms," as is this study, the comfortable Ours is usually the canonical Milton, easily lionized because of his impressive works. Certainly my great enjoyment of Milton's works is evident on every page; however, I believe I have struck the balance of valuing both the English and Spanish works on their own terms.

This chapter's single illustration is emblematic of the careful ambivalence that I strive to place into relief and that Milton seems to elicit among later Spaniards (see Figure 1). This enchanting sketch from Prieto's *Milton | El Paraíso perdido* (1972) accompanies the passage describing Eve's creation from Adam's side in *Paradise Lost* that begins "and took / From thence a rib, with cordial spirits warm, / And life-blood streaming fresh" (PL 8.465–75). The

Figure 1. Gregorio Prieto's "Sketch 3, Adam's Back, Eve's Profile," in *Milton | El Paraíso perdido* (1972). (Fundación Gregorio Prieto; image courtesy of Harvard University Libraries)

sketch is a more artistic and more relevant illustration than the famous Jastrow rabbit-and-duck (1899) for emphasizing the importance of aspect shifts and the confounding difficulty of apprehending two aspects simultaneously.[42]

Prieto's sketch operates as does the Jastrow rabbit-and-duck in many ways. Its two figures face opposite directions. It similarly resists prioritizing one over the other: even though Eve is drawn in finer lines, she faces the audience; even though Adam faces away, he is drawn in bolder lines. Yet while both illustrations thus represent difference without priority and subordination, the Prieto is much more apt for a number of reasons. Foremost and at its most general, the sketch is apt because of its obscurity, as with so many elements of Milton's Spanish presence. Also apt is its sparse texture as sketch (in contrast to the density of the Jastrow rabbit-and-duck), which reflects the paucity of Spanish responses to Milton. Finally, Prieto's sketch adds in complexity what it removes in density, with its unbounded spatial focal point. Adam and Eve do not share the same outline; Eve's profile is both within *and* in front of Adam's back left shoulder, her breasts merging with *and* superimposed upon Adam's back rib cage, whence she will emerge *and* is emerging. And there, above Adam's neck, is a hand—Eve's hand?—independent of Adam, perhaps picking flowers, perhaps even embodied entirely in the flowers themselves. Prieto's flowers seem to float unsupported, so that even in the moment of Eve's creation, readers familiar with *Paradise Lost* are prompted to recall the later scene in which Eve, on the verge of the Fall, is described as "Herself, though fairest unsupported flow'r" (*PL* 9.432). The deceptively simple sketch is thus emblematic of the complex, uncanny presence of Milton among Spaniards.

A book-length analysis of the centuries-long Miltonic-Hispanic dialogue provides distinct and fundamental understandings about the complex conversation between British/Anglophone and Spanish/Hispanophone cultures and literatures. Much like our own times, the early modern period is defined by the large-scale reshaping of world visions through geographical and technological explorations, new international markets, and all the consequent effects of those activities on languages and literary developments.[43] And of course England and Spain were at the forefront of those reshapings.

Some sets of literature translate human activity and the history of ideas into accessible remains and inspire others to resuscitate those remains into vibrant afterlives. This book investigates one particularly apposite set of afterlives in the hands of some of Milton's most creative Spanish readers. In his foundational *After Babel: Aspects of Language and Translation* (1975), George Steiner singles out Milton as the epitome of writers who create bridges "between past and present, and between different tongues and traditions which were splitting apart under the stress of nationalism and religious conflict. With its English, Latin, and Italian verse, with its at-homeness in Hebrew and Greek, Milton's book of poems of 1645 illustrates, supremely, the created contemporaneity of ancient and modern and the unified diversity—coherent as are the facets of a crystal—of the European community as they derive from two hundred years of translation."[44] The main task of *Milton among Spaniards* is to demonstrate the bridges that Milton prompted with Spaniards over roughly three centuries and within overlapping literary domains: in chapter 1, in the Spanish Catholic Inquisition's lists of the eighteenth and nineteenth centuries; in chapter 2, in the full Spanish translations of Milton's epic from 1812 to 2005; in chapter 3, on the late nineteenth-century Spanish stage; and in chapter 4, in Spanish visual art from 1688 to the 1970s.

"How Shall I Relate"?

To pay due respect to the subjects of this study, I repeatedly asked myself the question that serves as this section's title, the question that the archangel Raphael asks himself as he prepares to tell Adam and Eve about the War in Heaven in *Paradise Lost* (*PL* 5.564). The question of *how* of course involves *what*. Inevitably, writing a story that spans roughly three centuries means that much has been left out.[45] For the sake of brevity and clarity, one of my earliest decisions was to include only Spanish works written in Latin and Castilian Spanish—elsewhere referred to simply as *Spanish*—thereby eliminating works in the other Spanish languages of Basque, Catalan, and Galician, despite exciting work that has been done and is yet to be done with those languages.[46] Another decision was to include works by only European Spaniards, to the exclusion of works by Spanish Americans. I quickly determined that works by Spanish Americans and, after Spain's dispossession of the Americas, Latin Americans necessitate a completely different study to frame them adequately.

The four chapters of *Milton among Spaniards* follow a general chronology from the seventeenth to the early twenty-first century, with Milton's Spanish reception moving from active rejection to adaptation to co-option to untethered and playful immersion. Chapter 1, "Heretic Milton, 'Of the Devil's Party' per the Spanish Catholic Inquisition," focuses on Milton's inclusion and permutations on the *Index librorum prohibitorum*. The first part of the chapter draws out the key issues of censorship from Milton's prose pamphlet *Areopagitica* (1644), so regularly invoked up through today in discussions of free speech.[47] The second part then demonstrates these issues at work in shaping the self-sustaining artifact of Milton as authorial figure and as "Anglus" (Englishman), as he is identified on the lists—but never "poeta." Why is Milton added in the 1707 index well after his death in 1674, one of the very few Englishmen who ever made it onto the Spanish Catholic lists? The answer is not part of the racier narrative about the Spanish Catholic lists as persecutorial tools. Instead, Milton's presence in these archives tells the tale of the Spanish Catholic Inquisition's unintentional contributions to the development of an international author-function, quite independent of embodied authors, much less of individual souls. Milton's entries include none of his Anglophone works or original poetic works: the 1844 index comes closest by including an Italian translation of *Paradise Lost*. In a sort of backhanded compliment, the Spanish Catholic Inquisition included and kept Milton on its lists because his name had sufficient and enduring international cultural standing, giving truth to Milton's own claim that "all Europe talks from side to side" ("To Cyriack Skinner," 12) about him. The chapter concludes by attending to representations of Milton by Spaniards as the power of the Spanish Catholic Inquisition declined.

While we might think that illicit works would be viewed as alluring and therefore lead Milton's proscribed works to be objects of desire, Spanish readers did not flock to the English originals or Spanish translations even after prohibitions were softened. To generate interest in Milton as part of the growing world literature canon, many Spaniards tried their hands at Spanish translations of *Paradise Lost* starting in the nineteenth century, the subject of chapter 2, "'As May Express Them Best': Spanish Translations of *Paradise Lost*." These translations make up for their delay with their number: at least nineteen distinct full Spanish translations of *El Paraíso perdido* from 1812 to 2005, a number approximated only by French versions. This chapter takes the rare opportunity that this number and its historical breadth afford to conduct a comparative translation description, a desideratum that James S. Holmes and other translation studies scholars enjoin. Closely reading key passages from a number of these translations puts into relief the specific linguistic dilemmas, religious differences, and cultural reading practices that Milton's translators confronted. By giving equitable attention to some of the most powerful as well as less successful poetic moments to be found in the various versions of *El Paraíso perdido* and to their paratexts—prefaces, notes, and commentaries—we are able to add to and calibrate our interpretations of Milton's epic and of Spanish literary production and reception.

Chapter 3, "'To the Well-Trod Stage Anon': Milton on the Spanish and

International Stage," focuses on the most fascinating of a curious cluster of three Iberian plays composed at the end of the nineteenth century that feature Milton as the main character: *Milton: A Dramatic Scene in One Act and in Verse*. The intrinsic and extrinsic features of this play coordinate to yield as many interpretive dilemmas and pathways as do those of Milton's own youthful drama, *A Mask Presented at Ludlow-Castle* (1634), a work given due attention in this chapter. My goal is to show that this finely crafted piece of dramatic art serves to extend the relationship between individuals who had the power to affect national and international policy. The play's chief figures produce a triangulated, transatlantic nexus, for *Milton: A Dramatic Scene* took an English icon as its protagonist; was written by Spain's Hermenegildo Giner de los Ríos, who would go on to be one of the country's most influential educational reformers of the twentieth century and a politician at local and national levels, as a councilman and member of Parliament in Barcelona (1903, 1909–18); and was dedicated to and performed for James Russell Lowell, the U.S. professor of Spanish and French at Harvard, cofounder of the Modern Language Association, internationally famed writer, U.S. ambassador to Spain at the time, and later U.S. minister to England. Compressed into the play are the cultural energies and political circumstances of the three countries at the time: the British Empire governed about 25 percent of the world population, Spain had restored its monarchy, and the U.S. was experiencing enormous commercial and cultural growth following its Civil War and Reconstruction. This heady context is captured in the play's impressive display of key Spanish verse forms that pay tribute to the Spanish stage's past Golden Age, and of a plot that aligns with the socially conscious zeitgeist of the Spanish stage's then-current Silver Age.

We move from stage to canvas with chapter 4, "'By Shading Pencil Drawn': Spanish Illustrations of *Paradise Lost*." Renaissance studies have a particularly strong tradition of visual-verbal textual studies and of international and transnational awareness. We readily think of Stephen Greenblatt's reading of Hans Holbein's painting *The Ambassadors* (1533) in *Renaissance Self-Fashioning: From More to Shakespeare* (1980). Studies of the nearly two hundred sets of illustrations of Milton's works have also been long standing and full, with a heavy concentration on those by British (William Blake and John Martin) and French (Gustave Doré) artists, as well as recent work on U.S. and women artists. But Spanish visual representations have been underexplored by and large, even though illustrations by the Flemish-Spanish artist John Baptiste de Medina are present in the first Anglophone illustrated edition of *Paradise Lost* (1688). This chapter sheds light on the Spanish elements that have failed to register in discussions of this set of well-known illustrations and of the internationally ubiquitous art by Doré in the first fully illustrated Spanish prose and verse translations of *Paradise Lost*, published in 1873 and 1883. The showcase of this chapter is the set of seventeen sketches in the exclusive Spanish edition of *El Paraíso perdido* (1972) by Gregorio Prieto, a member of the Spanish Generación del 1927 that includes the famed poet and dramatist Federico García Lorca and the 1977 Nobel Prize in Literature laureate Vicente Aleixandre, both of whom figure in the surprising web of these sketches' circulation. It is my hope that the brief close reading of just one of Prieto's sketches earlier in this introduction amply demonstrates the rich interplay of the works of Milton's early modern English pen and the Spanish modernist's pencil.

Milton among Spaniards concludes with the epilogue "Juan Milton, el Inglés," in which I clarify some of the main trends that emerge from the preceding chapters' cumulative story and some of the especially promising work that it might prompt. It is with the sense of such future work, or sequels, that I return "Yet once more" (*Lycidas*, 1) to the famously sequeled work with which this introduction begins. *Don Quixote* stands, truth be told, as a wish fulfillment of sorts for this first book-length sally into contemporary "Criticisms" of the centuries-long Miltonic-Hispanic dialogue. *Milton among Spaniards* seeks to provide a similarly enriching vision of some aspects of Spanish culture, to be as careful in its handling of its titular namesake, and to prompt as welcoming a path for confronting difficult topics and themes about enduring human activities, values, and systems. With *Milton among Spaniards*, I seek to deepen our understanding of Spanish representations of one of the most influential figures of not only English literature but also world literature. Additionally, it is my hope that the exploration of the historical transformations of Milton among Spaniards will contribute to a capacious understanding of the important roles of literatures and criticisms in and for a variety of fields.

CHAPTER 1

Heretic Milton, "Of the Devil's Party" per the Spanish Catholic Inquisition

John Milton arrived in Spanish territories, if only briefly, in June 1639, when, "passing through Brescia to the Venetian frontier, he entered the Spanish Milanese territories."[1] Milton's works, however, waited about seven decades more before making any significant inroads into Spain. Enduring, if pejorative, testaments of their arrival appear in the Spanish Catholic Inquisition's lists of proscribed writers and texts, the *Index librorum prohibitorum*.[2] These entries played decisive roles in delaying the publication of complete Spanish translations of Milton's works, the topic of chapter 2. They also include the major political and symbolic elements that recur in Milton's afterlife in Spain, as epitomized on the Spanish stage and in illustrative art, the topics of chapters 3 and 4.

1. 1707 Marín Index: "* IOANNES MILTHONIVS, Anglus, Hæ- | retic. *Pro Populo Anglicano Defenfio, con- | tra Claudij Salmasij Defenfionem Regiam.* | Londini."

2. 1790 Rubín Index: "Milthonius (Joan.), Angl. I. *cl.*"

3. 1844 Palacios Index: "+ Miltonus (Joannes). Litteræ pseudosena- | tus anglicani, Cromwellii, reliquorumque | perduellium nomine, ac jussu conscriptæ, | (decr. 22 decembris 1700). | +—Il paradiso perduto: poema inglese, tra- | dotto in nostra lingua da Paolo Rolli (decr. | 21 de januarii 1732)" (see Figure 2).[3]

17

> * IOANNES MILTHONIVS, Anglus, Hæ-
> retic. *Pro Populo Anglicano Defensio*, con-
> tra *Claudij Salmatij Defensionem Regiam*.
> Londini.

> Milthonius (Joan.), Angl. 1. cl.

> ✠ Miltonus (Joannes). Litteræ pseudo-sena-
> tus anglicani, Cromwellii, reliquorumque
> perduellium nomine, ac jussu conscriptæ
> (decr. 22 decembris 1700).
> ✠ — Il paradiso perduto: poema inglese, tra-
> dotto in nostra lingua da Paolo Rolli (decr.
> 21 de januarii 1732).

Figure 2. Milton entries in the Spanish Catholic Inquisition's 1707 Marín Index, 1790 Rubín Index, and 1844 Palacios Index. (Courtesy of HathiTrust)

This chapter analyzes the literary and scholarly aspects of the censorial indexes of the Spanish Catholic Inquisition to be derived from Milton's entries, since these entries participate in the early shaping of Spanish readers' reception of Milton's writings. Equally important, they reflect the Spanish Catholic Inquisition's and Spanish readers' changing reading practices and concerns. Thus this study starts by examining *Areopagitica*. Milton's pamphlet against prepublication censorship, invoked so regularly internationally and up through today in discussions about access and censorship, serves as a touchstone to clarify key elements about reading, access, and censorial indexes and agents, particularly in relation to the Spanish Catholic Inquisition. The next step is ascertaining what Milton's entries tell us about how the Spanish Catholic Inquisition conceptualized its agency in relation to Spanish readers and how it read Milton and his works during its zenith in Continental Spain in the early eighteenth century to its decline in the mid-nineteenth century. The chapter concludes by attending to representations of Milton by Spaniards of varied temperaments in the wake of the Spanish Catholic Inquisition.[4]

Milton on the Spanish Catholic Inquisition

Milton's *Areopagitica* (1644) manifests a clear understanding of the Spanish Catholic Inquisition as an entity related to but distinct from the Roman Catholic Inquisition.[5] His pamphlet against prepublication censorship avoids the common, mistaken elision in popular and even some scholarly discussions about the two Inquisitions and attends to the divisions of labor typical of large censorial systems. Further, the pamphlet spotlights the scholarly branch, whose duty it was to construct and update the indexes, rather than the executive branch, whose duty it was to capture and prosecute heretics. Equally important, *Areopagitica* considers the messiness of textual censorship, so clearly displayed in Milton's entries on the Spanish Catholic indexes, discussed in the second part of the chapter.

Ernest Sirluck notes that, as a response to the Licensing Order of 1643, *Areopagitica* "gives the impression that licensing is a thoroughly un-English policy" (*CPW* 2.158). The repeated references in *Areopagitica* to the "Inquisition"—ten times as a noun, twice as a descriptor—constitute an effective rhetorical strategy of underplaying England's long history of book censorship by means of overplaying the history of foreign censorship (*CPW* 2.493, 503, 505, 507, 521, 530, 537, 538, 539 twice, 541, 568). But which Inquisition or Inquisitions? Sirluck maintains that "Inquisition" refers to the Spanish Catholic Inquisition, which held and continues to hold a powerful claim on the Western psyche: "Today the term Inquisition is more often than not used to mean the Spanish Inquisition; Milton appears to have used it in the same way; *cf.* pp. 502 ('Spanish Inquisition'), [529] ('the model of . . . Sevil'), and [569] ('this *authentic* Spanish policy')" (*CPW* 2.493n26).[6]

I maintain, however, that the pamphlet uses "Inquisition" variably, to mean both the general (Roman Catholic) and the particular (Spanish Catholic) Inquisitions. We should note that Sirluck's second evidentiary quotation replaces the name of a highly charged Italian site and a copulative, "*Trent* and," with an ellipsis (*CPW* 2.529). Erasing this sentence's reference to an Italian site and Roman Catholic metonymy undercuts the vision of the international, censorial system that Milton represents at this moment in the pamphlet. After summarizing ancient and early Christian censorship, Milton provides another copulative image of separate but allied entities. He describes the "stricter policy of prohibiting. Which cours *Leo* the 10, and his successors follow'd, until the Councell of Trent, and the Spanish Inquisition engendring together brought forth, or perfeted those Catalogues, and expurging Indexes" (*CPW* 2.502). The naming of the Florentine Pope "*Leo* the 10"—born Giovanni di Lorenzo de Medici (1475–1521)—signals just some of the internationalism of the Roman Catholic Inquisition.[7]

We can trace Milton's knowledge of a plurality of Catholicisms, including Spain's, to the Latin entry in his commonplace book on the "Prohibition of books when first us'd. The storie therof is in ye Councel of Trent Book

6," which records the independent activities of "Spanish theologians" that contradicted Roman Catholic authority (*CPW* 1.451). This is not to say that young Milton wholeheartedly praised Spanish Catholic independence. Ruth Mohl rightly notes the ambivalent tone toward Spanish Catholics: the entry about "the Spanish theologians has in it some Miltonic sarcasm as well as commendation" (*CPW* 1.452n6).

The examples of wrongheaded book censorship in *Areopagitica* incorporate the national governments that worked alongside the Roman Catholic Inquisition. Henry Kamen summarizes: "The Lateran Council of 1515, and in particular the Council of Trent in 1564, granted bishops in Europe a general power to license books for printing. . . . In England the government produced licensing laws in 1538, and in the 1540s various Italian authorities passed similar edicts. Spain came late into the field of controls."[8] Joseph Pérez notes similarly, "Spain was neither the only nor the first of the Catholic nations to draw up a list of works that the faithful were forbidden either to read or to possess. In this domain, the Sorbonne led the way in 1544, followed by the University of Louvain (1546) and the Republic of Venice (1549). The first Index issued by Rome dated 1551."[9] It is no wonder, then, that soon after the mention of Trent and Seville, *Areopagitica* quickly moves back to Italian territories.

In a pithy rhetorical masterpiece of sarcasm, Milton provides an example of book licenses, "the permissions on the flyleaf of his *Scisma d'Inghilterra*," published in the thrice-mentioned Florence: "*Vincent Rabatta* Vicar of *Florence*," "*Nicolò Cini* Chancellor of *Florence*," and "Friar *Simon Mompei d'Amelia* Chancellor of the holy office in *Florence*" (*CPW* 2.504n.64, 503–4). Milton had traveled to Florence a few years before the publication of *Areopagitica*, so the geographical emphasis is in part autobiographically based (*CPW* 2.504n64).[10] Additionally, Florence was a hub for the publication of works from Catholic countries. Works sent from Spain to Florence for publication would already have been approved by the Spanish Catholic Inquisition. The subsequent passage that describes an imprimatur page strengthens the Italian focus, with its use of Italian place-names and personal names: the "reverend Master of the holy Palace, *Belcastro* Vicegerent," "Friar *Nicolò Rodolphi* Master of the holy Palace," and the "5 *Imprimaturs* . . . seen together dialogue-wise in the Piatza of one Title page, complementing and ducking each to other with their shav'n reverences" (*CPW* 2.504). Leo Miller concludes from his search for a book with "5 *Imprimaturs*" that Milton would have found particularly apt that, until "another book with five imprimaturs is turned up, we may conclude that the example of Galileo's *Dialogo* is unique and supplied" the example.¹¹ This passage thus refers directly and indirectly to other Italian locales; to Rome via "the Roman stamp" and "holy Palace," and to Florence and Tuscany for readers aware of Galileo's *Dialogo* as the likely example, given Galileo's association with the former, where Milton records having visited Galileo sometime in 1638, and the latter, which Milton alludes to in his reference in *Paradise Lost* to Galileo as the "Tuscan artist" (*PL* 1.288).¹² The Italian emphasis could be due to the simple fact that Milton lived in a century of many short-lived Italian popes.¹³ The days of the only two Spanish popes, Callixtus III (Alfonso de Borgia, 1378–1458; r. 1455–1458) and Alexander VI (Rodrigo de Borgia, 1431–1503; r. 1492–1503), were long past.¹⁴

Rather than honing in on and deriding the Spanish Catholic Inquisition in particular, *Areopagitica* reinforces the perception of the international nature of Roman Catholicism. The phrase "Jesuits and *Sorbonists*" in *Areopagitica* concisely refers to a multinational consortium (*CPW* 2.519). The Jesuits were among the most active orders in Catholicism's extra-European colonizing efforts and in the establishment of learned societies on the European Continent. Likewise, while the Sorbonne (f. 1257) was founded as a theological school in Paris, it was an influential academic institution that attracted students from throughout Europe, including Protestant countries.¹⁵ Finally, Milton lambasts Lambeth House, the residence of the archbishop of Canterbury, because of English practices analogous to Continental Catholic ones. For readers in the know, the British presence might have been strengthened also through the reference to a publication "approved by Belcastro and Rodolphi." Miller finds the likely candidate to be a 1628 book about the Scottish Kirk by the "Papist" George Conn, *Georgii Conaei De Duplici Statu Religionis Apud Scotos Libro Duo. Ad Illustrissmum Principem Franciscum S.R.E. Card. Barberinum Magnae Britanniae Proctectorum. Romae. Typis Vaticanus. M.DC.XXVIII*.¹⁶

One Catholic practice not adopted by the religious powers in Milton's homeland, of course, was the production of postpublication censorial indexes, which smacked of servility and custom. Sirluck suggests that Milton uses the terms "Popery" and "open superstition" to "cover the two aspects of Roman Catholicism" that are intolerable (*CPW* 2.179). Randy Robertson similarly avers, "Milton's strategy of pairing censorship with popery, licensing with papal infallibility, was brilliantly calculated to galvanize his countrymen's anti-Catholic bigotry."¹⁷ In *Areopagitica*, Milton uses "papacy" and the related "popery" in developing his arguments against overreaching prepublication censorship to tap into historically based fears and realities about closet Catholics at home.¹⁸ "There be Protestants and professors who live and dye in as arrant an implicit faith, as any lay Papist of Loretto," he warns (*CPW* 2.543–44). If unchecked, these forces could lead to the censorial practices to be found abroad: "The Popes of *Rome* engrossing what they pleas'd of Politicall rule into their owne hands, extended their dominion over mens eyes, as they had before over their judgements, burning and prohibiting to be read, what they fansied not" (*CPW* 2.501; see also 2.492). Yet, in the last section of *Areopagitica*, Milton claims that not only Catholic censorial indexes and practices but all outward attempts of suppressing "corruption" are "vain and fruitlesse" (*CPW* 2.523).

Milton "excludes Catholics from toleration," even in the sense of "to be let alone," much less affirmatively accepted, as John Leonard cogently demonstrates.[19] Further, he characterizes Catholics of any national stripe as contemptibly unattractive—a characterization we will see at work vice versa in the Spanish Catholic Inquisition's representation of him. *Areopagitica* does not dwell on gory images of the bloody hands of the "Popes of *Rome*" in violent action against particular humans. Instead of forefronting policing agents of censorial institutions with swords in hand, Milton calls readers to attend to other weapons: "The shop of warre hath not there more anvils and hammers waking, to fashion out the plates and instruments of armed Justice in defence of beleaguer'd Truth, then there be pens and heads there, sitting by their studious lamps, musing, searching, revolving new notions and idea's wherewith to present, as with their homage and their fealty the approaching Reformation" (*CPW* 2.501, 554). Indeed, throughout *Areopagitica* Milton minimizes mention of the executive branches of censorship and of the violence enacted on individuals who take strong stands for religious freedom, especially in the recent past.[20] His response to this intranational licensing act minimizes references to physical force. In the early *refutatio*, punishments are quickly stated in general terms: "I deny not, but that it is of greatest concernment in the Church and Commonwealth, to have a vigilant eye how Bookes demeane themselves, as well as men; and thereafter to confine, imprison, and do sharpest justice on them as malefactors." The potential for maleficent men to bear the brunt of "sharpest justice" is redirected onto lively "Bookes." Similarly, rather than dwelling on the specifics of "the open cruelty of *Decius* or *Dioclesian*," who persecuted early Christians in various and extreme ways, Milton looks to the insidious process of "secretly decaying the Church" by depriving early Christians from studying Greek literature (*CPW* 2.492, 509).

The pamphlet does not key in on fearsome executors of the censorial mandates but rather, for example, on "2 or 3 glutton Friers," mocked members from the scholarly branch of the Inquisition. English "inquisiturient Bishops" who follow risible papist practices are similarly represented as portly porters, snatching up "the rare morsell" (*CPW* 2.503, 507, 506). More generally, the scholarly ministers of censorial systems are buffoons who "thought to pound up the crows by shutting his Parkgate." The licensor, who would "be made the perpetuall reader of unchosen books and pamphlets, oftimes huge volumes," and act as a "pupil teacher," provokes not fear but contempt. Near the end of the pamphlet, Milton cites his visit to "the famous *Galileo* grown old, a prisner to the Inquisition, for thinking in Astronomy otherwise then the Franciscan and Dominican licensers thought" (*CPW* 2.520, 530, 533, 538). But Milton neither overstates nor fully exploits the threat of violence surrounding Galileo.

All these contemptible figures are analogues to an English bureaucracy that Milton forecasts, should the Licensing Order stand, for the immense "new labour" needed for cataloguing "all scandalous and unlicen't books already printed and divulg'd," reviewing all "forrein books," making "expurgations, and expunctions," and tracking and persecuting "all those Printers who are found frequently offending" (*CPW* 2.528, 529). His vision of such an England is not too far off from the reality of "*Trent* and *Sevil*," which stumbled regularly under their bureaucratic weight, as described in the next section of this chapter. By the end of its power in the first half of the nineteenth century, as Raymond Carr argues, the Spanish Catholic Inquisition "was an ineffective irritant, slow and erratic in its procedures; it merely put up the price of books, forcing readers to all sorts of subterfuges in order to consume often outdated heresies. Even a pious man like [Gaspar Melchor de] Jovellanos [1744–1811] could feel bitterly at the attempts of the Inquisition to sabotage his plans for establishing a modern technical institute at Gijon."[21]

Two primary elements from this discussion of *Areopagitica* facilitate our approach to Milton's entries on the 1707, 1790, and 1844 Spanish Catholic Inquisition's indexes of prohibited works and authors. First, Milton's mindfulness about the existence of the two related but separate entities of the Roman Catholic Inquisition and Spanish Catholic Inquisition alerts us to the plurality of Catholicisms that the two series of indexes reflect. As we turn to the indexes themselves, the most significant form of this plurality is not between the international Roman Catholic Inquisition and the national Spanish Catholic Inquisition but rather between early eighteenth- and mid-nineteenth-century Spanish Catholic concepts of heresy. Second, Milton's focus on and representation of the scholarly branch rather than on the executive branch of the Spanish Catholic Inquisition enriches our appreciation of the practical and theoretical shifts recorded in the indexes that paralleled the practices of trial and torture, since they too so thoroughly shaped Spanish reading practices. The self-representations of the scholarly agents constructed in the prefatory materials of the indexes and of their relationship to other Spanish readers accords with the changes to be found in the entries themselves. As to be expected, these self-representations are quite contrary to Milton's comic depictions.

Milton on the Spanish Catholic Indexes

The preceding discussion of *Areopagitica* emphasizes the effects of censorship on individuals and nations, multinational concerns, the nature of censoring agents, and the weight placed on books rather than human agents per se. These same matters are epitomized in the Spanish Catholic Inquisition's indexes in which Milton's name appears.

Milton had nothing to fear from those indexes for a variety of reasons: he was not an identified heretic until thirty-three years after his death, and he was not a resident of Spanish territories, within reach of its executive branch. He had more to fear from individuals and institutions elsewhere for heresy ("theological or religious opinion or doctrine maintained in opposition . . . to the . . . orthodox doctrine") combined with treason ("violation by a subject of his allegiance to his sovereign or to the state").[22] Rubén Benítez notes that France, the homeland of Claude Saumaise (Salmasius), one of the prime targets of Milton's *Pro populo Anglicano defensio*, acted quickly in censuring the regicidal tract: it was among the books condemned to the fire in Paris in 1651.[23] Henry Redman Jr. notes its similar destiny in southern France the same year by order of the Parlement de Toulouse.[24] It was not only Milton's *Pro populo Anglicano defensio* but also his *Eikonoklastes* that the English House of Commons ordered burned nearly a decade later, in June 1660. Two months later, King Charles II issued an Official Proclamation against these two works for "contain[ing] sundry Treasonable Passages against Us and Our Government, and most Impious endeavors to justifie the horrid and unmatchable Murther of Our late Dear Father [King Charles I], of Glorious Memory."[25] Informal charges in England against Milton were also abundant upon the Restoration, as in the six-page *Character of the Rump* (1660):[26] "*John Milton* is their [the Commonwealth's] Goos-quill Champion, who had need of *A Help meet* to establish any thing, for he has a Ramshead, and is good only at Batteries, an old Heretick both in Religion and Manners, that by his will would shake off his Governours as he doth his Wives."[27] The second earl of Bridgewater, who played the role of the Elder Brother in Milton's early drama *A Mask* when he was eleven years old, disdained *Pro populo Anglicano defensio*: "He wrote in the margin: '*liber igne, auctor furca, dignissimi*' ('the book deserves the fire, the author the gallows')."[28] Both the book and its primary human agent merit postpublication violence here. The Continental community was not always in such accord with England, in general or in relation to English authors. For example, Christopher Marlowe, whose works were burned in England's Bishops' Ban in 1599, is not on any of the Spanish Catholic indexes under review.[29]

The very existence of the Spanish Catholic Inquisition's indexes instantiates a national division within a once unified concept and practice of Christendom, in accordance with the international (Roman) and national (Spanish) censorial systems represented in Milton's *Areopagitica*. Pope Sixtus IV sanctioned the establishment of a Spanish Catholic Inquisition in 1478, roughly three-quarters of a century before it published its first index. As Henry Kamen notes, "The first printed Index to be used in Spain, issued by Inquisitor General Valdés in September 1551, was no more than a reprint of one compiled by the university of Louvain in 1550, with a special appendix devoted to Spanish books."[30] Likewise the next Spanish Catholic index, the 1583 Quiroga Index, was heavily influenced by the 1564 Roman Catholic index issued by the Council of Trent. The Spanish Catholic Inquisition slowly took on a more active role in researching new entries for subsequent indexes. This scholarly activity within the Spanish Catholic Inquisition represented, as Alfredo Vílchez Díaz notes, a "cambio de mentalidad de una España medieval, varia, estructurada en células aisladas, a una España renacentista, recién unida, centralizada en manos reales, y necesitada del control del Estado y de los monarcas para conseguir la integración total que éstos pretenden" (change of attitude from a medieval Spain that was varied, structured in isolated cells, to a Renaissance Spain, recently united, centralized in royal hands, and requiring control by the state and monarchs to achieve the total integration that they seek).[31] It should be remembered that, while Henry VIII (r. 1509–1547) formally severed England's ties with the Roman Catholic Church in 1534, the Catholic Philip II of Spain (r. 1556–1598) warred against Pope Paul IV (r. 1555–1559) in 1556.

The frontmatter of the indexes expresses the role of the Spanish Catholic Inquisition as both a religious and a national-political institution in Spain's newly united territories, its independence from the Roman Catholic Church, in a manner different in degree from but similar in kind to the English crown's. Published between the Roman Catholic indexes of 1681 that lists Pope "Innoc XI.P.M." on its title page and of 1758 that lists "Benedicti

XIV Pontificis Maximi" lies the Spanish Catholic Inquisition's 1707 Marín Index, with its title page advertising "Pro Catholicis Hispaniarum Regnis, Philippi V.Reg.Cath." The title page refers to a Spanish monarch and makes no reference to the then-current pope, Clement XI (r. 1700–1721). Likewise its prefatory material features Spanish inquisitors.

The Spanish Catholic Inquisition, on the front and indeed the frontier lines of Christendom, increasingly relied on its own resources to shape its readers, citizens, and coreligionists. Henry Lea notes one prominent example of the Spanish Catholic Inquisition's independence at the beginning of the seventeenth century. The Roman Catholic Inquisition solicited the Spanish Catholic Inquisition to include Galileo in its indexes, to be in accordance with its own. But the Spanish Catholic Inquisition refused.[32] We can add another difference: the 1664 and 1726 Roman Catholic indexes do not list Milton, but the 1707 and 1764 Spanish Catholic indexes do.[33]

How do English authors and texts, and by extension Milton and his works, factor among the external dangers that Spain perceived? The answers can be gathered in part by the national ascriptions of the authors or languages of the entries. In the 1707 Marín Index, "Class I" entries consist of the names of heretical authors whose entire oeuvre is prohibited and tampered works by Christian authors that need expurgations: "Prima classis auctorum damnatæ memoriæ, quorum Opera edita, & edenda sunt prohibita: nisi expurgata, aut, quod videantur innoxia, nominatim permittantur" (First class of authors of damned memory, whose published and forthcoming Works are prohibited: but individual works are permitted which have been expurgated or else because they seem harmless).[34] "Class II" lists the authors of works requiring expurgation or careful attention: "Secunda classis. In qua certorum avctorum libri aut prohibentur, aut expurgantur, aut cautione, explicationeve adhibita, notantur" (The second class, in which the books of certain authors are either prohibited or else expurgated or else are marked by the addition of a caution or an explanation).[35] This is where we find, for example, *Don Quixote* and directions regarding one passage from the novel: "MIGUEL de Cervantes. | Su segunda parte de *Don Quixote*, cap. | 36. al medio, *borrese* las obras de caridad que se hacen floxamente, no teinen merito, ni valen nada" (MIGUEL de Cervantes. | Its second part of *Don Quixote*, chap. | 36. in the middle, *erase* the works of charity that are done lazily do not have merit, they are worth nothing).[36] Finally, "Class III" is for anonymous and corporate works, either prohibited or requiring expurgation. A particularly germane example from the "M III. Class" section in the 1707 Marín Index is the twenty-three-line entry for a work that is often ascribed to Milton but remains of dubious ascription: *Manifiesto del Protector de Inglaterra . . . causa contra España*.[37] This Spanish-language work, originally published in 1655 in Latin, English, and Spanish under the authority of the Cromwellian government, possesses no ascription of national origin in the index.

As in many less provocative, collaborative works updated over centuries, like the *Dictionary of National Biography*, the Spanish Catholic indexes are rife with discrepancies, as to be expected in a work compiled by many hands over centuries.[38] The indexes haphazardly deploy national and religious identities as well as authors' occupations, sometimes omitted, at other times highlighted. Some entries in the 1707 Marín Index have information on the authors but not their works. The 1790 Rubín Index is consistently sparse, as one can note readily from its Milton entry: it includes only Milton's name in Latin, nationality, and heretical class, reflecting what seems to be an overall attempt in that index to make the work more user-friendly for the merchants, booksellers, censors, and other members of the Spanish book trade. The 1844 Palacios Index then adds information, and not reinsertions but rather new matter, as we can again observe readily from the Milton entry, in what must have been the result of an enormous amount of work.

According to Joseph Peréz's analysis of the 1559 Valdés Index, most of the 701 texts are in Latin (446), with vernaculars represented, for example, by Spanish (65), Flemish (50), German (13), Portuguese (12), and French (10). English texts are absent. My analysis of the first volume in which Milton's name appears, volume 1 of the two-volume 1707 Marín Index, indicates that only 2.67 percent of the roughly 3,076 entries in Class I and II are authors identified as "Anglus" (see Appendix A).[39] The list of prohibited Class I and II authors whose works are listed in their vernaculars in the 1707 Marín Index are Spanish (195), Italian (35), French (32), Portuguese (16), Flemish (6), English (2), and German (1).

This dearth of English entries demonstrates the rather exclusive nature of Milton's presence in the series. It should not, however, be attributed solely to national animosities. England's peripheral cultural status in the early modern period also accounts in part for the low level of cultural commerce between England and Spain during the period. As Thomas Corns avers, Milton himself, "as a fairly well-travelled humanist intellectual," recognized that, in "the seventeenth century England was positioned on the edge of European consciousness, its language rarely understood outside mercantile ports with direct links to England, its towering literary achievements unconsidered by the French or Spanish or Germans or Italians (though the Dutch evidently had some enthusiasm for its works of popular piety in translation). Occasionally, a play of Shakespeare had been translated; there's a Dutch *Taming of the Shrew*, for example. Latin works by English authors did fare better."⁴⁰ That said, while the English were perceived and represented in Spain as peripheral culturally and linguistically, the opposite is the case politically. Plus, each and every entry in the indexes represents a danger according to the Spanish Catholic Inquisition and thus to be taken seriously. Milton might be considered particularly dangerous given that the works listed in his entries are in Latin and Italian, languages quite accessible to many Spanish readers. Some Anglophone works by and about other English politicians and writers would have been provocative for Spanish readers but inaccessible linguistically to many, as in the case of "*Fvlko Grevil, Theliffe Ofthe Renovud- | ne, Senior Phillip. Cidnæy."⁴¹

As one of the main co-creators of the 1707 Spanish Catholic index, the inquisitor Vidal Marín certainly depicts the indexes as major weapons in a battle between good and evil that is as ferocious as Milton depicts in the War in Heaven in *Paradise Lost*, as insidious as Satan's temptation of the Son in *Paradise Regained*, and as tragic for individuals and nations as encapsulated in *Samson Agonistes*. Correlatively, Marín constructs the roles of the institution's scholarly members as heroic against the visible signs of invisible evil, in contrast to Milton's risible depiction in *Areopagitica*: "La Continua malicia de los hereges, procura afear la hermosura de la Iglesia, desde que naciò, no lo han conseguido, no lo conseguiaràn, aunque armados de todo el veneno del Infierno" (The Continual malice of heretics seeks to deform the beauty of the Church since it was born; they have not achieved it, they shall never achieve it, though they be armed with all the venom of Hell).⁴² Marín represents the Church as needing protection so that it avoids the same fate as Milton's Truth in *Areopagitica*. Milton's Truth "came once into the world with her divine Master, and was a perfect shape most glorious to look on: but when he ascended, and his Apostles after him were laid asleep, then strait arose a wicked race of deceivers, who as that story goes of the *AEgyptian Typhon* with his conspirators, how they dealt with the good *Osiris*, took the virgin Truth, hewd her lovely form into a thousand peeces, and scatter'd them to the four winds" (*CPW* 2.549). Marín takes it as a unified institutional body's job—his and that of the three other inquisitors named in the preface, as well as the cadre of Spanish Inquisition officials—to protect the souls of the Church's flock. The express purpose of the index is clear: to be "en beneficio publico de los Catholicos, y a fin de quitarles las ocasiones que el demonio, y sus Ministros les ofrecen con libros, tratados, y escritos, que son los Maestros que á todas horas enseñan, y persuaden sus errores" (of public benefit to Catholics, and with the end of removing from them the occasions that Hell and its Ministers offer them with books, texts, and writings, which are Teachers that teach at all hours, and persuade with their errors).[43] While *Areopagitica* similarly personifies books, it repeatedly refutes the efficacy of institutional control for removing occasions of sin. Milton instead defines the appropriate agents to be a diffuse group, the "sad friends of Truth" (*CPW* 2.549). Marín and Milton share a passionate commitment to the unity of a beleaguered ideal and to their nation's citizens, but they would fulfill such a commitment by nearly opposite means.

As we explore the rationale and effects of censoring foreign—and, in Milton's case, foreign and deceased—writers, we round out the important critical accounts of the Spanish Catholic indexes that have garnered the lion's share of their study, accounts of the harassments and punishments meted out to native heretic authors, *conversos*, booksellers, and other targets of the Spanish Catholic Inquisition's executive branch. Limiting and redirecting Michel Foucault's mid-twentieth-century question, we might ask: What is an author insofar as the Spanish Catholic indexes are concerned? Scholars familiar with the indexes gather quickly that the authors listed are not necessarily heretics. The logic is not inconsistent, given the high incidence of counterfeit and defective publications. Pirated and poor quality publications account in part for the repeated explanations by many authors of the early modern period for their decision to publish their works: Sir Philip Sidney, Sir Thomas Brown, and Sir Isaac Newton use the humility *topoi* and Cervantes and others burlesque. Since their beginnings in the sixteenth century, the prefaces of the Spanish Catholic indexes indicate that the names of some authors are included not because the authors were heretics but because their works had become heretical at the hands of others who corrupted their works:

> Se advierte, que quando se hallaren en este Cathologo prohibidos, o expurgados algunos libros de sugetos de gran Christianidad, y Santidad conocida en el mundo; no es porque los tales Auctores se ayan desviado del sentir de la Santa Iglesia Romana . . . sino porque, ò son libros que falsamente se los han atribuido, no siendo suyos, ó por hallarse en los que lo son algunas palabras, y sentencias agenas, que con el mucho descuydo de los Impressores, ò con el desmasiado cuydado de los Hereges se las han falsamente impuesto.

> (We warn that when some prohibited or expurgated books on the great topics of Christianity or of world-renown sanctity are found in this Catalogue, it is not because those Authors had strayed from the

sense of the Holy Roman Church, . . . but rather because either they are books that have been falsely attributed to them, not being theirs, or some alien words or statements in them due to the great carelessness of the Printers, or with the great carefulness of Heretics that have been falsely added.)⁴⁴

This is the case with St. Augustine, Gregory the Great, and other Church Fathers listed in the indexes. Because of the varied reasons for inclusion, the 1707 Marín Index specifies the authors deemed heretical, authors like "Hæ- | retic" Milton. Finally, the tripartite classification system of the Spanish Catholic indexes into Class I, II, and III, as already described, reflects the Spanish Catholic Inquisition's recognition of the independent nature of texts produced through corporate control or once they were out of their authors' possession.

Like the Spanish Catholic Inquisition, Milton acknowledges the prevalence of tampered works by Church Fathers. In *Of Reformation* he asks with scholarly scorn, "Who is ignorant of the foul errors, the ridiculous wresting of Scripture, the Heresies, the vanities thick sown through the volums of *Justin Martyr, Clemens, Origen, Tertullian,* and others of eldest time?" He summarizes a "threefold corruption": "1. The best times were spreadingly infected. 2. The best men of those times fouly tainted. 3. The best writings of those men dangerously adulterated" (*CPW* 1.551, 549).⁴⁵ George N. Conklin notes Milton's repetition of this sentiment in *De doctrina Christiana*: the Old Testament as much as "the New Testament, has been liable to frequent corruption, and in some instances has been corrupted, through the number, and occasionally the bad faith of those by whom it has been handed down."⁴⁶ This is to say that texts transformed from the direct products of authors to cultural constructs at each step along the book trade.

The Spanish Catholic Inquisition was well aware of its bureaucratic shortcomings and by extension the great room for error in casting judgment on the status of individuals' souls based on texts that circulated under their names. The preface to the 1707 Marín Index laments that some texts are entirely banned rather than expurgated because the latter would be too time-consuming given the institution's limited resources: "Las mezclas que han hecho de sus errores con los Padres, no se refieren por ser innumerables, esto con tan atenta malicia, que sino es prohibiendo todo el libro, no se puede distinguir lo malo, de lo bueno" (The mixings that they have made through their errors with the Church Fathers, which are not referenced because they are innumerable, this with such attentive malice, that all the book is prohibited, the bad cannot be distinguished from the good).⁴⁷ This is the practical, bureaucratic side that Milton articulated in *Areopagitica*: "Good and evill we know in the field of this World grow up together almost inseparably; and the knowledge of good is so involv'd and interwoven with the knowledge of evill, and in so many cunning resemblances hardly to be discern'd, that those confused seeds which were impos'd on *Psyche* as an incessant labour to cull out, and sort asunder, were not more intermixt" (*CPW* 2.514). What Milton's passage characterizes as a burdensome and all but futile task, the Spanish Catholic Inquisition took as its ideal, albeit an unfulfilled one.

Perhaps reflecting its recognition of its human limitations, the scholarly branch of the Spanish Catholic Inquisition prescribed firm consequences for offenders, but certainly not as severe on individuals' earthly existence as brutal imprisonment or death. Per the 1707 Marín Index, the punishments for individuals possessing any books after ninety days of the publication of the list, because they are in a state of "pecado mortal, que es cierta (por la inobediencia avràn cometido) incurran en pena de excomunion serenda" (mortal sin, which is certain [for the disobedience that they will have committed], they incur as penalty just excommunication), as well as removal of their books and a fine of "seiscientos ducados aplicados por tercias partes, à gastos del Santo Oficio, Juezes, y denunciador, y otras penas" (600 ducats payable in three payments, for the expenses of the Holy Office, Judges, and accuser, and other troubles).[48] We must clearly acknowledge that, whatever the intent or letter of the law of the scholarly branch of the Spanish Catholic Inquisition, "the letter killeth," as St. Paul well notes and himself too well experienced, and as has been well documented in terms of the executive branch of the Spanish Catholic Inquisition.[49] No corporal consequences, of course, can result for deceased authors and authors outside of national territories, such as Milton.

Authors or, more rightly stated, author-functions also become cultural constructs through the various forces within the book trade, like the Spanish Catholic Inquisition. For example, none of the indexes labels Milton a "poeta," used for well over one hundred other writers in the first volume of the 1707 Marín Index. Milton's entry in that index lists only a prose work; the 1790 Rubín Index no works; the 1844 Palacios Index a prose work and a poetic work, the latter the Italian translation of *Paradise Lost* by Paolo Rolli. Regular users of the Spanish Catholic indexes would have reserved judgment on wherein lay the heresy of the Italian translation: the author, the poem's original publication, an insidious Italophone translator, unintentional corruptions in the Italophone translation, or the creator(s) of the original or Italophone editions' paratexts. In any event, all three indexes present a narrow and unattractive figure of Milton. As Neil Forsyth observes, Anglophone readers have known Milton as primarily the great English epic poet, his political republicanism taken up by the Romantics and then by scholars in the late twentieth century.[50] In contrast, both early and later Spanish references to Milton regularly represent him as a political figure, his prose deemed heretical for its censure of hierarchy and its pro-Protestant stance in international politics, and thus of interest primarily to historians and theologians. Milton's works were assuredly "of the Devils party," according to the Spanish Catholic Inquisition, but not interestingly so.[51]

In the 1790 Rubín Index, Milton's works do not appear assuredly or even easily heretical. The enlarged prefatory material includes the section "Señales parra la calidad de la Censura" (Signals for the nature of the Censure) that advises general users that "Aquellos Autores, cuyos Libros están todos prohibidos, se señalan, poniendoles una estrellita (*), ó con esta señal i. cl. (i.a Classis ó i.a Clase)" (Those Authors whose Books are all prohibited are signaled by placing a little star [*], or with this sign 1. cl. [1.ª *Classis* or 1.ª Clase]).[52] Certainly the plurality of signals introduces confusion for users familiar with the asterisks used in the 1707 Marín Index to signal heresy per se, not prohibition more generally—users who might not even think to refer to the new preface. Further confusion is invited by another new sign in this index, that of a hand with a pointing finger, which signals that the works and authors are prohibited for both general readers and those who "tienen licencia de leer Libros prohibidos" (have a license to read prohibited Books).[53] While licenses by the Spanish Catholic Inquisition permitting individuals to read prohibited authors and works had existed for some time, the direct mention of such licenses advertises the Inquisition's recognition of different types of Spanish Catholic readers. Such a conception of diversity rather than uniformity among Spanish readers is in line with the spectrum of readers that Milton tacitly refers to in *Areopagitica*: the "worthy man" like Dionysius Alexandrinus and the "wise man" like himself, whom he contrasts with "the fool" and "childish man" whom no means will hinder from "his folly" (*CPW* 2.511, 521).

Two changes in the 1790 Rubín Index reconceptualize and represent authors less as human agents than as author-functions: the use of modern orthography and the use of surname rather than first name to organize the lists.[54] While these changes may seem inconsequential, they result in a vastly different reading experience. The first change results in a *J* rather than an *I* to start Milton's first name. This and similar changes, such as the use of "w" rather than "vv," removes the sense of historical depth implied by the previous indexes' orthography. The second change depersonalizes the author and reduces the intimacy created in seeing all those Ioanni together. These changes contribute to the overall prioritizing of the textual author-function over perdurable individual souls. The distancing between author and text, with an emphasis on the latter, is cannily similar to the process that Nicholas McDowell notes in Milton's representation of the two: "The displacement of Heresy from the individual to book is apparent . . . in the famous images of books as martyrs in *Areopagitica*."[55]

This distancing extends into the 1844 Palacios Index. While that index returns to a more in-depth approach, it does not reintroduce the designator "Hæ- | retic" into the Milton entry. The earlier personal charge of heresy against "IOANNES MILTHONIVS" in the 1707 Marín Index concentrates attention on an individual author and an individual soul, countermanding Milton's assertion in *Pro populo Anglicano defensio* that he wrote the work as a corporate spokesperson for the Interregnum government: "The leaders of our state have authorized me to undertake this task" (*CPW* 4.305). The greater interest in the lives of books, and by extension their interactions with current readers, than in the spiritual state of authors is pithily summed up in the difference of meaning between the marks preceding Milton's name on the 1707 Marín Index and the 1844 Palacios Index. The asterisk in the former marks Milton as a heretical author; the cross in the latter simply marks the entry as being also present on the Roman Catholic index: "Los libros prohibidos por S. Santidad segun el índice impreso en Malinas, que se han intercalado en sus respectivos lugares en el presente, llevan delante este signo +" (The books prohibited by His Holiness the Pope, according to the index published in Mechelen, that have been collated in their respective places in the present edition, have in front of them this sign +).[56] Thus the 1790 Rubín Index and 1844 Palacios Index participate in the construction of modern forms of reception that situate authors within their historical roles and emphasize networks of power relations, overriding attention on individuals and individual souls.

Without the descriptor "Hæ- | retic," the 1844 Palacios Index reflects more accurately the corporate nature of Milton's works, or better said of works attributed to the author-function Milton. Milton's name functions as it does in current electronic catalogues, or indexes, as a cipher to be decoded actively by users. For example, like the 1844 Palacios Index, many electronic catalogues list Milton as the author of *Literae pseudo-senatus* (1676), printed two years after his death. These catalogues often include the corrective note that the work is a "surreptitious publication of dispatches written by Milton in his capacity of Latin secretary to the Council of State, between the years 1649 to 1659."[57] This work, which attracted much interest in England

and abroad both immediately and later, bears no publishing identification in its first three issues.⁵⁸ Essentially the wily work leaks high-level government information from the mid-seventeenth century. The full title of the posthumously published "LITERÆ | *PSEUDO-SENATŪS ANGLICANI,* | *Cromwellii,* | Reliquorumque Perduellium | nomine ac jussu con- | scriptæ | A | JOANNE MILTONO" (Letters Written by John Milton in the Name and by the Order of the So-called English Parliament of Cromwell and Other Traitors) subordinates Milton's agency to that of the Interregnum government.⁵⁹ The original title page reinforces the precedence of England's Lord Protector Oliver Cromwell as authorizing agent through the larger front size used for his name, the use of the ablative rather than genitive for Milton's name, and the use of "conscriptæ" to describe Milton's participation.⁶⁰ Electronic catalogues variously ascribe authorship of the work to Milton, "Lord Protector (1653–1658; O. Cromwell), England and Wales," the corporate body of the "Council of State, England and Wales," and a combination of these.⁶¹ The work is not cross-listed in the 1844 Palacios Index by its title or under "Cromwell"—there is no Cromwell entry. Despite these connotative and denotative niceties, *Literae* did indeed circulate under Milton's name. The 1844 Rubín Index entry thus reflects and perpetuates the impression that, in his role as an early modern English government official, Secretary Milton wielded a high level of cultural capital.⁶²

The second entry in the 1844 Palacios Index, *Il Paradiso perduto,* further demonstrates the unwieldy, international nature of authorial representation.⁶³ Listed with *Literae, Il Paradiso perduto* indicates the growing international, multilingual commerce that the Spanish Catholic Inquisition was facing: the Latin of *Literae* for the educated elite in the Western world at large, the Italian for a large community of Italophone readers, including many Spaniards. What is equally important is what is *not* listed on the 1844 Palacios Index. Is *Pro populo Anglicano defensio* simply no longer available in Spanish territories, or is it no longer considered heretical? Both options are equally viable. Vílchez Díaz argues, "Los últimos años del siglo contemplan un cambio" (The last years of the [eighteenth] century evince a change) that is "drástico en el mundo occidental. Cae el concepto de monarquía de origen divino y incluso el de monarquía a secas" (drastic in the Western world. The concept of a monarchy of divine origin, including absolute monarchy, falls by the wayside).⁶⁴ There is also the matter of the absence of the English *Paradise Lost* and two full Spanish translations of the epic. The verse translations by Escóiquiz of 1812 and by Benito Ramón de Hermida Maldonado of 1814 were both published well before 1844.⁶⁵

We might assume the reason for the absence of these Spanish translations, which indeed were authorized in Spain, to be that they did not ruffle the feathers of the Spanish Catholic Inquisition as did Rolli's Italian *Il Paradiso perduto*. Indeed, the Escóiquiz translation, which has remained the most widely circulated Spanish translation, is avowedly Catholicized, as detailed in chapter 2. The preface indicates that the translator, a Catholic priest in King Ferdinand VII's inner circle, actively removed all elements "ridiculas é indecentes contra los ritos y usos de la Iglesia católica, propias de la secta en que había nacido Milton, y que léjos de acrecentar el mérito del poema, lo desfiguran" (ridiculous or indecent, contrary to the rites and practices of the Catholic Church, characteristic of the religious sect into which Milton had been born, but which far from increasing the work's merit disfigure it).[66] In contrast, the Italian translation maintains Milton's scandalous parts.[67] While Rolli's *Il Paradiso perduto* translates rather faithfully Satan's famous blaspheming phrase "Better to reign in Hell, than serve in Heav'n" (*PL* 1.263), Escóiquiz's *El Paraíso perdido* omits it.[68] Similarly, while Rolli's *Il Paradiso perduto* contains Milton's passage of Adam and Eve engaging in prelapsarian sex (*PL* 4.736–70), the Escóiquiz follows up Adam and Eve's bedtime hymn to God with "Y en brazos de la paz, y la inocencia, / Al plácido descanso se entregaron" (in the arms of peace, and innocence, / They surrendered themselves to placid sleep).[69]

The decree dates, however, lead us to another likely or contributory reason for the absence of the two full Spanish translations: "22 decembris 1700" next to *Literae* and "21 de januarii 1732" next to *Il Paradiso perduto*. The preface to the 1844 Palacios Index indicates that it includes entries that the Spanish Catholic Inquisition had reviewed through 1805 and that the Roman Catholic Inquisition had reviewed through 1842. While both Inquisitions could act swiftly by means of decrees, like the English monarchy's 1660 edict censuring Milton's *Pro populo Anglicano defensio*, the indexes were notoriously delayed in being updated. Thus, if editions of *El Paraíso perdido* had made their way into Spanish or Roman inquisitors' hands, delays in the review of texts could result in an open passport for them to "[walk] the town a while," to echo Milton's sonnet about another one of his incendiary prose works that was anathema to nineteenth-century Catholicism, *Tetrachordon*, on the subject of divorce ("A book was writ of late," 3).

Two last matters regarding the 1844 Palacios Index reflect the interaction of the Spanish polity and its Inquisition. First, this index's unusually long delay in review and publication makes sense given the especially tumultuous political scene in early nineteenth-century Spain.[70] Second, its very publication testifies to the agency of the audience of the indexes. In 1812 Napoleon's designated head of Spain, Joseph I (r. 1810–1813), abolished the Spanish Catholic Inquisition, and the institution never regained power.[71] Yet some portions of the Spanish reading public actively sought guidance from their homeland's storied censorial institution in order to avoid works that might scandalize. Kamen notes that the decree of September 7, 1558, banning the introduction of all foreign books in Spanish translation, was thorough and effective and "remained theoretically in force until the end of the ancien regime."[72] The indexes were not just regulatory or optative on the part of censorial institutions but also reflective of reader reception.

Reading Milton in the Wake of the Spanish Catholic Inquisition

By exciting fear, whether political or spiritual, censorial institutions stifle some would-be casual readers from embroiling themselves in dangerous engagements and spur others to brave acts of reading, translation, and publication. Some Spaniards, however, evaded the fears and reprisals associated with the Spanish Catholic Inquisition for reading Milton's works. Benítez provides an important survey of partial translations of *Paradise Lost* and Miltonic presence within elite Spanish circles from 1750 to 1850. Here I focus on two testaments published in the decades preceding the 1790 Rubín Index and on two published after the 1844 Palacios Index, since they capture some important ways that Spanish elites engaged with Milton within their specific religious and social contexts in the decades of the Spanish Catholic Inquisition's waning institutional power.

The first two texts testify to Spaniards' recognition of the Western European canonization of Milton as "poeta," *pace* the indexes' withholding of that designator from Milton's entries. The cosmopolitan Enlightenment writer José de Cadalso y Vázquez (1741–1782) advertised his reading of *Paradise Lost* in the commercially successful satire *Los eruditos a la violeta, ó, curso completo de todas las ciencias dividido en siete lecciones para los siete dias della semana, con el Suplemento de este* (The Sciolists, or, a Complete Course of All Knowledge Divided into Seven Lessons for the Seven Days of the Week, with a Supplement for It; 1772). For Tuesday's topic, "Poesía, y Retórica" (Poetry, and Rhetoric), Cadalso provides a transhistoric, international list of works by the Greek Homer, Latin writers such as Virgil and the Ibero-Romans Lucan and Martial, the Spanish poets "Juan de Mena, Boscan, Garcilaso, Leon, Herrera, Ercilla, Mendoza, Villegas, Lope, Quevedo, &c," and many French and Italian writers before reaching Milton and Shakespeare:

De los Poetas Ingleses abominad á la francesa, diciendo que su Epico Milton deliró, quando puso artillería en el Cielo, cuando hizo hablar á la muerte, al pecado, &c. y no llamareis un punto menos que feróz á la Melpomene, que inspiró á Shakespear sus dramas lúgubres, fúnebres, sangrientos, llenos de Splin, y cargados de densos vapores de Tamesis, y de las negras particulas del Carbon de piedra.

(Of the English Poets condemned by the French, saying that Milton's Epic became nonsense when he put artillery in Heaven, when he made death talk, and sin, &c. and you would hardly use a term less than fierce Melpomene, who inspired Shakespeare in his gloomy dramas: dismal, bloody, full of Spleen, and charged with the dense vapors of the River Thames, and the black particles of Coal.)[73]

Nonetheless Cadalso concedes the necessity for any erudite Spaniard to know sections of *Paradise Lost* (although not any of Shakespeare's works). He thus provides in his ample "Suplemento" (63–156) to the text of *The Sciolists* (1–63) select portions of the epic in English followed by his Spanish translations for memorization, which he recommends in order to impress folks with a show of erudition. Cadalso constructs a pompous persona that assumes all his readers have the time and means to travel internationally, as he did, including to England. He suggests his readers memorize passages from others of Milton's works that they might find lying around either at home, where they would be protected by their well-heeled exceptional status, or abroad, beyond the reach of the Spanish Catholic Inquisition.

Yet for all the playful tone of the essay, details from the Spanish translations in Cadalso's work indicate either active or passive self-censorship. Benítez notes Cadalso's good selection for translation, the opening invocation (*PL* 1.1–49) and the dialogue between God the Father and the Son (*PL* 3.135–57, 167–72, 266–72), since "la invocación constituye un resumen de todo el contenido de la obra y el diálogo proporciona al lector católico una muestra de la grandiosa figuración del Dios Padre y de su relación con el Hijo. Se evitan en cambio, los aspectos de la obra más discutibles teológicamente, entre ellos la figura y los actos de Satán" (the invocation constitutes a summary of the whole content of the work and the dialogue supplies the Catholic reader with an example of the magnificent figuration of God the Father and his relationship with the Son. In turn, the most theologically debatable aspects of the work are avoided, among which the figure and actions of Satan). Benítez adds provisos: "No obstante, Cadalso vierte literalmente el verso «till one greater Man / restore us», idea que ha sido considerada una negación de la divinidad de Cristo" (Notwithstanding, Cadalso translates literally the verse 'till one greater Man / restore us,' an idea that has been considered a negation of the divinity of Christ), as does "the heav'ns and earth / Rose out of Chaos" (PL 1.9–10), with its heretical implication of the existence of matter prior to Creation.[74] Cadalso's selection is indeed much less incendiary than any of Milton's proscribed prose or passages from the epic that focus on Satan.

Cadalso's selection is not, however, as doctrinally and politically neutral as, for example, a French work of roughly the same period, a 1,940-line imitation of *Paradise Lost* by Anne-Marie Du Bocage, *Paradis terrestre* (1748). Christophe Tournu avers that "the two clear changes that Du Bocage made to Milton's original are deChristianizing and depoliticizing," managed through a focus on the marital union of Adam and Eve.[75] In constrast, Cadalso addresses the doctrinal matter of the divinity of Christ a second time in his brief selections. While he literally translates the ambivalent stance on the matter in the allusion to Christ in the invocation of book 1, as Benitez notes, he tilts toward a more doctrinally conservative coequality of God the Father and the Son in their dialogue in book 3:

> y el Hijo apareció, con nunca vista
> gloria, brillando en él su Padre todo
> con su virtud, y con su gloria misma,
> en su rostro el amor se vió divino.[76]

> Beyond compare the Son of God was seen
> Most glorious, in him all his Father shone
> Substantially expressed, and in his face
> Divine compassion visibly appear'd. (*PL* 3.138–41)

Milton's original differentiates between the Father and the Son, the latter characterized as a substantial expression of the former and thus countering the consubstantiality of these two members of the Trinity. Cadalso's translation is in greater accord than is Milton's original with Trinitarian doctrine through his translational choices of "con su virtud" (with his [the Son's] virtue) and "su gloria misma" (the same glory), especially given the repetition of "gloria" used one line earlier in describing the Son.

The staid four-volume, deluxe edition of *Don Quixote* (1780), published under the aegis of the Real Academia Española (Royal Spanish Academy), also exhibits active engagement with Milton the poet. The 102-page "Análisis del Quixote" defines the Spanish novel proudly as the "gloria del Ingenio Español, y precioso depósito de la propiedad y energía del Idioma Castellano" (glory of Spanish Ingenuity and precious repository of the power and energy of the Spanish language).[77] As part of its project to validate the cultural capital of this Spanish work, which the preface avers has in the "espacio de cerca de dos siglos" (space of close to two centuries) garnered "el mayor aplauso y estimacion entre las naciones cultas" (the highest applause and esteem among cultured nations), it refers to other canonical works in the world literature pantheon, like "*la* Eneyda *de Virgilio*," "*la* Jerusalen *del Tasso*," and "*el* Paraiso *de Milton*."[78] In the preface, Milton's epic poems are represented as strong works of world literature that Cervantes's works excel. For example, in explaining the "mayor dificultad" (major difficulty) in Cervantes's use of Don Quixote and Sancho Panza as the "dos personages solos en la mayor parte de su accion" (only two characters in the major part of story's action), it points to Milton as the only one "entre todos los poetas épicos" (among all the epic poets) who was able to "vencer una dificultad semejante" (overcome a similar difficulty) with Adam and Eve. Milton succeeded with the narrative dilemma by having the couple exhibit a wide range of emotions, "primero como dechados de perfeccion en el estado de la inocencia, y despues como exemplos de la infelicidad y miseria en el del pecado" (first as paragons of perfection in the state of innocence and then as examples of unhappiness and misery in the state of sin). This character depth is, however, a narrative strategy that Cervantes "buscó mucho ántes" (had found long before), in representing "Don Quixote unas veces discreto, otras loco, y manifestando succesivamente á Sancho como ingenuo y como malicioso" (Don Quixote sometimes as discrete, at other times crazy, and successively representing Sancho as ingenuous and as malicious).[79] Cervantes's *Don Quixote, Part II* also gets the upper hand over Milton's *Paradise Regained*. To exemplify the singularity of the excellent sequel (1615) to *Don Quixote* being even stronger than the 1605 original, the preface affirms, "Longino compara á Homero en la Odisea con el sol quando está en su ocaso, que conserva su grandeza, pero no tiene ni tanta fuerza, ni el mismo ardor. Igual censura han merecido el Paraiso conquistado de Milton, y los seis últimos libros de la Eneyda" (Longinus compares Homer in *The Odyssey* with the sun when it is in decline, which conserves its grandeur but does not possess either as much strength or the same ardor as does *The Iliad*. Milton's *Paradise Regained* and the last six books of *The Aeneid* have merited the same censure).[80]

While the tones of the Cadalso and Real Academia Española are vastly different, these two publications convey no apprehension about reading Milton's poems and shift his role from the political realm to a literary canon. They thus participate actively in the re-creation of that very canon, which includes Milton's poetry, if with some reservations. Further, those reservations are voiced as based on literary, not confessional, assessments. Of course, religion does factor in with the Cadalso, as shown, as does nationality, with the claim that the "Anglus" Milton and Shakespeare are predisposed to "nonsense" and "Spleen." Similarly, the Real Academia Española retains the association of texts and authors' personal characteristics in citing Milton's age as a factor in the lack of vigor in *Paradise Regained*.

It is impossible to determine if Cadalso's and the Real Academia Española's articulation of assessments based on literary standards mask confessional assessments or seek to humor conservative readers and institutions. Two writers of nineteenth-century Spain who clearly evince continuing preoccupations with authors' and readers' souls, heresy, and the close relationship of authors and texts are the poet Luis Alfonso Roman Martínez y Güertero (d. 1874), who wrote under the pseudonym Larmig, and the woman of letters Emilia Pardo Bazán (1851–1921).

Martínez y Güertero spent some years in London and, upon his return to Madrid until his suicide, was active in the Spanish literary scene of the time. His "Querellas del vate ciego" (The Blind Poet's Complaints), featuring Milton, circulated widely in a collection of poems by the luminaries of that Spanish literary scene. Pardo Bazán cites Martínez y Güertero's poem favorably in her literary criticism on Milton a decade later.[81] The 428-line "Complaints" represents the aged Milton on a walk with his beloved daughter Deborah and voicing regrets for his personal, political, and religious past. His rueful reflection on the execution of Charles I and his correlative disavowal of his regicidal prose and heresy could be a wish fulfillment for the Spanish Catholic Inquisition and for Romantics, including France's Alphonse de Lamartine.[82] For nine Sicilian quatrains (four pentameter lines rhyming *abab*), Martínez y Güertero's Milton recalls with pathos Charles I from the start of the civil wars, in which he trades his "corona" (crown) for "bruñida malla" (burnished mail [armor]), to his appearance with "su mirar severo" (his severe gaze) on the scaffold.[83] It is this Milton that merits the elevated title of "vate"—in the poem's title and sprinkled throughout—a role beyond that of "poeta," denied Milton on the Spanish Catholic Inquisition indexes. Martínez y Güertero transforms the apex of Milton's production in that role, *Paradise Lost*, into a coded confession of the author's misguided religious faith and political role. One can only speculate that Martínez y Güertero would have extended this salvific characterization in his unpublished last poem, "The Daughters of

Milton," which he is recorded to have shown his friend Núñez de Arce the day before his suicide.[84]

The heresy and nationality that the Spanish Catholic Inquisition linked to Milton are also concerns in Pardo Bazán's *Los poetas épicos Cristianos* (The Christian Epic Poets; c. 1880). Like Cadalso a century earlier, Pardo Bazán had traveled to London. She engages with the original English *Paradise Lost* in her "ensayos de critica biográfica" (essays of critical biography) on Dante, Tasso, Milton, Klopstock, and Chateaubriand.[85] She agrees with Cadalso's characterization of England as an ascetic, hard homeland for literature, especially in contrast to Spain, with its gentler citizens and institutions: "Nuestra Inquisición es espantajo de chiquillos, terrorífica pero inofensiva silueta esbozada sobre la pared, si la comparamos á la horrible tragedia de la Gran Bretaña, donde salieron á escena los titanes y las furias" (Our Inquisition is a scarecrow for children, a frightful but inoffensive shadow cast on the wall, if we compare it to the horrible tragedy of Great Britain, where titans and furies came onto the scene).[86] She describes the good disposition of Catholics, "la tolerancia exquisita, la cordialidad intelectual que han reinado siempre en la ciudad de los Pontífices" (the exquisite tolerance, the intellectual cordiality that have always reigned in the city of Popes), that Milton received in Rome during his European tour (1638–39): "Abrieron de par en par al joven poeta protestante las puertas de la Biblioteca Vaticana y sus tesoros, y le ofrecieron la amistad de los hombres más insignes de aquella época" (They spread wide open the doors of the Vatican Library and its treasures to the young Protestant poet, and they offered him the friendship of the most distinguished men of that era).[87]

Both the English Royalists and the Puritans of Milton's era stand in contrast to such ecumenical hospitality. Pardo Bazán harnesses the negative connotations of the word "inquisition" onto the Parliament's *"speaker,* [William] Lenthall" (she uses the English term) who set up "las víctimas de la Inquisición política, ó sea la *Cámara estrellada"* (the victims of the political Inquisition, which is to say the *Star Chamber*), and she repeats Thomas Macaulay's story of the soldiers led by Ironsides Oliver Cromwell: "Nunca se vieron jugadores ni borrachos, ni se oyeron blasfemias, ni se cometieron latrocinios ó impudicias" (No gamblers or drunkards were ever to be seen, no blasphemy was heard, no larceny or immodesty was committed). In contrast, the sight of "una imagen de Nuestra Señora, pintada en un vidrio, les enfurecía como al toro a el rojo trapo, infundiéndoles ansia de destrucción y delirio de muerte" (an image of Our Lady, in stained glass, infuriated them like a bull to a red cape, filling them with thirst for destruction and deathly delirium).⁸⁸ Milton's familial inclinations only intensified such national predispositions, according to Pardo Bazán, who infers that the firm adherence by Milton's father to Protestantism against his family's Catholicism "debió de influir mucho en la formación del carácter del hijo y comunicarle la firmeza" (had to influence greatly the formation of the character of his son and transfer to him a strong determination).⁸⁹ Finally, like the Real Academia Española (and the French critic Hippolyte Taine, among others), she points to Milton's biography to undermine the literary achievement of his masterwork *Paradise Lost*: "Cuando Milton anciano realiza el poema meditado desde la juventud, sus facultades están amortiguadas y yertas; la fuerza plástica de las imágenes ha disminuido" (When the aged Milton completes the poem, meditated on since his youth, his faculties are muffled and stiffened, the flexible power of imagery has diminished).⁹⁰

Given her focus on epic poetry, she mentions Milton's "prosa amazacotada, agria, casuística, dogmática" (heavy, sour, caustic, dogmatic prose) and other poetic works only in passing.⁹¹ On the one hand, she voices high regard for Milton's epic in the work's preface and participates actively in the international construction of world literature, as does the Real Academia Española. For example, she states that she found herself unable to include the masterwork of the Spanish Golden Age poet Fray Diego de Hojeda, *La Christiada* (1611), in her collection of essays because, upon studying it for the project, "empezó á parecerme un poema de tercer orden, indigno de figurar en la misma serie que Milton, y, sobre todo, que Dante" (it started to appear to me a third-tier poem, unworthy to figure in the same series as Milton and, above all, as Dante).⁹² On the other hand, similar to Cadalso and the Real Academia Española, she grants Milton's position within the Western canon with decided reservations: "Homero fué tan superior á Virgilio, como Dante á Milton y Milton á Chateaubriand" (Homer was as superior to Virgil as Dante to Milton and Milton to Chateaubriand).⁹³ Her rhetoric of literary evaluation, in textual conversation primarily with Taine and the British essayist Macaulay, is slowly replaced over the course of the seven chapters in "Milton" with religious characteristics specific to "la raza Latina" (the Latin race). She defines Dante's *Divine Comedy* as an artistic expression of the essence of Catholicism and *Paradise Lost* the essence of the Reformation: "En sentimiento y pensamiento; en impulso y vuelo genial; en imaginación, corazón y alma, Dante es fruto del Catolicismo, como Milton de la Reforma" (In feeling and thought; in impulse to genial flight; in imagination, heart, and soul, Dante is the fruit of Catholicism as much as Milton of the Reformation); both are "poetas-tipos y hombres-tipos de sus respetivas razas y religiones" (poet-types and human-types of their respective races and religions).[94]

As a whole, Pardo Bazán's assessment would leave her Spanish readers unenthusiastic about reading Milton's epic but willing to do so for cultural refinement, much in the vein of Cadalso's readers. She characterizes *Paradise Lost* as a work of national importance but ultimately unengaging to Spanish readers because, "a pesar del juicio de Macaulay, no contamos á *El Paraíso perdido* entre las producciones más insignes del espíritu humano" (notwithstanding Macaulay's judgment, we do not count *Paradise Lost* among the most significant productions of the human spirit).[95] She limits Milton's "fit audience . . . though few" (*PL* 7.31) to English readers:

> En efecto, para Inglaterra se escribió *El Paraíso perdido*. . . . En asunto y estilo, el poema era cortado á la medida de la nación. A una raza empapada en la Biblia ofrecía Milton la Biblia adaptada al siglo XVII y despojada desu sospechosa vehemencia oriental de su poesía primitiva, fuerte, perfumada como la mandrágora.
>
> (Essentially, *Paradise Lost* was written for England. . . . In matter and style, the poem was shaped for the nation. Milton offered to a race saturated in the Bible a Bible adapted for the seventeenth century and divested by its suspicious oriental vehemence of its primitive, strong poetry, perfumed like a mandrake.)[96]

She goes further than does the Real Academia Española in its account of the tepid nature of *Paradise Regained* as the frail work of an old man. According to Pardo Bazán, Milton's poetic power "parece amenguado y reducido, sea por los años, sea por la acción de fuerzas de distinto orden, de índole más intelectual y ética que artística" (appears diminished and reduced, be it due to his years, or due to the action of powers of a distinct order, of a temper more intellectual and ethical than artistic).[97] Further, Milton's poetic powers cannot be catholic, which is to say universal, because they are Protestant: "Un artista *completo* no puede ser protestante. Católico ó pagano, sí; protestante, no" (A *complete* artist cannot be Protestant. Catholic or pagan, yes; Protestant, no).[98] Thus, in the concluding sentence of the essay, she ironically instantiates Milton's assessment in *Areopagitica* that all books will serve the "discreet and judicious Reader . . . to discover, to confute, to forewarn, and to illustrate" erroneous material (*CPW* 2.512–13): "Milton, protestante y puritano, afianza en nuestro corazón y nuestra fantasía de latinos el sentido católico; Milton, intérprete de un ideal que no es el nuestro, nos lleva con ímpetu redoblado hacia nuestro constante ideal" (Milton, Protestant and Puritan, calls together the Catholic essence in our heart and our imagination as Hispanics; Milton, interpreter of an ideal that is not ours, returns us with redoubled impetus to our constant ideal).[99] As much as Martínez y Güertero's characterization of a penitent Milton in "The Blind Poet's Complaint" seems like a wish fulfillment for the stated aim of the Spanish Catholic Inquisition of overturning heresy, Pardo Bazán's final analysis of Milton's English, Protestant epic reads like a consolation for its scholarly branch that, even after its demise, some members of the Spanish elite could take up their work of projecting a tepid view of the canonical Milton.

Conclusion

The Spanish Catholic Inquisition was a protean, unwieldy network that greatly impacted the multilingual commerce of books, authorial representation, and reader reception, as Milton's *Areopagitica* argued national and international censorial institutions were capable of doing. The scholarly branch of the Spanish Catholic Inquisition was part of a religionational institution that was, in turn, part of a larger international organization, both full of bureaucratic shortcomings. Nonetheless the Spanish Catholic Inquisition was successful by and large in its intent to suppress the circulation of Milton's works in Spain through its unique set of indexes. In the eighteenth and nineteenth centuries it advanced an unattractive figure of Milton among Spanish readers, especially in regard to his incendiary political prose works in Latin during a period when elite readers were regularly trained in that lingua franca. We find versions of that figure enduring in the works of elite Spanish readers of the late eighteenth and nineteenth centuries, as the institution's power waned and as the use of vernacular languages throughout Europe waxed. Milton's optimistic vision in *Areopagitica* of an England with open access to books bustling with informed citizen-readers engaging in "much arguing, much writing, many opinions" contrasts with Spaniards' tepid reception of his works when those works had free passage in Spain beginning in the nineteenth century, when the power of the Spanish Catholic Inquisition waned (*CPW* 2.554). It would be an overstatement, however, to say that Milton remained in "dark oblivion" (*PL* 6.380) among Spaniards, as did other authors listed on the Spanish Catholic indexes. A more judicious assessment is that Milton's unexciting characterization trumped his infamy so that he was not a darling of a rebellious Spanish readership upon the decline of the Spanish Catholic Inquisition.

The Spanish reception of Milton's works upon the censorial institution's decline contrasts with the English reception of censored books in the early modern English book trade. According to Stephen Dobranski, when specific books were "burnt publicly," their demand increased.[100] David Norbrook notes a similar dynamic with "anti-clerical texts" in Catholic Italy: "The more zealously the Inquisition tried to control the production of books in Italy, the more enthusiastically did printers elsewhere try to meet the demand."[101] The referent of Norbrook's "Inquisition" is of course the Roman Catholic Inquisition, not the Spanish Catholic Inquisition. The Roman Catholic Inquisition superintended the literary histories of Italy and most other Catholic countries, in general and in terms of Miltonic reception.[102] Because those other Catholic countries interacted directly as a network with a shared central node, their literary histories are much more related to each other than they are to that of Spain, which was superintended by the related Spanish Catholic Inquisition.[103] Spain stood near but not among that specific network, contributing to a cultural isolation that the series of indexes sought to create and that later Spaniards would seek to counter, as well as to a cultural ambivalence that subsequent chapters explore.

CHAPTER 2

"As May Express Them Best"
Spanish Translations of *Paradise Lost*

Spanish translations of Milton's works have done little to inspire Spanish general readers or scholars to embrace or dedicate their energies to the most established canonical early modern English writer after Shakespeare. This is not a result of lack of Spanish translations of Milton's works, especially of *Paradise Lost*.[1] While no full Spanish translations of Milton's epic were published until the nineteenth century, they make up for their delay with number: at least nineteen distinct full Spanish translations of *El Paraíso perdido* emerged from 1812 to 2005 (see Appendix B).[2] It is a sum approximated only by French translations, which number eighteen.[3] The proximity in the number of Spanish and French translations of *Paradise Lost*, however, does not extend to their reception or contributions to Milton studies. Despite the high number of distinct versions of *El Paraíso perdido*, their sales, impact, and circulation have been consistently lower than those of *Le Paradis perdu*. In her Spanish introduction for would-be twenty-first-century Hispanophone readers of Milton's epic, Anna K. Nardo rightly states, "Se dice que *El Paraíso perdido* es el poema más importante que nadie se ha leído" (It is said that *Paradise Lost* is the most important poem that nobody reads).[4]

Why the negligence on the part of general Spanish readers and critics, despite so many translations? As demonstrated in chapter 1, the Spanish Catholic Church that superintended Spanish reading habits until the mid-nineteenth century contributed to the limited and tepid reception of Milton in Spain by its inclusion of his name in its infamous lists of proscribed texts and authors, the *Index librorum prohibitorum*. These proscriptions, however, are insufficiently explanatory after the Spanish Catholic Inquisition's influence waned, much less so when we consider the Anglophilia and bibliophilia that Spaniards displayed in the late eighteenth and nineteenth centuries.[5] E. Allison Peers demonstrates that Edward Young and Thomas Gray were "sources of inspiration," or at least attribution, for Spanish writers as much as for other Europeans in the eighteenth century.[6] Peers's discussion of those authors includes two translators of Milton's *Paradise Lost*: the cosmopolitan Enlightenment writer José de Cadalso y Vázquez (1741–1782), whose partial translation is discussed in the previous chapter, and Juan Escóiquiz, whose full verse translation is central to this chapter. Further, Spanish translations of Shakespeare's plays from the eighteenth century onward by native translators such as Leandro Fernández de Moratín, Marcelino Menéndez y Pelayo, and Guillermo Macpherson y Hemas, and British Hispanophiles like Jaime Clark, have earned the praise of Hispanophone critics, circulation among readers, appreciation on the stage, and secure positions on library shelves.[7] We also possess moving Spanish translations of the English religious poems of John Donne, as highlighted in Antoine Berman's *Towards a Translation Criticism: John Donne*.[8] Finally, Francisco Lafarga cites the publication of the two first full Spanish translations of *Paradise Lost* of 1812 and 1814 as correlative to the "no menos de cuatro versions de los *Salmos* de David" (no fewer than four versions of the *Psalms* of David), published, with permission, between 1785 and 1800 as evidence of the flourishing of religious publications in Spain at the end of the eighteenth and beginning of the nineteenth century.[9]

Lafarga's contextualization rightly calls attention to the complicated nexus of "linguistic, literary, and socio-cultural" as well as "contextual, intertextual, and situational elements" endemic to translations and their reception, as James S. Holmes and others have so cogently outlined.[10] The sociocultural certainly springs to the fore with Milton's Spanish translations given the well-known political animosities between early modern England and Spain and the unavoidable Anglo-Protestant nature of Milton's works. The fact that a number of Spanish translations of *Paradise Lost* emerged during Spanish regime shifts—the adoption of the Spanish Constitution (1812–13), the end of the First Spanish Republic (1873–74), and the end of Francisco Franco Bahamonde's dictatorship (r. 1936–1975)—is suggestive. However, other translations emerged in years that were relatively uneventful in Spanish politics.

We do well, thus, to heed Holmes's call to create a solid foundation for a "translational sociology" that might account for reader reception of Spanish translations of *Paradise Lost* by making good progress on the earlier "phase" of a "comparative translation description, in which comparative analyses are made of various translations of the same text."[11] The question then shifts from "Why the negligence on the part of general Spanish readers and critics, despite so many translations?" to "What can we learn from the textual products of some of Milton's most attentive Spanish readers, which is to say his translators?" This chapter provides an answer through comparative analyses of the texts and paratexts of a number of Spanish translations of *Paradise Lost* and shows that we can learn much from them about Spanish reading practices, our own reading practices, and Milton's epic.

While my analyses are extensive, they do not aim to be comprehensive given the sheer number of Spanish translations of Milton's epic, the variety of types of translations, and matters of access. Instead the first Spanish verse translation of Milton's epic, by Juan Escóiquiz of 1812, and first Spanish prose translation, attributed to Cayetano Rosell of 1873, garner the greatest attention because they have remained the most often cited and sold in Spain and most available in the Hispanophone and Anglophone worlds through today.[12] Attending to various versions of *El Paraíso perdido*, we encounter shared linguistic dilemmas and resolutions, great variety clustered around passages that address thorny religious matters, and uneven shifts in literary-cultural conventions related to epic tradition. The translators of Milton's epic display, appropriately enough, an independence that does not render discussion of their works by eras salient. This chapter is thus organized into three sections focused on linguistic dilemmas, religious concerns, and literary-cultural elements.[13]

By way of preface and to exemplify the overlap of these three elements, which will be otherwise muted for the sake of clarity, we can look to the first six lines of the freighted opening invocation of *Paradise Lost*. On the linguistic level Spanish translators face phonemic, syllabic, and connotative dilemmas in Milton's tour de force description of the effects of "man's first disobedience,"

> whose mortal taste
> Brought death into the w o r l d, || and all our woe. (*PL* 1.2–3, emphases mine)
>   1   2 3 4   4 3 2 1

All Spanish translators must accept the impossibility of replicating both the nearly uniform monosyllables and the alliterated "w" sounds. Spanish words tend to be syllabically longer than English ones, and, even though the donor language (the language in which a work is originally written) of English and the receptor language (the language into which the translation is taking place) of Spanish share Latin as a contributing source language, English, unlike Spanish, imported the "w" sound.[14] Escóiquiz opts for producing the alliterative effect with "d" and "n" sounds, Manuel Álvarez de Toledo with "m" and "t" sounds:

>   Escóiquiz: cuyo bocado,
>   Desterrando del mundo la inocencia
>   Dió entrada á los dolores, y á la muerte.
>   Álvarez de Toledo: cuyo fruto
>   Trajo al mundo la muerte y todo mal.[15]

Neither, however, replicates the four consonantal sounds directly preceding the caesura of line 3 and the sounds' reversal following it, as indicated by the reverse enumeration below the quotation of the English. Milton's poetics aurally represents the content of the epic, the changed dynamic from a pristine world into a still recognizable but toppled fallen world. A mimetic effect is possible, as we can see by versifying, so to speak, and slightly changing the Rosell prose translation:

>   Rosell: cuyo funesto manjar
>   trajo la muerte al *m*u*n*do y to*d*os *n*uestros *m*ales. (emphases mine)[16]
>   1 2 3   3 2   1

Despite the success of that aural replication, Rosell's first half line, "cuyo funesto manjar" (whose disastrous eating), fails to replicate the pun of Milton's original "mortal," meaning both *human* and *deadly*, even though the Spanish word *mortal* is readily available.

Milton's word-level, linguistic choice of "mortal" is rife with a central religious argument contained in the opening invocation and the epic as a whole. He uses the word six times in book 1 and thirty-two times in the entire epic, including in the invocations to books 1, 3, and 7, and perhaps most chillingly as Nature responds to "the mortal sin / Original" by weeping (*PL* 9.1003–4).[17] This first "mortal" stands between "man's" and "one greater man" (*PL* 1.1, 4), linked intimately through meaning and alliteration. The first "man" is most directly Adam but also all humankind—all "mortal" readers—and the "greater man" Jesus, who will "Restore us, and regain the blissful seat" for all mortals (*PL* 1.5). Many translators, including Benito Ramón Hermida de Maldonado, Rosell, and Bel Atreides, increase the affiliation between "man's" and "greater man" by translating both as "hombre"—the latter variably uppercase—driven by the fact that Spanish does not form the possessive through additions to the stem word, as is the case with the English possessive *'s*. Such a translation is not necessary, obvious, or uniformly utilized. For example, Escóiquiz clarifies the identity of the "greater man" with his translation, "el hijo del Eterno" (the son of the Eternal).[18] Álvarez de Toledo creates an even greater poetic division and emphasizes the general sense of the former with "Del pecado primero de los hombres" (Of the first sin of men) and the latter "Otro" (Other). Álvarez de Toledo's translation is accompanied by the English on facing pages, which can aid careful readers to apprehend the visual and verbal homology of the original—unfortunately, the English verse line in the Álvarez de Toledo volume possesses the first of its many typos, this one providing the unintentional vision of someone who cuts food into small pieces: "till one grater Man."[19] While less satisfying poetically, Escóiquiz's and Álvarez de Toledo's translations of "greater man" are more religiously conventional, since they reduce the heretical potential of a poetic line that, as Rubén Benítez notes, "ha sido considerada una negación de la divinidad de Cristo" (has been considered a negation of the divinity of Christ).[20]

Certainly a religious impetus can be attributed to Escóiquiz's term since his endnotes defend the divinity of the Son and argue for Milton's belief in the Trinity. However, literary-cultural significances also inhere in the term "man." With the use of "man" in the first verse line and repetition in the fifth, Milton calls attention to his imitation and extension of the convention of epic invocations. The foundational first verse line of Virgil's Latin *Aeneid* is "Arma virumque cano" (Of arms and the man I sing); the first two verse lines of Ludvico Ariosto's Italian *Orlando Furioso* "Le donne, i cavalier, l'arme, gli amori, / Le cortesie, l'audici imprese io canto" (Of ladies, knights, arms, love, / Courtesy, and daring feats I sing), with its elite and contextualized type of men; and the first verse line of Edmund Spenser's English *The Faerie Queene* "Lo I the man, whose Muse," combined with "And sing of Knights and Ladies" delayed to the fifth verse line.[21] Milton's English predecessor Spenser plays with the epic invocation in introducing ambiguity as to the agent, the narrator "I . . . Me" or the muse, who also appears in line 7. Milton displaces Spenser's bifurcations of "man" from narrator or muse to humankind, Adam, or Jesus and the agent in the sixth line, the "Heaven'ly Muse."

Escóiquiz proves himself as conservative with literary conventions as with religious matters. His translation begins in Virgilian mode with "Canto" (I sing). Rosell blends translational fidelity and flexibility with his translation's opening, "Canta, celeste Musa, la primera desobediencia" (Sing, heavenly Muse, the first disobedience), maintaining the verb in its conventional place of the first line but reflecting Milton's displacement of agency to the muse. Both Álvarez de Toledo and Atreides use the second-person verb in the sixth line in their translations at the turn of the twentieth-first century. Certainly the presence and tradition of epic conventions from especially Latin and Romance-language epics, like *The Divine Comedy*, and French translations and criticisms of *Paradise Lost* exerted a powerful force in Spanish translations of *Paradise Lost* in earlier periods. They were certainly at the fore for the translators of the two most enduring editions of *El Paraíso perdido*. Escóiquiz begins his own original epic, *México conquistada* (1798), in close accord with *The Aeneid* with "Las armas canto y el varon Hispano" (Of arms I sing and the Spanish man); Rosell published his Spanish translation of *La divina comedia* the year before his Spanish translation of *El Paraíso perdido*.[22] The translational choices of placement and agent are not to be explained simply by historical periods, with Escóiquiz and Rosell representative of eighteenth-century Spanish translators and Álvarez de Toledo and Atreides representative of the turn of the twenty-first century: Escóiquiz's contemporary Hermida uses the second-person singular verb and delays it further than the original, to line 9.[23] This brief analysis gives a sense of the translational diversity of the numerous translations of *El Paraíso perdido*.

Prefaces to Spanish translations of *Paradise Lost* often cite translational failure rather than translational diversity as their raison d'être. For example, in the preface to his 1914 Spanish prose translation of *Paradise Lost*, Juan Matéos opines, "Apenas habrá idioma moderno de país culto, en que el inmortal poema de Milton no tenga varias traducciones en prosa o verso. Tampoco escasean en español, mas por desgracia la calidad no corre pareja con el número" (There is scarcely a modern language in any cultured country in which Milton's immortal poem does not have various translations in prose and verse. Nor are they wanting in Spanish, more the disgrace that the quality does not equal the number).[24] We might hesitate to take the well-worn claim of the "mala calidad de la[s] versión[es] existente[s]" (bad quality of existing version[s]) at face value and instead credit it to translators' attempts to muster interest in their own work.[25] Such assessments, however, are not limited to Milton's translators. They are evidenced by low Hispanophone engagement with Milton's epic and are articulated regularly by Hispanophone literary critics. Benítez's close readings of the first two full Spanish verse translations provide sound justification that the Escóiquiz translation contains many passages that "leen bien y mantienen una considerable calidad en cuanto a la sonoridad de los versos. Pero en relación con el contenido, el traductor no tiene el menor respeto por el pensamiento del poeta" (read well and maintain a considerable quality insofar as the sonority of the verses. But in relation to the content, the translator does not have the least respect for the poet's thought) and that the Hermida deserves to be excused despite the fact that it possesses "algunos garrafales errores" (some awful errors) and displays a "manejo del verso libre o rimado ... tan deplorable que en su lectura se pierde toda la belleza y la sublimidad del poema inglés" (handling of the free and rhymed verse ... so deplorable that the reading loses all the beauty and sublimity of the English poem).[26]

This study does not shy away from calling attention to such matters as plain errors, as already done in pointing out the plentiful typos that mire one translation. I do not, however, engage in a blame game of Milton's translators. Indeed I call attention to some particularly excellent translational successes, and I hope that readers will share my appreciation for the dexterity that translators exhibit in the face of Milton's prosody, ideas, and reputation. Primarily my aim is to indicate the interrelated conundrums in translating *Paradise Lost* into Spanish as a foundation for accounting, in part, for the low reception of the high number of these translations, endeavoring to parse distinct translational elements rather than to focus solely on the lightning rod of religious divisiveness.

Linguistic Dilemmas

Some lexical choices in Spanish translations of *Paradise Lost* are impossible to explain, and there is always the difficult matter of register, whether based on translators' facility with the donor language or on readers' ears as based on idiosyncratic, regional, or historical contexts. For the matter of register, we can turn in brief to the "Hail wedded love" passage, in which Milton contrasts Edenic married sexuality to postlapsarian sexuality, with its "bought smile / Of harlots, loveless, joyless, unendeared, / Casual fruition" (*PL* 4.750, 765–67). Rosell understates Milton's reference as "la sonrisa venal de falsas, insípidas é impúdicas mercenarias" (the venal smile of false, insipid, and unchaste mercenaries), which is vague enough to include harlots and pimps.[27] Esteban Pujals uses the generalizing singular in his otherwise grammatically and denotatively accurate rendering, "sonrisa de la meretriz" (harlot's smile).[28] Álvarez de Toledo shocks by going to the other extreme in his rendering, "risas que se compran / De putas sin amor" (laughs purchased from sluts/whores without love). Álvarez de Toledo is uncompromising in his rendering of Milton's use of the word "harlot" after the Fall: "the harlot-lap / Of Philistéan Dálila" becomes "la ramera / Filistea Dalila" (the whore / Philistian Dalila). Further, the "bevy of fair women" becomes "Bellas hembras" (Beautiful females)—the term "hembras" can be used to refer simply to "females" but is also used with offensive connotations that align women with female animals (PL 9.1060–61, 11.582).[29] Atreides nicely retains the focus on the bodily relationship between Samson and Dalila by utilizing the Spanish popular expression "seno meretricio," which replaces the "lap" with the "seno" (breast) and means something like the heart of carnal sin.[30]

Two linguistic matters that are explicable, significant, and recurrent in a number of Spanish translations of *Paradise Lost* are prosody and grammatical gender. The majority of Spanish translations of *Paradise Lost* are verse, and thus their translators have to deal with the epic's prosody. The first two verse translations, by Escóiquiz and Hermida, vary from trimeters to alexandrines, with Escóiquiz tending toward the longer end. Milton gives heightened attention to prosody in "The Verse," the prose paragraph added to the epic's frontmatter in 1668 upon the request of the printer Samuel Simmons to explain to readers "why the Poem Rimes not."[31] Milton's definition—"the measure is English heroic verse without rime"—hints at a resolution for achieving translational fidelity in English-to-Spanish translations of the work.[32] George Puttenham's *Art of English Poesy* (1589) records the alliance between English heroic verse and "verses alexandrine," and the usefulness of the latter for translations of English into Romance languages since the average syllabic lengths of words tend to be shorter in the donor language.[33] In the preface to his translation, Enrique López Castellón asks, "¿En qué metro castellano debe verterse el pentámetro inglés?" (Into what Spanish meter should English pentameter be made?) and concedes that there is no right decision between "endecasílabo castellano . . . o el alejandrino de catorce" (hendecasyllabic Spanish . . . or the alexandrine of fourteen) syllables.[34] He limits the best choices to those two and, like Pujals and Álvarez de Toledo, uses hendecasyllabic meter for his translation.[35]

Part of the wit of the comment about *Paradise Lost* by the eighteenth-century British critic Samuel Johnson, that "None ever wished it longer than it is," rests on a chief distinguishing feature of *Paradise Lost* within the epic tradition.[36] At 10,565 lines of decasyllabic blank verse, it is brief for an epic. Milton's younger contemporary Andrew Marvell appropriately marveled at how Milton unfolded in such a "slender Book his vast Design" and at the poet's nimble utilization of English "Number, Weight, and Measure."[37] English, even when displaying more partiality to its multisyllabic Latin base than to its succinct Anglo-Saxon base, can be concise, cramming considerable content into the iambic pentameters that took hold of the early modern English stage and of course into the decasyllabic blank verse of *Paradise Lost*. While octosyllabic, hendecasyllabic, and hexameter lines are relatively common in Spanish poetry, they tend to contain fewer words and less content than their English equivalents.

Despite these obstacles, Hermida, Álvarez de Toledo, and Atreides manage to approximate Milton's original verse-line count. As to be expected, a byproduct of such concision is that details, including those of plot, setting, and description, sometimes get cast aside. Álvarez de Toledo's and Atreides's translations adhere as much as possible to the verse lines of the original English on facing pages, but Hermida's verse translation achieves its brevity through selective excision of many portions of the original and some additions. For example, while Milton's twenty-six-line invocation to book 1 becomes only twenty-five lines in the Hermida, Eve's modified sonnet in book 12 (*PL* 12.610–23), in which she expresses her bittersweet readiness to leave Paradise, becomes twenty lines. The Atreides shows the most expert handling of Eve's final modified sonnet. He maintains the same number of verse lines and makes the most of his choice of "amétrico trocaico" (ametric trochaic) verse.[38] The first ten lines of Eve's sonnet vary from twelve to fifteen syllables; the last four lines are fifteen, fifteen, sixteen, and eighteen syllables, giving a sense of reluctance and weight to the second half. Atreides again utilizes this technique shortly after, in the last lines of the poem:

> Tenían todo el mundo ante sus ojos, en que hallar
> Remanso ameno, y la Providencia como guía.
> Cogidos de la mano y con lentos pasos vagabundos
> A través de aquel Edén su senda solitaria comenzaron.[39]

> The world was all before them, where to choose
> Their place of rest, and Providence their guide:
> They hand in hand with wand'ring steps and slow,
> Through Eden took their solitary way. (*PL* 12.645–49)

Atreides builds the lingering effect in making the last two lines, of sixteen and eighteen syllables, follow upon two shorter lines, of fourteen and fifteen syllables. It should be noted that prose translations can also reflect Milton's prosody and style. For example, the Rosell prose translation comes close to matching the relative length of Eve's sonnet, which, given the nature of prose rather than verse, requires another form of comparison.[40] The Rosell renders the fourteen lines of the 649 lines total in book 12 in roughly 40 percent of one page of his eighteen pages. Both the original and the Rosell are thus nearly equivalent, at about 2 percent of book 12.

Increasing verse-line length is an established concession in English-to-Spanish translation; increasing the number of lines less so. In justifying his 1986 *El Paraíso perdido*, Pujals chastises the prolixity of the still-utilized Escóiquiz translation: "Escóiquiz tiende constantemente a la amplificación" (Escóiquiz tends constantly to amplification).[41] Pujals's claim does not simply reflect modern preferences for concision, as is evident by the "Nota de la editora" (Editor's note) in Hermida's 1814 Spanish verse translation:

> Habiéndose publicado otra traduccion del *Paraiso perdido* al tiempo mismo que esta, y siendo aquella voluminosa y esta pequeña, lo que podrá dar lugar á imaginarla incompleta. Se previene que la concision que se advierte, consiste en que no tiene tantas notas ni tanto prólogo, y está impresa sin luxo, y en que su exactitud es tan escrupulosa, que consta casi del mismo número de versos que el original de Milton.

> (Another translation of *Paradise Lost* having been published at the same time as this one, and that one being so long and this one brief, may give rise to imagine this one incomplete. One is forewarned that the concision noted lies in the fact that it does not have as many notes or as long a prologue, and this printing [is published] without extravagances, and in that its fidelity is so scrupulous that it consists of nearly the same number of verses as Milton's original.)[42]

This forewarning has a solid foundation. The Escóiquiz translation has twice as many verse lines as Milton's original, with mixed results. For instance, the amplification of Milton's original twenty-six-line invocation of book 1 to forty-eight lines still omits important elements, like the "Aonian mount" (*PL* 1.15). In another, the lengthening of Eve's fourteen-line modified sonnet (*PL* 12.610–23) to twenty-two lines substitutes one kind of promise for another. Escóiquiz's forgoing of the sonnet structure erases the promise inscribed in the very sonnet form, the promise that humans can create beauty and order in the postlapsarian world. But Escóiquiz renders Eve's final words in a way that aligns them even more closely with Adam's than in the English original. The brevity in the original of Adam's last speech of twenty-one lines (*PL* 12.553–73) and his rushed descent to Eve (*PL* 12.606–8) combine with Eve's final lines to imply, subtly and powerfully, at once their individual differences (Milton's Eve is more formal) and the reunited nature of the married couple, in contrast to their divisive behaviors after the Fall but before their respective visions "Portending good" (*PL* 12.596). The verbal unity of the couple's last words in Escóiquiz's *El Paraíso perdido* is even closer, with both their final dialogues rendered in nearly the same number of lines and in the same number of consonantal rhyme endings: Eve's with *aabbccddee fghfhg ijijkk* and Adam's with *abbaccdede ffgghh ijjikkj*.[43]

Nearly two centuries after Escóiquiz's translation, Castellón also elects, ultimately, to increase line numbers. He explains, "Mi «traición» ha sido aumentar en mi traducción el número de versos originales, que pasa de 10.565 a 13.663. A mi juicio es el menor de los costes posibles si queremos asegurar una lectura amena, atractiva y, sobre todo, comprensible" (My 'treason' has been to augment the number of the original verses in my translation, which passes from 10,565 to 13,663. In my judgment it is the smaller of the possible costs if we want to ensure an amenable, attractive, and, above all, comprehensible reading). Castellón justifies his inability to retain the verse-line count in part on his resulting ability to retain material that his predecessors had silently cut, as did Hermida and Pujals, both of whom disapproved of Escóiquiz's prolixity. Castellón locates the availability of this linguistic choice in more tolerant religious practices:

> En mi respaldo, diré que las dos mejores traducciones del poema que conozco, la de José María Boix i Silva, en Barcelona, Alfa, 1953, y la de Esteban Pujals en Madrid, Cátedra, 2001, recurren también al endecasílabo, el primero en catalán, el segundo en castellano, y son muy respetosos con el original, a diferencia de trabajos antiguos donde la censura católica amputada por su cuenta los versos de Milton que estimaba injurioso para la Iglesia de Roma.

> (In my defense, I would say that the two best translations of the poems that I know, that of José María Boix i Silva, in Barcelona, Alfa, 1953, and the one by Esteban Pujals in Madrid, Cátedra, 2001 [orig. 1986], also use hendecasyllables, the first in Catalan, the second in Spanish, and they are very faithful to the original, with the difference of old works in which Catholic censure amputated per its determination from Milton's verses what it deemed injurious to the Roman Church.)[44]

Another obstacle for translators of *Paradise Lost* into Spanish and any Romance language is the near absence of grammatical gender in English. This characteristic is nugatory neither in general nor in relation to *Paradise Lost*. Indeed it is a matter that Milton's translators regularly mention. For example, Atreides notes of his translation of "Th' infernal Serpent; he it was" (*PL* 1.33) as "La infernal Serpiente [f.], él [m.] fue," that "rompo la concordancia con el género femenino del nombre *Serpiente* para seguir a Milton" (I break the concordance of the feminine gender of the name *Serpent* to follow Milton).⁴⁵ Further, the required gendering of objects and places in Spanish detracts from some of the effects that Milton creates through sparse use of optional English grammatical gendering of objects and places. Elsewhere I have described the losses of Milton's subtle yet powerful implications on gender roles in Escóiquiz's translation of book 2.⁴⁶ In brief, Milton creates a subtle but powerful alliance in the account by the beleaguered character of Sin of the immediate aftermath of the birth of her son Death:

> I fled, and cried out *Death*;
> Hell trembled at the hideous name, and sighed
> Through all her caves, and back resounded *Death*. (*PL* 2.787–89)

A bitter moment of sisterhood between Sin (the allegorical concept and character) and the nearly personified feminine Hell (the allegorical concept and place) is lost in this passage owing to Spanish linguistic constraints: the male character Death is rendered by the feminine singular "La Muerte" and Hell as the masculine plural "Los abismos."⁴⁷

This linguistic dilemma only adds to the religious and literary-cultural difficulties that readers in many languages have found with the scenes in books 2 and 10 featuring Sin and Death. Since I have elsewhere discussed the scene in book 2 with a focus on Escóiquiz, I focus here on book 10. Escóiquiz was sufficiently discomfited by his inability to find an adequate replacement for the standard Spanish grammatically feminine term for Death, La Muerte, that he justified his choice to retain it in the preface:

> Entre otras dificultades que he encontrado para traducir con alguna propiedad este poema á nuestra lengua, me ha ocurrido una, que consiste en no tener en castellano otra voz del género masculino, que signifique la muerte, que la de fallecimiento, que es absolutamente impropia para nombrarla personificada, como se nombra en el poema ingles. . . . Pues, para salir de este embarazo siempre que hay inconveniente en darla su nombre femenino, del arbitrio de nombrarla por un epiteto del género masculino que la convenga, como el de mónstruo, esqueleto, etc.

(Amid other difficulties I have encountered in translating this poem into our language with some propriety, I have come upon one that consists of not having in Spanish another term of masculine gender that signifies death except for pass away, which is absolutely improper to name the personification, as it is named in the English poem. . . . Thus, to overcome this obstacle, whenever it is inconvenient to give it its feminine name, I have used my discretion to name *her* by an epithet of masculine gender that suits *her*, such as monster, skeleton, etc.) (emphases mine)[48]

Tellingly, this explanation evinces the very grammatical dilemma it describes: the twice used "la" (her) refers to the male character Death. To add to the gender trouble, the character of Death is always present in the poem with his mother, Sin, the standard Hispanophone word for which is masculine, el Pecado. Escóiquiz does not directly address this grammatical problem, but he does render Sin as the singular feminine La Culpa (Fault). Conversely, Dionisio Sanjuán and Castellón do explain their choice of the grammatically feminine La Culpa for the female character Sin with notes on the first use of the character's name.[49]

Into the twentieth and twenty-first centuries, Spanish translators of Milton's epic continued to contend with how best to manage the opposition of the two characters' grammatical gender and gender characterization. Antonio Fuster and Atreides take advantage of the reduction in the use of articles in their twentieth- and twenty-first-century translations and delete the articles *el* and *la* that regularly precede "Pecado" and "Muerte," respectively. Álvarez de Toledo also deletes the articles, part of his translational technique of "implicación evidente" (evident implication) that he uses to achieve hendecasyllabic lines.[50] In three separate notes, Pujals, who uses "Pecado," advises readers of the gender trouble: in his first mention of the two characters in the preface, when Sin informs Satan of her and Death's identities in book 2, and when they reappear at the portal of Hell in book 10.[51]

Milton reintroduces Sin and Death after their long absence in the narrative sitting "Within the gates of Hell" (*PL* 10.230), awaiting the return of Satan from Paradise:

> Sin opening, who thus now to Death began.
>   O Son, why sit we here each other viewing
> Idly, while Satan our great author thrives
> In other worlds, and happier seat provides
> For us his offspring dear? (*PL* 10.234–38)

Escóiquiz judiciously anticipates his Spanish readers' need for a reminder of the grammatical gender trouble and thus moves up the reference to Death's being a male character from the direct address of "Son" to the previous line introducing the dialogue: "La Culpa al fin, se vuelve al hijo fiero, / Y así le dice" (Fault at last turns to her wild son / And this is what she says to him)— *le* can refer to "him" or "her," but the context slants it toward the masculine.[52] Atreides does not provide an additional lead-in but does start Sin's dialogue with "Hijo mío" (My son).[53] Further, Escóiquiz remains true to his prefatory remarks of using other monikers for Death, in rendering the lead-in to Death's response to his mother, "Whom thus the meagre Shadow answered soon" (*PL* 10.264). Escóiquiz avoids the common, feminine-gendered word for shadow, *la sombra*, and instead opts for "El esqueleto negro y descarnado" (The black and defleshed skeleton), the masculine endings of the two, rather than one, adjectives of the noun reinforcing the character's male gender.[54]

Rosell and Sanjuán show far less attentiveness and accuracy in their references to Sin as a female character and Death as a male character in book 10 than they do in book 2, where they name the pair "el Pecado" and "la Muerte" and "la Culpa" and "la Muerte," respectively. In book 10, both mistake in their rendering of the opening of Sin's address to "la Muerte" by having Sin address Death as "hija mía" (my daughter). The mix-up of the progeny as daughter rather than son is reinforced in both translations when Sin refers to Death shortly thereafter as my "sombra inseparable" (f., "inseparable shadow").[55] Rosell's and Sanjuán's translation of "Idly" perpetuates the problem, although to different effects. Rosell uses the plural masculine adjective *ociosos* (slothful), which must refer to at least one male. By default—given that the adjective comes directly after "hija mía"—"el Pecado" (Sin) must be that male, as is reinforced by the masculine article *el*. This causes great confusion given that Sin goes on later in the same speech to refer to "nuestro padre" (m., "our father") Satan, thus conjuring a past homosexual union between el Pecado and Satan that gave rise to their daughter, la Muerte.[56] Sanjuán renders the adjective for "Idly" in its plural feminine form, *ociosas*, thus rendering both Sin and Death female.[57] Rosell corrects the progeny's gender in Death's response, spoken by the grammatically masculine "el descarnado Esqueleto" (m., "the defleshed Skeleton"), and later when Satan refers to his "á la vez hijo y nieto" (m., "simultaneously son and grandson"), Death. But Sin's gender troubles remain: Satan views "su digno y encantador hijo, el Pecado" (m., "his noble and enchanting son, Sin"), then addresses her/him as "Hija querida" (f., "beloved daughter").[58]

By way of transitioning from linguistic conundrums to religious matters, we turn in brief to Álvarez de Toledo's rendering of the book 10 passages involving Sin and Death. Álvarez de Toledo uses uppercase "Pecado" and "Culpa," without their articles, for the character Sin, and "Muerte" for the character Death.[59] But he sometimes uses lowercase, thus denoting the nature or quality of sin and death rather than the characters Sin and Death, which incorporate the nature and quality of their names. For example, as the pair set to embark for the postlapsarian world, Milton's Sin tells her son, Death, "Thou my shade / Inseparable must with me along: / For Death from Sin no power can separate" (PL 10.249–51). Soon thereafter Satan boasts to Sin and Death about the impending growth of "this new kingdom . . . / Through Sin to Death exposed by my exploit" (PL 10.406–7). Álvarez de Toledo's translations—"No hay fuerza que separe culpa y muere [sic]" (There is no power that separates sin and death) and "Al pecado y la muerte lo destino" (through sin to death I destine it)—alter the meaning while retaining the logical sense and subtly highlighting the religious claims.[60]

Religious Matters

Whether due to avowed self-censorship, a commitment to domesticating translational methods, or their interpretations of the epic, Spanish translators have confronted Milton's overt and nuanced representations of religious figures, themes, and ideas, then have had to grapple with how to make them comprehensible and palatable to Spanish audiences, which have been largely Catholic or at least familiar with Catholic doctrine.[61] Many Spanish translations of *Paradise Lost* greatly revise Milton's religious claims. Escóiquiz and Atreides in particular alert readers in their paratexts to their religious commitments rather than simply making silent emendations.

Escóiquiz concludes his "Prólogo del traductor" (Translator's Prologue) by stating that he actively self-censored due to religious scruples: "Debo, por último, advertir, que nada he cercenado del original en mi traduccion, sino algunas alusiones, que el célebre Delille ha omitido tambien en su traduccion francesa, como ridiculas é indecentes contra los ritos y usos de la Iglesia católica, propias de la secta en que había nacido Milton, y que léjos de acrecentar el mérito del poema, lo desfiguran" (I should warn, in conclusion, that I have severed nothing from the original in my translation, except for some allusions, which the celebrated [Jacques] Delille has also omitted in his French translation, as ridiculous or indecent, contrary to the rites and practices of the Catholic Church, characteristic of the religious sect into which Milton had been born, but which far from increasing the work's merit disfigure it).[62]

The statement sounds a bit chastising, but Escóiquiz's thirty-two endnotes tell another story, one similar to the salvific, ecumenical one of Martínez y Güertero's poem "Querelles del vate ciego" (The Blind Poet's Complaint), discussed at the end of chapter 1. In Escóiquiz's notes, Milton figures as a poet who has been misunderstood as making heresies that are, in fact, artistic responses to the exigencies of narrative and topic; the linguistically antithetical translator, Escóiquiz's contemporary Hermida, shapes such a similar religious reconciliation through the paratexts of his *El Paraíso perdido*.[63] For example, the endnote to Escóiquiz's translation of Milton's description of the fallen "angel forms" (*PL* 1.301), "Su cuerpo" (His body), advises that, "Milton, como lo hemos advertido en el prólogo, los supone también corpóreos, porque sin esta ficcion era imposible hacerlos figurar en una obra de imaginacion, cual es un Poema Epico" (Milton, as we have warned in the Prologue, imagines them as also corporeal, because without this fiction it would be impossible to represent them in a creative work, as is an Epic Poem).[64] Samuel Johnson found himself similarly compelled to voice his reservations about "Milton's design" in terms of the "agency of spirits," explaining that Milton "saw that immateriality supplied no images, and that he could not show angels acting but by instruments of action; he therefore invested them with form and matter. This being necessary was therefore defensible; and he should have secured the consistency of his system by keeping immateriality out of sight, and enticing his reader to drop it from his thoughts. But he has unhappily perplexed his poetry with his philosophy."[65]

Escóiquiz is perhaps most defensive of Milton in his endnote to God the Father's statement to the angels following the Son's volunteering to act as the sacrifice for humankind:

> But all ye gods,
> Adore him, who to compass all this dies,
> Adore the Son, and honour him as me. (*PL* 3.341–43)

After citing "san Pablo," as do some contemporary Anglophone editors, Escóiquiz avers:

> Como las expresiones de Milton, aunque conformes á esta sagrada autoridad, pueden dar motivo á que un lector ignorante, ó poco instruido en los misterios de nuestra religion, se figure que el hijo de Dios, en el modo de pensar de Milton, no fué reconocido ni adorado como Dios por los Angeles hasta aquella época, y en fuerza de un decreto espe-

cial de su Eterno Padre, error tan ajeno de Milton, como de cualquier católico enterado de la doctrina de la Iglesia; debo advertir al tal lector, que la adoracion del Verbo Divino y del Espiritu santo fueron siempre imprescindibles para los Angeles de la del Padre Eterno.

(Since Milton's expressions, even though they conform to this sacred authority, can give rise for an ignorant reader, or one insufficiently instructed in the mysteries of our religion, to imagine that the son of God, in Milton's way of thinking, was not recognized or adored as God by the Angels until that time and obligated by a special decree by his Eternal Father, an error as far from Milton as from any Catholic knowledgeable of the Church's doctrine, I should warn that reader that the adoration of the Divine Word and of the holy Spirit was always as essential for the Angels as was that of the Eternal Father.)[66]

The ecumenism that Escóiquiz extends to Milton constitutes a rhetorical move in the endnotes of subsuming Catholicism into "Christianity," a term used repeatedly near the end of the notes for books 11 and 12.[67] This paratextual tendency is in accord with the omissions and silent additions of Escóiquiz's translation, which make the epic not only less Protestant but also more Catholic.[68] The passage continued to trouble Spanish translators, like Sanjuán, who notes Milton's foundation in "la Sagrada Escritura y en la opinion de algunos célebres escritores" (Sacred Scripture and in the opinion of various celebrated writers) and who alerts readers that "algunos con fundamento" (some with foundation) have noted that the passage accords with the Latin dictum of "el día presente de Dios nec præteritu, nec futurum, sed præsens" (God's eternal day without past, without future, but present).[69]

In his preface Atreides also alerts readers to his conversely liberal interpretation of some of the religious aspects of the epic. He indicates his interpretive agreement with Michael Bryson's *The Tyranny of Heaven: Milton's Rejection of God as King* (2004), especially of God the Father as an unpalatable portrait of a divine monarch. However, contrary to Bryson's claim that "Milton deliberately presents" such a God in order "to attack the whole tradition of imagining God as a king," Atreides sets aside author intentionality and suggests that the characters of God the Father and Satan got away from Milton.[70] Atreides thus revamps claims by Voltaire and other early admirers of Milton from France, and argues that the "anómolo binomio" (binary anomaly) is a driving force behind the epic's continued power and relevance.[71]

It must be noted, however, that, in contrast to Escóiquiz's translation and endnotes, Atreides's do not emphasize the prefatory stance.

Translational variety is at the fore, as would be expected, in Spanish translations of the three passages in *Paradise Lost* that most overtly criticize Catholic dogma, figures, and practices: the Paradise of Fools passage; the passage on angelic digestion, with its provocative use of "transubstantiate"; and the terms "Pontifical" and "pontifice" upon Satan's return from Paradise to Hell. In book 3, as Satan travels from Hell to the created universe, Milton demonstrates his disdain of Catholic doctrines and figures in the imagined "Limbo large and broad, since called / The Paradise of Fools" (*PL* 3.495–96). The long passage begins with "Embryos and idiots, eremites and friars / White, black and grey, with all their trumpery"; ridicules those who disguise themselves in "the weeds of Dominic, / Or in Franciscan"; caricatures the vision of "Saint Peter at Heav'n's wicket"; then focuses not simply on ecclesiastical robes, like surplices, but also on the more obviously Catholic "Cowls, hoods and habits," trailed by "relics, beads, / Indulgences, dispenses, pardons, bulls" (*PL* 3.474–75, 479–80, 484, 490, 491–92). Alastair Fowler notes "a Catholic tradition which consigned *idiots*, cretins and unbaptized infants to a much-debated *limbo infantum*. The Franciscans maintained this limbo was situated above the Earth, in a region of light." He identifies the mendicant White Friars as Carmelites, Black Friars as Dominicans, Grey Friars as Franciscans, and the Austin (Augustinian) friars as Eremites.[72]

Hermida simply excises the anti-Catholic satire and adds an endnote: "Aquí omite el traductor algunos versos extraños al asunto" (Here the translator omits some verses extraneous to the matter).[73] Escóiquiz replaces it with a sixty-five-line passage that is, in part, a piecemeal collection of other sections of Milton's original. He begins his rendering with

No léjos moran, los que en su fecundo
Cérebro, cada dia un nuevo mundo
En idea construyen, más perfecto.

(Not far dwell those who in their fecund
Brains construct each day a new world
In theory more perfect.)[74]

The remaining verse paragraph satirizes the imperfect "ruina en ruina" (ruin upon ruin) created by limited human imaginations. The second verse-paragraph focuses on human avarice—"Otro, llevado de esperanza avara... Hallar creyendo aquel desconocido / Secreto de volver el plomo en oro" (Another, moved by avaricious hope ... Finds himself believing that unknown / Secret of changing lead to gold)—before turning finally to "otros locos, que allí ostentan / Un ambicioso lujo" (other madmen, who there parade / An ambitious luxury) but are left sad and weary.[75] Escóiquiz thus shifts the satire from Catholic duplicity to proud, self-deluding quests for individual glory and gain.

Two less religiously conservative prose translations make only minor changes to the passage. For example, the Rosell changes "Embryos and idiots" to "hipócritas ó dementes" (hypocrites or lunatics).[76] That translation and the one by Sanjuán both faithfully render the references to the Catholic orders and provide explanatory notes specifying that the colors refer to "Los Carmelitas, los Dominicos y los Franciscanos" (The Carmelites, Dominicans, and Franciscans).[77] Fuster's and Álvarez de Toledo's overriding strategy for verbal reduction results in Fuster's reducing the religious figures to the singular "hábito de un dominico o de un franciscano" (habit of a Dominican or a Franciscan) and Álvarez de Toledo's to "de dominico / O menor" (of Dominican / Or Franciscan).[78] Atreides's choice of ametric trochaic enables him to slow down the pace, which calls attention to the satire.

Escóiquiz and Hermida are thus more in keeping with English than Spanish company in their express distaste for the passage. John King notes:

> Milton unembarrassedly breaks epic decorum by attacking "trumpery," a familiar cant term from anti-Catholic propaganda. Objecting specifically to the scurrilousness of that word, Richard Bentley proposes that the Paradise of Fools passage is a spurious addition in his 1732 edition [of] *Paradise Lost*: "all this long description of the outside of the world, the Limbo of Vanity, was not Milton's own, but an insertion by his editor.... In its several parts it abounds in impertinencies.... 'Tis a silly interruption of the story in the very middle." (3.444–98n)[79]

A. W. Verity also chides that the "almost burlesque satire of the passage seems scarce in keeping with the dignity of an epic."[80] Frank Huntley seeks to recuperate the passage by advocating for a more generalized message, in inadvertent correspondence with Escóiquiz: "Milton justifies its inclusion and position ... by his whole plot, his cosmic setting, and his moral intention. Its anti-Catholicism, there by history, ceases to be topical as it is raised by Milton's artistry to become a symbol of pride—ill-matched."[81] Huntley's reading, like Escóiquiz's translation, would have readers focus on catholic rather than Catholic error.

Excision and variety are also to be found in the Spanish translations of the digression on angelic transubstantiation in book 5. After Adam, Eve, and Raphael exchange salutations and sit down to dine, Milton's narrator chastises "the common gloss / Of theologians" regarding angelic eating and represents Raphael sitting down to eat "with keen dispatch / Of real hunger, and concoctive heat / To transubstantiate" (*PL* 5.435–36, 436–38).[82] The verb calls up the doctrine of the transubstantiation of the Eucharistic bread and wine into Jesus's body and blood, a doctrine responsible for some of the sharpest disputes in the Protestant Reformation and Catholic Counter-Reformation. Hermida again excises (*PL* 5.433–43) and adds an endnote similar to the earlier one: "Se omiten aquí algunos pocos versos sobre la naturaleza angélica; mas propios de la curiosidad escolástica, que de un poema" (A few verses on angelic nature are here omitted, more suitable to Scholastic curiosity than to a poem).[83] Escóiquiz again replaces. He does not use the readily available Spanish verb *transubstanciar* but rather has Raphael conclude the pre-dinner pleasantries with a call to mealtime prayer that presses the distinctions between earthly and heavenly eating:

Agradeced en tanto, estos hermosos
Frutos conmigo, como la figura
De aquella dicha deliciosa y pura,
Que con nosotros gozareis gloriosos.

(Meanwhile, be thankful with me for these beautiful
Fruits, like the figure
Of that delicious and pure joy [i.e. of Heaven, previously described],
Which with us you, glorious, could savor.)

Escóiquiz has them then immediately set to eat, without the narrative interruption: "[Raphael] Acabó, y comenzaron su comida / Gustosa y limpia" (He concluded, and they began their meal / Delicious and pure).[84] From the context, "they" can refer to either the angel and the couple or only the couple. Rosell and Sanjuán maintain Milton's representation of angelic eating but avoid the freighted verb *transubstanciar*.[85] Atreides and Castellón use the word *transubstanciación*.[86] In line with the religious freedom he perceives newly available in his era, Castellón goes further with a lucid note about this passage's reference to "el docetismo de Marción" (Marcion's Docetism), specific biblical passages, and "el problema aristotélico del cambio de una substancia en otra" (the Aristotelian problem regarding the change of one substance into another).[87]

Amid the many extensions of this one use of this one word, the matter most related to Catholicism is the image of the table, the locus where Eucharistic transubstantiation traditionally takes place; its significance also emerges in relation to Spanish illustrations of *Paradise Lost*, as discussed in chapter 4. John King has brought attention to how, in book 5, the "repetition of the word table, previously unnoted by commentators, focuses attention upon Eucharistic satire."[88] Milton's narrator refers to the "table" at which the archangel Raphael and the couple dine (*PL* 5.Argument, 391, 392, 443), and Raphael also refers to "this table" in Eden and to the heavenly "tables" at which angels eat (*PL* 5.391, 632). There is yet another element, again previously unnoted by commentators, that attentive translators would readily discern: "table" and "transubstantiate" occur only in book 5 of Milton's original. Sanjuán's and Atreides's translations accurately capture the original's uses in book 5 with *mesa*, yet while Atreides refrains from using the word in other books, Sanjuán uses it inaccurately yet logically and movingly, in rendering the narrator's lament at the beginning of book 9, the Fall book, "No more talk where God or angel guest / With man, as with his friend, familiar used / To sit indulgent, and with him partake / Rural repast" (*PL* 9.1–4). Sanjuán renders the last portion "ya no acudirán éstos a sentarse a su mesa" (they [God and angels] will no longer go to sit at their [humans'] table).[89]

Escóiquiz's and Rosell's translations are uneven on the matter. Escóiquiz retains Milton's word choice in the Argument and in Raphael's description of "las suntuosas mesas" (the sumptuous tables) of Heaven, but simply removes the reference to the Edenic eating site. Instead he refers to the event or the food, "festín" (banquet).[90] In erasing the table(s) that subtly yet pointedly comment on the Eucharist, Escóiquiz eschews Milton's large poetic strategy in book 5 of generating a liberal view of Christian Eucharistic union by narratively representing a figure of divine good—Raphael—communing easily, freely, lovingly with the figures of human good, Adam and Eve.

The treatment of this passage in the Rosell translation warrants a brief discussion of the overlap of the religious and the literary-cultural, or aesthetic. The Rosell uses the word for Raphael's references but omits the narrator's references. Both this and the Sanjuán use the word in book 9, rendering "Rural repasts" as "campestre mesa" (rural table).[91] The Rosell *El Paraíso perdido* was originally published under the same cover as a Spanish translation of *Paradise Regained*.[92] In *Paradise Regained*, tables emerge especially powerfully in book 4. Jesus derides the poor quality of Satan's temptations, then tells Satan that, to make his "majestic show / Of luxury" more effective, he "shouldst add to tell / Their sumptuous gluttonies, and gorgeous feasts / On citron tables or Atlantic stone" (PR 4.110–15). Even more impressive is the table that shows up soon thereafter, when the angels swoop down and "before him [Jesus] spread / A table of celestial food" (PR 4.587–88). The powerful image of the table at the end of *Paradise Regained* represents a regaining of paradise and another level of the communion of divine good and human good in the person of Jesus and thus ties it together with *Paradise Lost*. The connection between the table(s) of book 5 of *Paradise Lost* and book 4 of *Paradise Regained* would have been lost for Spanish readers, however, even had the Rosell translation been more consistent with translational choices in *Paradise Lost* because the Spanish translation of *Paradise Regained* uses *mesa* three times in book 2 to match the original's use (PR 2.340, 384, 402), but only once at the very end of book 4 rather than twice.[93]

Spanish translators handle the last of Milton's three most overt references to Catholicism in *Paradise Lost* using similar strategies. After the Fall, Milton has Sin and Death construct a "work by wondrous art / Pontifical," which is referred to again shortly thereafter as "this new wondrous pontifice" (PL 10.312–13, 348). Editor John Leonard equitably provides the three related meanings of the adjective "pontifical"—"bridge-building (OED 6), with a pun on 'papal' (OED 2) or 'episcopal' (OED 1)"—and appropriately homes in on the prominent, satiric connotation: "The Pope's title *Pontifex* was taken to mean that he was a bridge-builder between this world and the next."[94] Leonard notes one meaning of "pontifice" as "bridge" and calls attention to the fact that the word "already existed as a variant of 'Pontifex' meaning 'Bishop' or 'Pope.' In this sense, Satan himself is the *wondrous pontifice*."[95]

Puente, which inscribes the Latin root of "pontifical" and "pontifice," is the common Spanish noun for "bridge." Thus, excising the adjectival "pontifical" can be justified on purely aesthetic and logical grounds. This is the route taken by Hermida and Rosell in their use of *puente* without an adjective for "art / Pontifical" and by Escóquiz and Sanjuán for "pontifice."[96] Atreides's maintenance of the adjective warrants his revision of the noun to avoid redundancy, based on obvious aesthetic grounds: "Ya con arte milagroso prolongaran su labor / Pontifica" (Thus with miraculous art, they prolonged their labor / Pontifical).[97] Atreides's placement of the noun at the end of a line and the adjective at the start of the next line imitates Milton's prosody and its mimetic quality of bridging two lines. Certainly the English original of these passages on the facing pages of Atreides's and Álvarez de Toledo's translations can alert readers to the pointed anti-Catholic jibe. The Rosell and Castellón employ notes to do so. In the former, the note for "art / Pontifical" articulates a clear interpretation of "pontifical" as a reference to the Catholic pope, not to a Protestant or Catholic bishop, and an equally clear irritation. In the text, Rosell has Sin and Death construct "su puente con maravilloso arte" (their bridge with marvelous art) and later renders "this new wondrous pontifice" as "nuevo y admirable puente" (new and admirable bridge).[98] In the note to the first passage, Rosell expounds, "Con arte *pontifical*, dice aquí el autor, jugando ridículamente del vocablo, porque *pontifex* viene de *pons* y *facere*, y segun Varron, *quia sublicius pons á pontificibus factus est primum, et restitutus sæpé*. Y si, como otros creen, aquí alude aquí al poder papal, la ocurrencia es todavía de peor gusto" (With art *pontifical*, says the author here, playing ridiculously with vocabulary, because *pontifex* comes from *pons* and *facere*, and according to Varo [quoting the Latin], *for by them the Bridge-on-Piles was made in the first place, and it was likewise repeatedly repaired by them*. And if, as others believe, he here alludes to papal power, the occurrence [of such a pun] is even more in poor taste).[99]

Castellón's translation and notes cooperate to render Milton's tone and allusive jibe. Castellón translates the first passage as:

El Pecado y *la* Muerte *con*cluyeron,
con arte magistral, su gran hazaña:
una colgante y *p*étrea *p*asarela. (emphases mine)

(Sin and Death concluded,
With magisterial art, their great exploit;
A hanging and stony footbridge.)

Castellón captures Milton's parodic tone through various choices: while elsewhere he drops the gendered articles that contradict the characters' gender, he retains them here; he places the redundant *con* close to one another; he deflates the structure into a footbridge or perhaps even, more eerily, a gangplank; and he uses two uncommon words beginning with the "p" sound for a forced alliteration rather than the common word that also starts with a "p," *puente*. Castellón footnotes the passage, "Milton dice textualmente «art pontifical», arte para la construcción de puentes, pero también demonización del «pontífice» católico, presentándose como constructor de un puente entre este mundo y el cielo" (Milton says textually 'art pontifical,' the art for the construction of bridges, but also a demonization of the Catholic 'pontifice,' presenting himself as a constructor of a bridge between this world and heaven).[100]

While Rosell invokes aesthetics in his note and Castellón balances aesthetics in his translational and paratextual choices, Escóiquiz makes a translational choice that enriches the aesthetic and religious extensions of this passage, albeit at the expense of strict fidelity to the content of Milton's original. Escóquiz uses "un puente inmenso" (an immense bridge), "arco" (arch), "espantoso / Puente" (fearsome / Bridge), and "obra fuerte" (strong work).[101] With "arco," Escóiquiz strengthens a light echo in Milton's original, between this visual image set amid the "waves" at the border of Hell and Chaos and the visual image of the "triple-coloured bow" after the earthly "flood" that concludes the next book, book 11 (*PL* 10.311, 11.897, 893). Escóiquiz translates Milton's rainbow as "Ese arco inmenso" (that immense arch).[102] The association of the parodic image of the "puente inmenso" that Sin and Death construct for sinners' easy access to Hell and the arch that God brings to signal his bridging "cov'nant" between God and humankind is made all the stronger in the Escóiquiz translation because, while Milton invests no color in Hell's bridge and describes the rainbow as "triple-coloured," Escóiquiz invests no color descriptions at all in either image (*PL* 11.898, 897).

Literary-Cultural Reading Practices

Going beyond the practice of expurgation of some of the books listed in the Spanish Catholic Inquisition's *Index librorum prohibitorum*, some Spanish translators of *Paradise Lost*, and translators of Milton's works into other languages, have taken the liberty of making "small Improvements," as did the eighteenth-century British editor Richard Bentley.[103] The results are mixed in relation to the religious ends. The interplay of the translations and their notes indicate the translators' and presses' awareness of religious sensibilities as just one component of Spanish reader reception. Perforce in an epic poem based on Genesis, religious elements also inhere in the broadest category resonant with Spanish translations of *Paradise Lost*, the literary-cultural or aesthetic, the context for which is transhistoric and international, nowadays often called world literature. It is within this broad context that Naoki Saiki cautions against possessing a "static view of translation in which difference is substantialized; we should not yield to the reification of translation that denies translation its potentiality to deterritorialize. Therefore it is important to introduce difference in and of language in such a way that we can comprehend translation not in terms of the communication model of equivalence and exchange but as a form of political labor to create continuity at the elusive point of discontinuity in the social."[104] My claim in this section is that the simultaneous political labor and literary-cultural work of Spanish translations of *Paradise Lost* position Spain among the republic of letters, as reflected in the translations themselves and as expressed in the translations' verbal paratexts (I specify verbal paratexts since visual paratexts are reserved for chapter 4).

It is with these matters at the fore that we return to Juan Matéos's lament in the preface to his 1914 Spanish prose translation of *Paradise Lost*, "There is scarcely a modern language in any cultured country in which Milton's immortal poem does not have various translations in prose and verse. Nor are they wanting in Spanish, more the disgrace that the quality does not equal the number." Matéos echoes a cultural urge expressed nearly a century before, in the paratexts of the first two published editions of *El Paraíso perdido*. Escóiquiz articulates his translation of "una obra de las más célebres en el Orbe literario" (one of the most celebrated works in the literary World) as the result of his drive to act "con alguna utilidad para mi patria" (in some service for my country). His recognition that the poem has been "traslado ya en casi todos los idiomas de la Europa" (translated already into almost all the languages in Europe) implies a desire to be competitive or up to date internationally. So does his decision to include "las eruditas notas de Addisson, y algunas mias, que aclarasen las dificultades que habían de ocurrir al comun de los lectores" (the erudite notes of Addison, and some of mine, that clarify difficulties that may occur to the common reader), so important because "el asunto de que trata el poema, es uno de los más misteriosos, delicados é importantes de nuestra religion cristiana" (the matter that the poem covers is one of the most mysterious, delicate, and important of our Christian religion).[105] Explanatory paratexts, in the form of prologues, commentaries, and notes, are indeed significant vehicles for translational function that benefit readers' denotative understanding of the poem. They must also be understood as functioning culturally to place readers in an international conversation, given that Addison's notes were included in highly regarded English, French, and German editions of the epic.

Hermida strikes a similarly patriotic note but also a very personal one in the opening paratext. He describes *Paradise Lost* as "conocido en todo el mundo por sus traducciones, y solo desconocido en lengua española" (known throughout the world through its translations, and unknown only in the Spanish language). He reflects his appreciation of world literature and his agency in it when he explains his exclusion of any external notes in his edition to the fact that even such fans as Voltaire and Delille have greatly misunderstood Milton's poem, going so far as Frenchifying it so that Adam and Eve "se han convertido en un petimetre y en una madama de Paris" (have been converted into a fop and a madam of Paris). Hermida also expresses personal passion for the beauty he finds in Milton's epic and the respect he has for the "ilustre Milton, angel en tu figura, sobresaliente en tu talento, sabio en las lenguas orientales y el las vivas de Europa" (illustrious Milton, angel in your figure, audacious in your talent, knowledgeable in the Eastern languages and the living languages of Europe), to whom he addresses the "Dedicatoria que hace el traductor a los manes de Milton" (Dedicatory that the Translator Makes to Milton's Soul). Hermida effuses, "Todo tu poema respira la admiracion de la divinidad y se exfuerza en descubrirnos sus caminos" (All your poem breathes forth admiration for the divine and works to uncover for us its paths).[106] He even finds a winsome pleasure in turning to his *El Paraíso perdido* in his old age after years of government service, just as Milton turned to his *Paradise Lost* in his. Explanations like these, of national service and near reverie, are in sharp distinction from those in prefatory materials in other eighteenth-century Spanish translations of works considered entertainment reading, like Samuel Richardson's *Pamela*, or contemplative reading, like Edward Young's "Night Thoughts." Hermida's expressed passion, it must be noted, is rare even among Milton's translators, but it is not unique: we know of the cases of the Czech translator Josef Jungmann, the Serbian translator Milovan Djilas, and the Mexican translator Francisco Granados Maldonado.[107]

We can track an uneven shift in the cultural affiliation manifest in the opening paratexts of Spanish editions of *Paradise Lost*. Sanjuán does not offer his own prefatory material for his 1868 edition, which instead begins with Spanish translations of the "notas de Addisson, Saint-Maur y otros" (notes by Addison, [Nicolas-François Dupré de] Saint-Maur, and others). Similarly, the 1873 Rosell edition is without a translator's preface but instead begins with a Spanish translation of "La vida de Juan Milton por Roberto Vaughan" (The Life of John Milton by Robert Vaughan).[108] Given the absence of translators' prologues in the Sanjuán and Rosell editions, readers cannot readily determine whether the implied cultural affiliations are those of the translators or the presses. Further, in their brief introductions, the translators from the turn of the twenty-first century—Álvarez de Toledo, Atreides, and Castellón—do not directly explain their motivations for producing yet more translations of *Paradise Lost*. Earlier Spanish translations that have been republished at the turn of the twenty-first century—Escóiquiz, Rosell, and Sanjuán—drop the English- and French-derived paratexts. Starting in 1971, the Mexican powerhouse Porrúa Press added to the opening paratext of its edition of the Sanjuán *El Paraíso perdido* an introduction by the Mexican priest, critic, and writer Joaquin Antonio Peñalosa.

Paratexts both initiate readers into and are dependent on the translators' and presses' participation within specific literary circuits. It is unfortunate when such circuits malfunction and when significant numbers and types of impediments and errors appear and persist. Detracting from the function of the notes of some early editions of *El Paraíso perdido* are their length and errors. The 1812 Escóiquiz edition has a daunting 129 pages of opening paratexts before readers get to the 228 pages of books 1–3 in the first volume of the three-volume edition; the 1873 Rosell edition has 66 pages of opening paratexts preceding its 291 pages of books 1–12. Presses quickly recognized that the opening paratextual materials were taxing for or ignored by readers, and certainly cost-inefficient, since they regularly removed them from republications. Moreover some paratextual material is simply incorrect and remained uncorrected in later printings. For example, the "Biografía" in the Escóiquiz cites the first publication date of *Paradise Lost* as 1669 rather than 1667, and the "Biografía" in both the Escóiquiz and Sanjuán refer to "la muerte de Cárlos II, decapitado en 1648" (the death of Charles II, beheaded in 1648), when it was Charles I who was beheaded.[109] (While the death of Charles I was on January 30, 1649, per the New Style calendar, the 1648 date could be a vestige of the Old Style calendar or an error.) Also consistent and repeated in many editions are variant spellings, such as "Addisson" for Addison. These are far from nugatory matters for readers and scholars who might be interested in following up on references, not only in the days before electronic catalogues but also today, when some electronic search engines are not set up for "fuzzy" searches, that is, searches for near equivalents of keywords.[110] Then there is the case of the Álvarez de Toledo edition misnaming the author "John F. Milton." Nothing in the preface or notes provides justification for the middle initial, which is without basis.[111]

The translations and paratexts in Spanish editions display their participation in literary circuits that include, first, primarily ancient Western, French, and British cultures and, eventually, also Italian, U.S., and Latin American ones. Many "improvements" in Spanish translations of *Paradise Lost* coincide with areas of French and English unease over Milton's decorum and taste, as expressed by, among others, Addison, Johnson, C. S. Lewis, and Voltaire. For example, Escóiquiz expurgates Satan's exciting, blasphemous—but not specifically anti-Catholic—line "Better to reign in Hell, than serve in Heav'n" (*PL* 1.263). The renderings of that titillating line by Rosell, Matéos, Fuster, Álvarez de Toledo, Castellón, and others are surprisingly uninspiring. The one by Atreides is rhythmically and denotatively accurate: "Mejor reinar en el Infierno que servir en el Empíreo." The aural echo of *empire* in "Empyrean" (*Empíreo*) justifies the word's use, although, it must be stated, the more common word for "Heav'n", *Cielo*, would have created an evocative assonant rhyme with *Infierno* and would have linked nicely with Atreides's use of *cielo* nearby, in lines 1.244, 255, and 270.[112]

Escóiquiz explains his displeasure with Satan's heresies as being based on literary or aesthetic principles rather than religious ones, as do some of his French and English counterparts. He suggests that Milton is compelled to make Satan less "odioso á los lectores, que la repugnancia con que lo mirasen, disminuyese el interés del poema" (hateful to readers, because the repugnance with which they view him diminishes interest in the poem).[113] In another note Escóiquiz seethes at Satan's blasphemous view of the threat he posed to God the Father in the War in Heaven (*PL* 1.103–17):

> Esta blasfemia, como todas las demás de la misma especie, que se encontrarán en los discursos de Satanás, y los de sus secuaces, en la extension del poema, no son mas que un efecto de su desesperacion; pues como se verá por otras expresiones, puestas igualmente en su boca, todos ellos estaban bien ciertos de su debilidad, y de su absoluta dependencia de Dios, y así todas las injurias y horrores que vomitan contra él, no son mas que falsedades, reconocidas por los mismos que las profieren, y nacidas de su soberbia obstinada y de su ódio injusto.

> (This blasphemy, like the rest of this species, which are to be found in Satan's discourses, and those of his minions, throughout the poem, are no more than an effect of his/their desperation; as will be seen in other expressions, also put in his/their mouth, all of them [the fallen angels] were very certain of their weakness and of their absolute dependence on God, and thus all the injuries and horrors that they vomit against him are no more than falsehoods, recognized as such by the very speakers that proffer them, and born of his/their obstinate pride and his/their unjustified hatred.)[114]

Addison is more temperate but no less firm in his conviction that the fallen angels are God's and humankind's "professed enemies."[115] While contemporary scholars avoid such value-laden assessments, Escóiquiz's comments are in keeping with the text's stinging label of Satan as the "Arch-Enemy" (*PL* 1.81) and with readers who, whether they find Satan engaging or repulsive, recognize his logic as faulty and his role within the text as incendiary and antihuman.[116]

Decorum and taste may also account for the disfavor with Milton's representations of divinely sanctioned sex. Milton introduces prelapsarian human sex with Adam and Eve engaging in "the rites / Mysterious of connubial love" (PL 4.742–43) after evening prayers. The use of "*rites* to mean marital sex was a commonplace warranted by St. Paul's account (Eph. 5.32) of the bodily union of husband and wife."[117] Further, it is clear from the reference to the products of bodily union as "human offspring" (PL 4.751) and the prevention of "adulterous lust" (PL 4.753) that Milton "dignifies sex by having Adam and Eve make love before the Fall."[118] Escóiquiz's translation praises "wedded love" (PL 4.750) but does not represent Adam and Eve as engaging in sex. As Escóiquiz would have it, after their evening prayers, "Al plácido descanso se entregaron" (To peaceful rest they resigned themselves) and "en su lecho dormian" (in their bed they slept).[119] While current Catholic doctrine asserts that Adam and Eve did have sex in Paradise, the *Catechism* of the Council of Trent from 1566 "concluded that it was 'quite certain' that there was no sexual 'consummation' before our first parents sinned."[120] Escóiquiz's decorous exclusion of Adam and Eve having sex in Paradise thus also reflects this erstwhile Catholic dogma and belief.

Escóiquiz's and Hermida's translations also excise Milton's representation of angelic sexuality. Escóiquiz's twenty-two-line translation of Milton's original ten-line description by Raphael of angelic sex (PL 8.620–29) ends with a Dantesque sense of angelic spiritual communion:

> Con otro sér el nuestro se reune,
> Y en él con Dios, á cuya union divina
> Toda otra pura union nos encamina.
>
> (Our being unites with another being,
> And in it (i.e., the newly united being) with God, towards which
>   divine union
> Every other pure union leads us.)[121]

Hermida's nearly coeval verse translation is briefer (six lines) and equally measured. Hermida's Raphael supplies the reassurance "Saber te baste somos venturosos" (It suffices you to know us happy) through a pleasure that is "mas colmado" (more abundant).[122] Sanjuán's prose translation also reduces but rather accurately renders the lines Hermida omits.[123]

Especially up to the mid-twentieth century, Spanish translations of *Paradise Lost* tap into and seek to expand the cosmopolitanism of their intended

Spanish readership. They are also mindful of and influenced by literary traditions within Hispano-Catholic culture and integrate domesticating strategies, a common translational set of techniques that conform to the (imagined) receptor culture. The insertion of poetic Marian devotion is certainly clear in Spanish translations of Milton's references to the Virgin Mary, devotion to whom is less prominent in English literature than in Spanish literature.[124] In book 5, Raphael salutes Eve:

> Hail mother of mankind, whose fruitful womb
> Shall fill the world more numerous with thy sons
> Than with these various fruits the trees of God
> Have heaped this table. (PL 5.388–91)

Raphael's salutation alludes to the biblical Gabriel's salutation to Mary: "And the angel came in unto her, and said, Hail, *thou that art* highly favoured, the Lord *is* with thee; blessed *art* thou among women. . . . Thou shalt conceive in thy womb, and bring forth a son."[125]

Milton's three-and-a-half-line passage spurs Escóiquiz to a sixteen-line salutation that captures the fervor of the extensive Hispano-Catholic Marian literary tradition:

> «¡Salve! le dice el Angel: (venturosa
> Palabra, que ha de ser en lo futuro
> A otra Eva, á la purísima María,
> Repetida, y con suerte más dichosa;
> Pues que esta divina Eva la cabeza
> Quebrantará de la infernal serpiente,
> Y la esposa de Adán, por su flaqueza,
> Será engañada lastimosamente.)
> «¡Salve, la dice, pues, ¡oh tú fecunda
> «Madre de los humanos, destinada
> «A poblar esta esfera dilatada!
> «La multitud de perlas, con que inunda
> «Sus campiñas la aurora, y las estrellas
> «Innumerables, cuyas luces bellas
> «El Cielo alumbran, á tu descendencia
> «En número darán la preeminencia».

> ("Hail!" the angel says to her: (fortunate

Word as will be in the future
To another Eve, to the most pure Mary,
Repeated, and with better luck;
Since this divine Eve will crush
The head of the infernal serpent,
And the wife of Adam, for her weakness,
Will be pitifully deceived.)
"Hail!" he says to her, "thus, oh, you, fecund
"Mother of humankind, destined
"To populate this wide sphere!
"The multitude of pearls, with which the aurora
"Inundates her landscapes, and the stars
"Innumerable, whose beautiful lights
"Heaven illuminate, to your descendants
"Will cede preeminence in number.")[126]

The narrator's glee that the "Hail" to Eve will be "repeated" to Mary is reflected poetically in the repetition of Raphael's "Hail" at the beginning and directly after the narrative digression. The repositioning of the metaphors to the celestial realm also explicitly echoes Dante's *Divine Comedy*, with which Spanish readers would be familiar.

Hermida extends Raphael's three and a half lines to nine, but the extension is in part due to his inclusion of elements of the introduction to the salutation into the salutation itself, such as the single reference to "María bendita" (blest Mary). Hermida's repetition of "Ave" (Hail) and use of exclamation points are emphatic.[127] Castellón too repeats "Salve" (Hail) and uses exclamation points. Even the circumspect Atreides—who keeps to three and a half lines, has Raphael say "Salve" only once and refrains from using exclamation points in Raphael's salutation—uses an exclamatory "¡Salve!" in the introduction to the salutation. The overall effect of this Marian enthusiasm is Raphael's appearing to be much more excited about meeting Eve than Adam; the five and a half lines of Raphael's greeting to Adam (*PL* 5.372–77) is translated regularly with fidelity and without exclamation points.

Other translators keep closer to the original than does Escóiquiz in rendering the passage on the Virgin Mary in the archangel Michael's later account of future history. Milton's Michael subordinates Mary's role in the Incarnation to God's in the use of "but": "A virgin his mother, but his sire / The power of the Most High" (*PL* 12.368–69). Escóiquiz's Michael levels and perhaps even reverses the emphasis. The translation presses the point and mystery of Mary's maternal virginity at greater length—and adds a crying baby Jesus:

«Que de una Vírgen las entrañas puras,
«Sin dejar de ser Vírgen han parido,
«Y en el establo pobre está llorando,
«De quien Dios es el Padre,
«Y una hija suya inmaculada madre.»

("That from a *Virgin*, her pure loins,
"Without ceasing from being *Virgin*, have given birth,
"And in a poor stable is crying
"One whose Father is God
"And, a *daughter* of his, his immaculate *mother*.") (emphases mine)[128]

Escóiquiz brackets the single reference to God the Father within four references to Mary. He also activates Marian devotional poetry by his choice of the word "immaculate," a word that never appears in the original epic but often appears in Hispano-Catholic Marian poetry. The Immaculate Conception—the belief that Mary was wholly without sin from her conception onward—was sustained for centuries by various Church Fathers, including Origen, Theodotus, St. Augustine, and John Duns Scotus, and became Catholic doctrine in 1854, within a half-century of Escóiquiz's translation.

Domesticating translational practices also involves the omission of literary conventions that are not particularly strong in the receptor language and culture. Given that Bible reading was restricted in early modern Spain per institutional constraints and given the reduction in reading epics in contemporary Western countries after the early modern period, Milton's Spanish translators would not necessarily have biblical allusions and epic conventions at the fore. Or perhaps they felt comfortable in reducing them given the minor effect the allusions might have on Spanish readers, who were far less directly familiar with the Bible than were their English counterparts. In any event, erase these allusions and conventions they did. The translational case of Milton's tour de force mimesis of word, action, and free will at the end of book 10, in the scene of Adam and Eve's repentance, is a chief example. Milton's fallen Adam suggests to Eve that they "to the place / Repairing where he judged us, prostrate fall / Before him reverent" to repent for their disobedience with "humiliation meek" (*PL* 10.1086–92). Immediately following the seven-line passage, the narrator describes the couple's action, again in seven lines, with only the necessary minor grammatical variations: they "to the place / Repairing where he judged them prostrate fell / Before him reverent" with "humiliation meek" (*PL* 10.1098–1104). This nearly exact repetition is anticipated intratextually by the repetition in God the Father's prophecy of just such a conversion in his conversation with the Son, that he will

> soften stony hearts
> *To pray repent, and bring obedience due.*
> *To prayer, repentance, and obedience due*
> Though but endeavoured with sincere intent,
> Mine ear shall *not* be slow, *mine* eye *not* shut. (*PL* 3.189–93, emphases mine)

Escóiquiz, Hermida, Rosell, Fuster, Castellón, and Atreides do not replicate Milton's careful ending of book 10. Since Escóiquiz states in his preface that he drew from Delille's French translation for his work and since Delille's *Le Paradis perdu* does reproduce the passage's original mimesis of language and action, we must attribute to Escóiquiz either deliberate choice to avoid the repetition or carelessness.[129] The Rosell translation uses "devotamente" (devotedly) for the first use of "reverently," then "reverentemente" (reverently) for the second. He deviates from standard Spanish word order by placing the adjective first in "contritos corazones" (contrite hearts) for the first use, only to use the normative order, "corazones contritos," for the second use. While he leaves the first passage a single sentence, he splits the second into two sentences, and though the first passage contains forty-two words, the second contains forty-seven.[130] Álvarez de Toledo renders the two seven-line passages in nearly the same number of lines. But even he diverges from the symmetry of Milton's original without gaining any positive effects in meaning or sound: he varies the wording of the first four lines of each passage but then replicates the near-exact repetition in the last lines of each passage.

Pujals is rare both in providing an equivalent and profoundly moving rendering of the passage and in calling attention in a brief note to the repetition and its aesthetic effect as emphasizing the depth of Adam and Eve's repentance and signaling the first operation of grace.[131] He does not, however, cite its precedence as both "Homeric formula" and biblical echo, as does, for example, John Leonard in his edition.[132] While Castellón does not replicate the passage's symmetry in his translation, he does call attention to biblical precedence:

Milton con su sensibilidad de dramaturgo, cuida especialmente el final de cada libro, como se busca en el teatro crear una buena impresión . . . [para] el espectador cada vez que desciende el telón. Con ecos bíblicos de *Isaías 16, 9*; de *Jeremías 9, 1* y del *Salmo* penitencial 51, 17, esta repetición persigue resaltar la profundidad del arrepentimiento de Adán y Eva, que los lleva a poner en práctica punto por punto lo que han pensado hacer; las acciones ratifican, así, exactamente, las palabras.

(Milton, with his sensibility as a dramaturge, takes special care with the endings of each book, just as in the theater one looks to create a good impression . . . [for] the spectator each time that the curtain descends. With biblical echoes of *Isaiah 16:9*, of *Jeremiah 9:1*, and the penitential *Psalm 51:17*, this repetition aims to exalt the profundity of Adam and Eve's repentance, which leads them to put into practice, point by point, what they have thought to do; the actions ratify, thus, the words exactly.)[133]

Missing in this note citing three Old Testament passages is reference to not only the Homeric tradition but also the key New Testament passage of contrition that describes an intent and subsequent action in nearly identical phrasing, the parable of the prodigal son who plans to state then states his repentance, "Father, I have sinned against heaven, and before thee, And am no more worthy to be called thy son."[134] As it turns out, Anglophone editions at the turn of the twenty-first century are also silent on this New Testament precedence.[135]

The notes of Spanish translations of *Paradise Lost*, especially in conjunction with their corresponding translated passages, are a treasure trove for readers seeking insights into Spanish reading practices. What did Spanish translators, presses, censors, and readers consider to be literary-cultural elements and influences and matters to be addressed in notes? Do these differ substantially from their Anglophone counterparts? Both English and Spanish editions include notes that clarify many of the same geographical places and historical figures. However, many references to poets and writers in the notes of Spanish translations of *Paradise Lost* are absent from major Anglophone editions. For example, accompanying Hermida's combined rendering of God's statement "what I will is Fate" and "Immediate are the acts of God" (*PL* 7.173, 176), "Su querer es obrar" (His will is action; italicized in the original), is the endnote "Esta expresion de Milton es repetida con frecüencia por santa Teresa" (This expression by Milton is repeated with frequency by St. Teresa) of Avila.[136] By contrast, both Fowler's and Leonard's Anglophone editions refer to Milton's prose *De doctrina Christiana*—the former also to "Augustinian commentators on *Genesis*" and Francis Bacon.[137] Also, Castellón includes in a note to the fallen angels' invention of the canon (*PL* 6.470–501) not the English, French, and Italian epic precedents common in Anglophone editions but rather a Spanish precedent: "Cervantes, contemporáneo de Milton, en el *Quijote*, I, 38, nos dice que el inventor de la artillería recibe en el infierno el premio por su diabólico invento" (Cervantes, a contemporary of Milton, tells us in the *Quixote* 1.38, that the inventor of artillery earns the prize in Hell for his diabolic invention).[138]

Other notes in Spanish translations reflect different sets of cultural concerns. For example, Sanjuán includes in a note on the "Pleiades" (*PL* 7.374) that appear at the end of the fourth day of Creation a reference to the Old Style calendar that starts the year on March 25, Annunciation Day, rather than January 1: these "siete estrellas . . . nacen con el Sol, en la primavera, deduciéndose de aquí que Milton ha adoptado la opinión de los que creen que este día de la Creación fue el 25 de marzo" (six stars . . . are born with the Sun, in the Spring, to be deduced from this that Milton has adopted the opinion of those who believe this day of Creation was March 25).[139] Editors Fowler and Leonard cite the Book of Job—the former also Ovid.[140] Castellón notes that the angel Michael's rhetorical question, "for on earth / Who against faith and conscience can be heard / Infallible? yet many will presume" (*PL* 12.528–30), is a statement "contra el dogma católico de la infalibilidad del Papa" (against the Catholic dogma of the infallibility of the Pope).[141] Fowler and Leonard note the religious attack on the "doctrine of papal infallibility," but also its intertextual relation to Milton's *Treatise of Civil Power*.[142] Elsewhere Castellón refers readers to non-English, indeed Catholic, art. For the passages in which God the Father calls Sin and Death "these dogs of Hell" and "My Hell-hounds" (*PL* 10.616, 630) as they near the postlapsarian world, Castellón writes, "Los dominicos fueron representados como «perros del Señor» en un fresco que Milton pudo haber visto en Santa María Novella de Florencia" (The Dominicans were represented as 'God's dogs/guard-dogs' in a fresco that Milton could have seen in [the Church of] Santa Maria Novella in Florence).[143] This religiously and biographically sensitive point complements Fowler's intratextual reference to "Sin's middle" in book 2 and Leonard's intertextual reference to an English work, Shakespeare's *Julius Caesar* 3.1.273.[144]

Studies of the disjunction and coherence of the notes in Anglophone and Spanish editions can enrich readings by Miltonists, world literature scholars, and, most important, general Spanish readers and students. Given that the global presence of Spanish continues to increase substantially, such work promises to have a sufficient readership to merit the effort, to contribute to larger studies that integrate other vernaculars, and to at last fulfill the stated aims of the many Spanish translators of *Paradise Lost*: to render the work's artistry to Spanish readers and to render Spanish readers full participants in world cultural networks.

Conclusion

This chapter takes its title (*PL* 5.574) from the archangel Raphael's conjecture about how to convey a massive story about one arena (Heaven) to an audience residing in another, albeit related, arena (Paradise). The "Divine interpreter" Raphael characterizes doing so as a "Sad task and hard" (*PL* 7.72, 5.564). Yet his task is rewarded by the Edenic couple, who "The story heard attentive, and was filled / With admiration" (*PL* 7.51–52). Certainly translating any story or work from one language and culture into another is a hard task, and in this chapter I have pointed out some of the "sad" falterings alongside the happy results by some of the linguistic, religious, and literary-cultural interpreters who have taken up the task of translating Milton's English epic into Spanish, albeit to less "attentive" and "admir[ing]" audiences. While no single edition of *El Paraíso perdido* has captivated me, I have found myself engaged aesthetically by specific passages in isolation and intellectually by analyzing the ten published full translations of *Paradise Lost* that I have been able to get my hands on.

Two main matters of these ten translations constitute the brief "translational sociology" which I shelved at the beginning of this chapter but with which I conclude it: limited access and its compensatory partner collaboration.[145] Reflecting in brief upon my research practices, rather than expurgating them, records another cause of low reader reception of *El Paraíso perdido* and some strategies for raising it. It is to be expected that access to older editions of *El Paraíso perdido* might be limited, even in today's globalized world with its electronic communication systems. Yet I was able to access four of the six editions (66 percent) published in the nineteenth century, in material and digital form (the Escóiquiz, Hermida, Rosell, and Sanjuán), a larger percentage than the six of thirteen (45 percent) published in the twentieth and twenty-first centuries (Matéos, Fuster, Pujals, Atreides, Álvarez de Toledo, and Castellón). For the latter, publishing and commercial practices contribute to my limited access.

In her excellent *Oculto a los ojos mortales: Introducción a* El Paraíso perdido *de John Milton* (Hidden from Mortal Eyes: An Introduction to John Milton's *Paradise Lost*; 2014), Anna Nardo recommends the Pujals (1986), Atreides (2005), and Castellón (2005) translations to new Hispanophone readers of Milton's epic.[146] Those would-be readers would have a hard time obtaining the Atreides and Castellón, which quickly became difficult to access in material or digital form. In summer 2016, Galaxia Gutenberg Press advised me that the Atreides edition was "agotado" (out of print) and would not be republished.[147] After first exhausting the usual means I regularly use in the U.S. of requesting a regional interlibrary loan from my campus library or purchasing at bookstores, the press, or online, in 2016 I emailed Atreides, who graciously provided me with the galley proofs via shareware. In 2017 Atreides's perseverance enabled him to regain the full rights to the translation so that he could publish it—minus the important endnotes—on Kindle.[148] Finally, in 2018, the National Library of Spain acquired a copy of the Atreides from which I could have requested digital copies of selections; fortunately my campus library extended its interlibrary loan so that I was able to research a copy from the University of Barcelona. Lack of reader demand does not seem to be the basis for the Atreides translation being out of print; Atreides explained, "The whole edition was sold out in no time, so there are no available copies. I myself have tried to get some more than once in recent times, but without success."[149]

My attempts at obtaining the Castellón in the U.S., in either material or digital form, proved unsuccessful, despite the U.S. having the second largest number of Hispanophones in the world. During the 2016–17 school year that I spent in Mexico through a Fulbright–García Robles Grant, I was able to access it at two disparate sites: a small city library in Oaxaca and at the famed library of the National Autonomous University of Mexico. Privilege and perseverance provided my access—a sharp contrast to the broad readership that Milton's Spanish translators have sought. This is to say that obstacles in a literary circuit that would fully include recent Spanish translations of *Paradise Lost* remain for persistent scholars, and certainly for general readers.

This chapter has left to others—and perhaps piqued their interest to accomplish—the work to be done on the political and literary roles of Milton's translators; Spanish translations of Milton's other poetry and prose works; the ebbs and flows of the publication of English-to-Spanish translations in the context of the publication of translated works worldwide; and so many other related and fascinating matters. Such work would be most effective if undertaken through international collaboration, since not all of the translations are readily available in one locale but rather are scattered worldwide, and many are out of print and unavailable for purchase. The collaboration of living Spanish translators and knowledgeable Hispanophone readers would take advantage of the international communication now available and activate individual agencies for the purpose of incorporating and affecting Spanish reader reception.

Milton's continued presence in the world literature canon has already been secured because of the works' archival strength, past influence, prestige, and, I would add, inherent poetic achievement. But his oeuvre remains to be reconfigured by the other valid measure of canonicity: current and future circulation and reading among not only those languages and institutions that have shaped the world literature canon to date but also Hispanophone Milton studies and readerships.[150] It is my hope that this chapter forms part of a foundation for translation studies—linguistic, literary, and sociocultural—that will not only account for the reasons why the efforts of so many Spanish translators have been stymied during the two centuries since the first full Spanish translation of *Paradise Lost* was published but will also create greater practical and theoretical pathways between existing and future Spanish translations of Milton's works and the would-be audiences who seek and would be grateful "to hear" (*PL* 8.3) Milton's works in Spanish.

CHAPTER 3

"To the Well-Trod Stage Anon"
Milton on the Spanish and International Stage

While Milton appears as a minor character in plays from the northeastern side of the Pyrenees in the nineteenth century, in the historical dramas *Cromwell* (1820) by Honoré de Balzac and *Oliver Cromwell* (1827) by Victor Hugo, he is the star of three plays from the southwestern side of the mountain range at the end of the same century:[1] the Portuguese play *Milton: Cómedia em um acto* (Milton: A Comedy in One Act; 1867) by Francisco Braga, the Spanish collaboration *El Paraíso de Milton, drama en tres actos y en verso* (Milton's Paradise, A Drama in Three Acts and in Verse; 1878) by Francisco Pérez Echevarría and Arturo Gil de Santivañes, and the Spanish drama *Milton: Cuadro dramático en un acto y en verso* (Milton: A Dramatic Scene in One Act and in Verse; 1879) by Hermenegildo Giner de los Ríos.[2] Each of these texts makes powerful if generally ignored statements about that era's Iberian stage and about the relationship between Spanish and British culture and literature. Giner de los Ríos's (1847–1923) *Milton*, however, is particularly rich intratextually, intertextually, and extratextually and therefore constitutes the primary focus of this chapter. My close reading of the play, combined with biographical and historical contextualization, complements the broad comparative translation description in the previous chapter of the at least nineteen full Spanish translations of *Paradise Lost* published over a nearly two-century period (1812–2005), both methodologies selected with deference to the objects of study.

This one-act and, by all appearances, one-performance play demonstrates how, two centuries after Milton's death, the English poet-statesman inspired a young Spaniard to attempt the difficult task of writing and staging a dramatic work in order to broker international relations. This play is but one of many multifaceted attempts at the end of the nineteenth century to use modern language studies and the arts to develop international relations, in this case triangulated, transhistoric, and transatlantic: *Milton: A Dramatic Scene* takes an English icon as its protagonist, was written by a Spaniard who would go on to become one of his country's major educational reformers, and was dedicated to and performed for the Smith Professor of Modern Languages at Harvard University, cofounder of the Modern Language Association (MLA), internationally famed writer, U.S. ambassador to Spain at the time, and later U.S. minister to England, James Russell Lowell. Compressed into the play are the cultural energies and political circumstances of the three countries at the time: the British Empire governed about 25 percent of the world population, the U.S. was experiencing enormous commercial and cultural growth following its Civil War and Reconstruction, and Spain had restored its monarchy and was creating what we might call the Silver Age of the Spanish stage.[3]

This chapter attends to the interplay of the dramatic work's external and internal elements, thus heeding the caution of the literary historian David T. Gies, "To study dramatic literature in nineteenth-century Spain totally removed from its personal, ideological, economic, and social context would be interesting, perhaps, but pointless."[4] Miltonists in particular may need no convincing on this point since Leah Marcus and others have made invaluable contributions to our understanding of Milton's early drama *A Mask Presented at Ludlow-Castle* (1634) by showing the interplay of the text's imagery and plot with the Egerton family's history, British local governance during the period, and the masque genre's development in English literature.[5] The first section of this chapter focuses on the play's context and on answering the questions "Why Milton?" and "Why a staged one-act drama?" The second section focuses on the play's permanent signs of sound and sense that evince its appeal as dramatic performance, and on answering the question that recovered texts, like *Milton: A Dramatic Scene*, rightly elicit, "But is it any good?" My answer for *Milton: A Dramatic Scene* is yes, and I support such an answer by focusing on prosody. Indeed the full title of the work, *Milton: A Dramatic Scene in One Act and in Verse*, signals the great importance that verse plays in this work. By attending to both context and text, we are able to appreciate the play's happy ending as a satisfying conclusion to the drama itself and also a wish fulfillment of sorts for the playwright to broker positive international relations between Spain, the U.S., and England.

Milton on the Spanish Stage

Hermenegildo Giner de los Riós's *Milton: A Dramatic Scene* is as unfamiliar to Hispanophone as to Anglophone audiences, despite its author's fame and concerted attempts to make it better known. Giner de los Ríos's renown in Spain rests primarily on his cofounding, along with his more famous brother, Francisco, the Free Institute of Teaching, which rehabilitated teaching methods and shaped liberal cultural politics in Spain. The brothers' educational practices and theories continue to be cited into the twenty-first century in Hispanophone pedagogy and culture, and Giner de los Ríos's Hispanophone translations continue to be used as standard texts in Spain. The National Library of Spain currently holds over one hundred of his works, thirteen of his books reside in the public library of Córdoba, Spain, and his translations continue to be republished.

Milton: A Dramatic Scene garnered neither immediate nor enduring recognition. The useful index of major Spanish newspapers of the nineteenth century, *Veinticuatro Diarios* (Twenty-four Dailies): *Madrid, 1830–1900*, does not mention its 1879 performance among the twenty-four entries related to Giner de los Ríos.[6] By contrast, Anfòs Par records numerous performances in Madrid and Barcelona starting in 1828 of another play featuring an English literary icon, *Shakespeare enamorado* (Shakespeare in Love).[7] Esteban Pujal's introduction to his Spanish translation of *Paradise Lost* (1986) also manifests the continued obscurity of the work. It mentions Echevarría and Santivañes's *Milton's Paradise* but not Giner de los Ríos's *Milton: A Dramatic Scene*.[8] This despite the fact that Giner de los Ríos mentions it in the section "John Milton" in his *Manual de literatura nacional y estranjera, antigua y moderna* (Manual of Literature, National and Foreign, Ancient and Modern; 1899), used widely for preparation for national public school exams: "Algunos episodios anecdóticos de su vida recogió hace años. el autor de estas líneas, en su drama *Milton*, estrenado con éxito" (Some years ago, the author of these lines pieced together some anecdotal episodes of his [Milton's] life, in his drama *Milton*, premiered with success).[9]

These "anecdotal episodes" of Milton's life reflect the young Giner de los Ríos's exposure to major British and European legends about Milton, and by extension Spain's participation in Western literary circuits, complicating claims about Spain's cultural isolation in this period. Giner de los Ríos's representation of an aged, blind, and downtrodden Milton, "fall'n on evil days . . . and evil tongues" (*PL* 7.25–26), accords with the figure of the forlorn Milton in the Echevarría and Santivañes play and throughout Europe and the Americas in the nineteenth century. Samuel Johnson's *Lives of the*

English Poets (1779–81) established the pathetic representation of the elder Milton that dominated Miltonic reception of the period as "poor and blind," "blind, and by no means wealthy": "Fortune appears not to have had much of his care. . . . In the civil wars he lent his personal estate to the parliament; but when, after the contest was decided, he solicited repayment, he met not only with neglect, but *sharp rebuke*; and, having tired both himself and his friends, was given up to poverty and hopeless indignation." Johnson moderates the potential for sentimental responses to Milton's supposed pecuniary straits, saying, "There is yet no reason to believe that he was ever reduced to indigence: his wants, being few, were competently supplied."[10] Recent scholarship lends credence to Johnson's proffered "yet." Carol Barton summarizes the evidence of Milton's Restoration condition as less pathetic: "As far as we can determine . . . the poet and statesman passed away as peacefully as he had lived those last few years, in the 'somewhat commodious' four-hearth dwelling. . . . His older nephew, Edward Phillips, says he 'had a very decent interment according to his Quality.'"[11]

Milton: A Dramatic Scene follows the titular character on the last day of his life, November 10, 1674, struggling in his relationship with the youngest of his three daughters, Débora, and against political threats, embodied in the Duke of York but aided by the English poet laureate William Davenant and the farm owner Abraham Clarke, based on the historical Milton's son-in-law.[12] In the play, Abraham laments that publishers "paid only ten pounds / for his [Milton's] *Paradise*," and Milton refers at various times to his financial straits.[13] The prefatory materials of late nineteenth-century republications of the most available Spanish translation of *Paradise Lost* at the time, Juan Escóiquiz's *El Paraíso perdido* (1812), describe Milton's pecuniary situation similarly:

> A pesar de las dificultades que su miseria y ceguera le ofrecian para procurarse la subsistencia, logró escribir su *Paraíso perdido*, que publicó en 1669. . . . Si no hubiesen sido siempre las grandes dificultades patrimonio de los grandes hombres (no hablo de guerreros), no podria creerse que solo despues de haber sometido su escrito al criterio de cuantos libreros ó editores habia en Lóndres en aquella época, no encontrase quien se lo tomase, hasta que dió con Samuel Simons, que se lo compró en quince libras esterlinas.

> (Despite the difficulties that his misery and blindness caused in providing himself with a subsistence, he succeeded in writing his *Paradise Lost*, which he published in 1669 [sic]. . . . If it were not for the fact that

great men (I do not refer to warriors) have always found it difficult to obtain a patrimony, it would be impossible to believe that it was only after he had submitted his work to the criteria of the many printers and editors that London had at that time, that he wasn't able to find anyone to take it, until he fell in with Samuel Simmons, who bought it from him for fifteen pounds sterling.)[14]

In her chapter "Milton" in *Los poetas épicos Cristianos* (The Christian Epic Poets; c. 1880), Emilia Pardo Bazán characterizes the Interregnum as a time when "empezaban para Milton los años tristes" (sad years began for Milton) due to political turmoil, his blindness, age, and family life.[15]

The three-page biography of Milton in Giner de los Ríos's *Historia crítica abreviada de literatura nacional y extranjera: Antigua y moderna* (Abbreviated History of National and Foreign Literature: Ancient and Modern; 1902) depicts the sad version of Milton's late life once again:

> Una hija suya sirvióle de amanuense para sus trabajos, cuando perdió por completo la vista á consecuencia de gota serena, producida, según creen algunos, por un exceso de labor durante la época de mayor hervor revolucionario, sirviendo de secretario á Cromwell. . . . Venida la Restauración, fué perseguido y encarcelado por los Estuardos, y aun habría perdido la vida, sin la intervención en su proceso del poeta Davenant, sirviente monárquico, que á su vez debió la existencia á Milton, en las azorosas circunstancias de la guerra civil.

> (One of his daughters served him as amanuensis for his works when he completely lost his sight as a result of amaurosis, produced, as some believe, by an excess of labor during the period of the major revolutionary happenings, while serving as secretary to Cromwell. . . . Upon the Restoration, he was persecuted and jailed by the Stuarts, and he even would have lost his life, without the intervention on his behalf of the poet Davenant, royal servant, who in turn owed his existence to Milton, in the heated circumstances of the civil war.)[16]

The characterization of Milton in various Spanish media at the end of the nineteenth century is consistent with the British, French, and U.S. characterizations most popular at the time.[17]

The image of Milton at odds with the women in his life is also pervasive in Spanish artistic works from the nineteenth century onward. Echevarría and Santivañes's *Milton's Paradise* embellishes this reputed feature with its invented romantic liaison between Milton's third wife, Elizabeth Minshull, and his young friend Richard Philarus. In the prologue to a republication of Dionisio Sanjuán's translation of *Paradise Lost* (1971), Joaquín Antonio Peñaloso resurrects another of Johnson's anecdotes, one that implies marital strife between Milton and Elizabeth:

> El nuevo gobierno se esforzó por ganar para su partido la pluma insigne de Milton, ofreciendole el antiguo puesto. No cedió ni a las presiones ni a los ruegos de la esposa: "Tu querrías pasear en tu carroza como otras mujeres, y tienes razón. Pero no menos razón tengo yo para querer vivir y morir como hombre de honor."

> (The new government [the Restoration monarchy] took pains to recruit to its side the illustrious pen of Milton, offering him his old post. He ceded to neither the pressures nor the pleas of his wife: "You would like to take rides in your large coach like other women, and that is a good enough reason. But no less reason do I have to want to live and die as a man of honor.")[18]

In Giner de los Ríos's play, Milton has been abandoned by his (unnamed) wife and is left with only his daughter Débora. In a soliloquy, he cries out about the vanity of seeking present calm through family comfort, male or female: "My brother follows the monarchy, / and my wife leaves me alone!"[19]

Truth is a bit more equivocal than the legend or the drama. Milton's brother, Christopher, differed from him religiously and politically, but John Shawcross and others have shown that the Royalist and Roman Catholic Christopher remained in contact with John through "his brother's last days," including drawing up his nuncupative will.[20] Also, it was about thirty years before Milton's death, the day on which the play *Milton: A Dramatic Scene* is set, that the historical Milton had been abandoned temporarily by his first wife, Mary Powell Milton (1625–1652). Starting about a month after their marriage in summer 1642, Mary returned from London to her family in Oxford and remained with them for nearly three years. We possess little information about the causes of the separation. Robert Fallon points out that "hostile armies tramped back and forth across the downs and pastures between London and Oxford, the King's capitol, effectively isolating the two cities from one another," thereby preventing Mary from returning "to her husband, even should she have wished to, about which there is considerable doubt."[21] We also know little about Milton's marriages to his second wife, Katherine Woodcock (d. 1658, m. 1656–1658), and third wife, Elizabeth Minshull (1639–1727, m. 1663–1674). But we do know that Elizabeth was at his deathbed and that Milton left the bulk of his estate to her.

The play's crisis and resolution hinge on a historically imprecise confluence on the signal day on which the play is set. Davenant (1606–1668) is brought back from the dead for melodramatic impact and, as I argue later, socioeconomic breadth among the "good guys." In the play, Abraham is Débora's suitor and Milton's friend, even though it is unlikely that the poet ever met the farmer and even though the farmer had become the historical Deborah's husband in June 1674, about five months before the play's setting. Finally, there is the matter of Milton's official release by the English government from retribution for regicide, release which he receives in the penultimate scene of the play: it had been granted to the historical Milton through Charles II's Act of Indemnity and Oblivion of August 1660, roughly fourteen years before the play's setting.[22]

The late nineteenth-century legends about Milton were received with as much interest as skepticism in Spain as elsewhere. The basis of the story of the Duke of York's antipathy toward Milton in the play dates from February 24, 1663, when the historical Duke of York reportedly told his brother King Charles II, "Brother, you are greatly to blame that you don't have that old rogue Milton hanged," and to a visit the same year to Milton to taunt him.[23] Pardo Bazán signals her recognition of the legendary nature of the titillating story even as she recounts it: "Cuéntase que el duque de York, hermano del rey y rey después bajo el nombre de Jacobo II, manifestó cierto día gran deseo de conocer personalmente al famoso Milton, y con la venia real, fue á visitar al poeta en su casa" (It is said that the duke of York, brother of the king and later king under the name James II, felt the great urge one day to meet personally the famous Milton and with royal permission went to visit the poet in his house).[24] Pardo Bazán also records the much less well known legend upon which the plot of Giner de los Ríos's *Milton: A Dramatic Scene* rests. After painting a chilling scene of a "temeroso Milton . . . viendo sus libros *Iconoclasta* y *Defensa del pueblo* quemadas por mano del verdugo" (fearful Milton . . . seeing his books *Eikonoklastes* and *Defence of the English People* burned by the executioner's hand) and "sabiendo que había sido desenterrado el cadáver de Cromwell para arrastrarlo por las calles y suspenderlo con cadenas de la horca, determinó esconderse" (knowing that Cromwell's cadaver had been disinterred in order to drag it through the streets and hang it with chains by the neck, he determined to go into hiding), she adds to the well-known story of Milton's temporary hiding that his friends spread "la noticia de la muerte del poeta, y llevando á hombros un ataúd vacío, lo escoltaron hasta el cementerio, fingiendo demostraciones de la pena de enterrar á Milton" (the news of the poet's death, and carrying an empty coffin on their shoulders, they escorted it to the cemetery, feigning demonstrations of sorrow at burying Milton).[25]

Giner de los Ríos packs in a number of other legendary details. Near the end of the play, when the Duke of York discovers Milton's true identity, Milton refers to himself as "Polyphemus," which Giner de los Ríos footnotes with "Milton was called *the new Polyphemus* by his enemies."[26] J. M. French's *Milton's Life Records* explains that the sobriquet was used during Milton's lifetime, and countless critical and popular commentaries use it. Further, Giner de los Ríos includes Deborah's reputation for beauty and her unique daughterly affection for her father. In the play, Abraham and the Duke of York both speak of Débora's lovely figure and voice. Her many outcries in the play reflect the story of the historical Deborah's emotional response to an illustration of her long-deceased father: "'Tis my father, 'Tis my father, I see him, 'tis him, and then she put her hands to several parts of her face, 'Tis the very man! here, here!"[27] In the afterword, Giner de los Ríos states that the production carefully re-created "the smallest detail with the costumes," so that the actors "dressed with entire fidelity to the epoch," "from the bourgeois Abraham, to the luxurious and elegant member of Parliament, and even the very laborers."[28]

Just as with Shakespeare's and other playwrights' anachronisms and invented material, there are a number of explanations for those that appear in this play. Given Giner de los Ríos's already emerging work in pedagogy and the social work of Spanish stage drama at the time, to be discussed shortly, cultural pedagogy accounts in part for the intense quantity of legend in this play. So does correlative audience interest. As for historical inaccuracies, we must consider not only artistic license, human error, and limited access to valid data but also a nineteenth-century European ethos surrounding the figure of the beleaguered blind English bard.

Complementing the play's integration of Milton's legend, life, and work for dramatic impact and international cultural prestige, Giner de los Ríos's early one-act *Milton: A Dramatic Scene* bears canny similarity to Milton's early *Mask*, from its performance time of roughly one and a half hours to its personal and occasional qualities. Critical work on *A Mask* provides us with a framework for gaining nuanced appreciation for a number of elements of *Milton: A Dramatic Scene*, as a select summary highlights.

A Mask was an entertainment commissioned for a specific occasion and at a specific location to celebrate a specific individual who held a political position: the celebration at Ludlow Castle on Michaelmas (September 29) 1634 of the 1631 installation of John Egerton, first earl of Bridgewater, as president of the Council of Wales. It involved an already famed artist, the music composer Henry Lawes, thirty-eight years old at the time, and a budding artist who would achieve later renown, Milton, then twenty-six years old. The performance of *Milton: A Dramatic Scene* on February 19, 1879, was about a year prior to the departure in February 1880 of the play's dedicatee, Lowell, to assume his new role as U.S. minister to England.[29] Just as the date of *A Mask* on Michaelmas and three years after the earl of Bridgewater's installation as president of Wales causes us to pause, readers may pause to wonder if *Milton: A Dramatic Scene*, "premiered on the night of February 19, 1879," doubled as an early birthday gift of sorts to mark Lowell's turning sixty on February 22, or if it was scheduled to precede the *carnaval* that year, from Friday, February 21, to Fat Tuesday, February 25. In that year Lowell's international stature was at its zenith: the elder statesman was then viewed both at home and abroad as one of the few U.S. literary authors worthy of note. The prominence of the thirty-one-year-old Giner de los Ríos in reforming Spain's educational system and culture, however, arose in his maturity, well after the play's premiere. As with the first publications of *A Mask* by Lawes and then by Milton, the dramatic narrative and paratexts of *Milton: A Dramatic Scene* resist closure in close readings. The narrative of *Milton: A Dramatic Scene* posits a valuation of human empathy and participation, as exhibited by Davenant and Abraham, rather than mastery and detachment, as exhibited by the Duke of York and his servant Charles.

The paratexts of both works highlight the occasional and cherished quality of their premiere performance. Lawes's 1637 publication of the work appeared with the informative title *A MASKE PRESENTED At Ludlow Castle, 1634:* On Michaelmasse night, before the *Right Honorable, Iohn* Earle of Bridgewater, Vicount *Brackly,* Lord Præsident of *Wales, And one of His Maiesties most honorable Privie Counsell;* was prefaced by a two-page encomium from "H[enry] Lawes" to "THE RIGHT HONORABLE IOHN *Lord Vicount* BRACLY, Son and heire apparent to the Earle *of Bridgewater, &c.*"; and concluded by calling attention to the individuals involved: "*The principall persons in this* Maske; were The Lord BRACLY, Mr. THOMAS EGERTON, The Lady ALICE EGERTON." The preface is at once politic and lovely in its recollection of the performance, including Bracly's "*selfe, and others of your noble familie*" and Lawes, who played "*your attendant* Thyrsis." Lawes writes that he made copies of the work so often that "it hath tir'd my pen to give my severall friends."³⁰

When Milton published *A Mask* in his *Poems . . . 1645*, he also called attention to the place and dedicatee in naming it *A MASK Of the same AUTHOR Presented At LUDLOW-Castle, 1634. Before The Earl of Bridgewater Then President of Wales*; reproducing the prefatory letter by Lawes; inserting "The Copy of a Letter Writt'n y Sir Henry Wootton, To the Author, upon the following Poem. *From the Colledge, this 13. Of April, 1638*"; and including "The Persons" or list of characters followed by the names of the main actors much the same as that at the end of the 1637 publication. Wotton's letter first praises the literary merit of the "dainty peece of entertainment," then contextualizes it as favored within an exclusive and sociable community. Before receiving the copy from Milton, he "had view'd it som good while before, with singular delight, having receiv'd it from our common Friend Mr. R. in the very close of the late *R's Poems*, Printed at *Oxford*, whereunto it was added (as I now suppose) that the Accessory might help out the Principal, according to the Art of *Stationers*, and to leave the Reader *Con la bocca dolce*."³¹

Many paratextual elements of *Milton: A Dramatic Scene* also evoke the deep, personal investments of its premiere performance. The title page graciously refers to the celebrated site of "the Apollo Theater," the main "actress Miss Antonia Contreras," and the dedicatee, "the Minister of the United States of America in Madrid, James Russell Lowell, Celebrated Poet, Corresponding Member of the Spanish Royal Academy."³² The Apollo Theater was a major cultural venue in late nineteenth-century Madrid. One indication of its importance is that the 1904 Nobel Prize in Literature laureate, Spanish playwright, and politician José Echegary premiered his well-received *En el puño de la espada* (At the Hilt of the Sword) at the Apollo just a few years prior, in 1875. Furthermore, Echegary dedicated his *O locura o santidad* (Insanity or Saintliness) of 1877 to Antonio Vico, who played the titular character in Giner de los Ríos's *Milton: A Dramatic Scene*. Vico was a "legendario actor" (legendary actor), whose superb acting made him the "gloria de la escena española" (glory of the Spanish scene).³³ Contreras's strong presence on the Spanish stage can be gathered from the fact that, five months after the February 1879 staging of *Milton: A Dramatic Scene*, she acted in *El Príncipe Hamlet*; she would go on to star as Desdemona in a Spanish modernization of Shakespeare's *Othello* in 1882, then to rejoin her *Milton: A Dramatic Scene* costar Vico in an 1893 staging of *Hamlet*.³⁴ After the close of the final scene is a page-long missive from the author offering gratitude to the many persons who made the performance possible, all of which chronicle the great efforts by Giner de los Ríos and his circle of acquaintances to impress and honor Lowell.

This and other compelling paratextual and extratextual elements suggest further answers for the questions posited at the beginning of this chapter: "Why Milton?" and "Why a staged one-act drama?" While there is much intriguing secondary evidence, my research uncovered no direct evidence to provide full and complete answers.[35] Well-founded if provisional answers center on the mutually energizing dynamic between dramatic art and international politics.

Giner de los Ríos's selection of the genre of drama must be considered against the backdrop of Spain's and the U.S.'s varied developments of their respective national literatures. Spain's national theater was in the midst of a renaissance, while the U.S. national theater was yet to gain substantial ground. The international renown of the Spanish theater, even beyond its Golden Age, is reflected in the once well-known story of how Lowell's post in Spain came about.[36] According to Lowell's friend, the U.S. socialist novelist William Dean Howells, Lowell was first offered the post of U.S. ambassador to Austria. In declining that post, he intimated his desire to be considered instead for the similar post in Spain by quipping to Howells, "I *should* like to see a play by Calderón," one of Lowell's favorite playwrights.[37] With the *refundaciones* (adaptations) of Golden Age plays in the mid- to late nineteenth century, the other Spanish theatergoers too would have recognized Giner de los Ríos's use of the verse as Calderonian and, perhaps, its tribute to Lowell's tastes.[38]

The nineteenth-century renaissance of Spanish drama was part of Spain's active attempts at a cultural rebirth. In addition to the restoration of famed theaters, as David Gies documents, the "number of new theatres that were built after 1867 . . . underlines the great public interest in public theatre in the second half of the century." In *Milton: A Dramatic Scene*, Giner de los Ríos celebrates both Spain's theatrical past and its present: the former with his use of the Spanish verse form of *décimas*, which calls attention to the historical glories of the Spanish stage and which are discussed in the next section; the latter in his choice of a one-act play, which calls attention to Spain's contemporary elan. The importance of Giner de los Ríos's first independent foray on the Spanish stage is underscored by Gies's assessment that Spaniards were intent on maintaining the tradition of a strong Spanish national theater because it had become, at the end of the nineteenth century, "inextricably linked with a national sense of self-worth. Honorable theater was, in many minds, one of the last vestiges of national glory. As Spain gradually sank into a political stupor, wracked with wars at home and abroad, and struggling to maintain a dignity that was strongly identified with the Golden Age, the theater became emblematic not only of the troubles facing the country, but also of its hope for recovery."[39]

Giner de los Ríos would likely have been familiar with Lowell's taste because the two had a sustained relationship during Lowell's ambassadorship in Spain. Upon his arrival in Madrid, Lowell quickly joined the intellectual circle of the eminent Spanish scholar, Anglophile, and Orientalist Pascual de Gayangos y Arce, who had corresponded with, among others, Lowell's predecessors in the Smith Chair of Modern Languages at Harvard, George Ticknor and Henry Wadsworth Longfellow. Gayangos's daughter Emilia explains the genesis of the relationship between Lowell and Giner de los Ríos: "When [Lowell] expressed a wish to perfect his knowledge of Spanish I recommended our friend Don Hermenegildo de los Ríos to read with him. They got on capitally, and became very friendly. Twice a week Mr. Lowell came to me for his Spanish lesson, an hour or more of most delightful converse on many subjects, including his life in Italy, Germany, and America, with reminiscences of days and evenings spent with Longfellow, Emerson, and others."[40] During his ambassadorship in Spain, Lowell wrote of Giner de los Ríos, "[He] comes to talk Spanish with me. He is a fine young fellow who lost a professor's chair for his liberal principles and is now a professor in the Free University they are trying to found here—the Libre Enseñanza. I like him very much and, though he doesn't look much like him, he reminds me often of Harry [Henry James]."[41]

As did many of Spain's well-heeled literati and harassed educators, Lowell supported the Free Institute that the Giner de los Ríos brothers initiated in 1876 to counteract the stultifying academic atmosphere wrought by the investigations by conservative Restoration clerics in state schools in Spain. Lowell, who worked tirelessly to promote educational reforms in the U.S. and internationally, wrote of his support for the brothers' ambitious educational project: "They have established by almost starving themselves the *Institución Libre de Enseñanza* at Madrid where young Spaniards may and do get modern ideas. They and those like them are the only Spaniards who are not hostile to England and English Liberal ways of looking at things. They are doing an excellent work as I know not by hearsay but by my own knowledge."[42] Like many intellectuals in both the U.S. and Spain, Lowell looked to the international powerhouse of England for progressive ideas, "Liberal ways of looking at things."

Lowell's and Giner de los Rios's parallel work for political and educational reform gets us a little closer to determining why Giner de los Ríos might have chosen to feature Milton, rather than a U.S. icon like Abraham Lincoln, whom Lowell had so stridently supported. Both Lowell and Giner de los Ríos acknowledged that their respective countries were considered culturally backward in the late nineteenth century, and each considered the other's home country as such. They looked instead to English figures as models. One response to "Why Milton?" is that Milton is an *English* model for the public intellectual, or the scholar-writer as citizen. Certainly, more than the protean figure of Shakespeare, Milton speaks to the progressive political, educational, and literary roles that Lowell and Giner de los Ríos were sketching for their nations.[43]

Lowell held a highly ambivalent view of Spain, as did many literati in the U.S. and Europe at the time. On the one hand, he esteemed Spanish works of past eras and alluded to them regularly in his popular poetry and prose; he promoted Spanish studies at Harvard, at a time when the classical languages garnered more prestige than did modern vernaculars; and upon his return from Europe, he donated to Harvard Library "688 volumes and 130 pamphlets," "mostly Spanish with a few English and Italian," that he purchased in Spain.[44] On the other hand, Lowell's Spanish ambassadorship "enabled him to see with greater certainty the Orientalism that he had felt already in Spain," as his biographer Claire McGlinchee records.[45] In one letter Lowell comments on the poor quality of texts available in Spain: "I bought the other day the photolithographic copy of the first edition of 'Don Quixote,' for the sake, mainly of [the Director of the National Library of Spain Juan Eugenio] Hartzenbusch's notes. But they are mostly worthless—of value mainly as collation. He doesn't understand his author in the least, whose delightfully haphazard style is too much for him."[46] In another letter Lowell laments, "You can't imagine how far I am away from the world here—I mean the modern world. Spain is as primitive in some ways as the books of Moses and as oriental. Spaniards have, I believe, every possible fault—and yet I love the jades for a' that! They find themselves in the midst of a commercial age, poor devils! with as little knowledge of book-keeping as the Grand Turk."[47]

While it is easy to dismiss Lowell for his participation in the construction of an "Orientalized, racialized, and primitivized Spain," it is important to contextualize his negative perceptions and articulations.[48] Lowell is equally critical of the cultural state of his beloved homeland. His frustration with the nascent state of U.S. literature is encapsulated in his long poem "A Fable for Critics" (1848). Perhaps the most famous lines from the poem today are those concerning Lowell's contemporary Edgar Allan Poe: "There comes Poe with his raven, like Barnaby Rudge, / Three fifths of him genius and two fifths sheer fudge." This passage is often extracted to demonstrate Lowell's hard feelings toward his fellow U.S. writer, overshadowing Lowell's overall purpose of using satire about the state of U.S. literature to prod U.S. writers to improve it. Indeed Lowell includes himself in the list of the nation's poetasters:

> There is Lowell, who's striving Parnassus to climb
> With a whole bale of *isms* tied together with rhyme,
> He might get on alone, spite of brambles and boulders,
> But he can't with that bundle he has on his shoulders,
> The top of the hill he will ne'er come nigh reaching
> Till he learns the distinction 'twixt singing and preaching.[49]

Elsewhere Lowell attributes in part the paucity of great U.S. literature to the country's historical belatedness and voices his great hopes for the future: "Yet I think we shall find the good of it one of these days in being thrown back more wholly on nature; and our literature, when we have learned to feel our own strength, and to respect our own thought because it is ours, and not because the European Mrs. Grundy agrees with it, will have a fresh flavor and a strong body that will recommend it."[50]

Lowell's assessment of his nation's literature aligns with those in Spanish histories of world literature and literary guides through the first quarter of the twentieth century. Giner de los Ríos includes U.S. literature only in an appendix in his *Manual of Literature*. He begins the section with this basic assessment: "La literatura norte-americana constituye, en realidad, un apéndice de la inglesa, con cierto carácter propio y peculiar que le distingue de la maternal, de igual modo que hay diferencias de lenguaje más que de pensamiento (aunque de éste también) entre las literaturas hispano-americanas y la española" (North American literature is really an appendix to English literature, with some of its own and unique character that distinguishes it from the mother literature, in the same way that there are differences in language more than in thought (although of this sort too) between Hispano-American and Spanish literatures). He explains that, because of Puritan asceticism and the business of building a country, "nada tiene de extraño que los colonos ingleses, no solo no fuesen protectores de las artes, sino, en cierto modo, sus enemigos declarados" (it is not at all strange that the English colonists not only were not protectors of the arts but, in some ways, were their avowed enemies).

He goes on to praise generously U.S. oratory, which he believes accounts in large part for the lack of strong U.S. poetry and drama:

Á manera de como en Grecia y Roma la vida pública determinó, como era consiguiente, el gran apogeo de la oratoria, en los Estados Unidos fué la elocuencia manifestación literaria de grandísima importancia desde la proclamación de la independencia, compartiendo los laureles la politica y la moral y la religión.

(In the same way that in Greece and Rome public life fostered, as it followed, the great apogee of oratory, in the United States eloquence was the literary manifestation of very great importance starting with the Declaration of Independence, politics and morality and religion sharing the laurels.)

Aligning the literary history of the U.S. and England with those of Greece and Rome is affirmative about the potential for a great U.S. literature. Giner de los Ríos plainly sees the "falta á los Estados Unidos desde los comienzos hasta el momento presente, la creación de un teatro nacional" (absence of the creation of a national theater in the United States from their beginnings until the present moment) but calls U.S. novelists "maestros" (masters) of that genre, a compliment he increases by claiming that they should be viewed as "compartiendo la gloria con Inglaterra y aun emulando á sus grandes escritores" (sharing the glory with England and even emulating their great writers).[51] Like Lowell commenting on Spain's literary culture, Giner de los Ríos gives a backhanded compliment to the U.S.'s.

The compliments to Lowell's literary tastes and international prestige, however, are unfettered in *Milton: A Dramatic Scene*. Giner de los Ríos reproduces Lowell's moralized Milton on the Spanish stage. Milton was one of Lowell's favorite English figures, one whose use and recognition in allusion signaled for Lowell membership in a Republic of Letters with England at its head.[52] In his edition of Milton's *Areopagitica* (1891), Lowell is unabashed in showing that he reads literature intimately for wisdom. He writes that Milton "is not so truly a writer of great prose as a great man writing in prose, and it is really Milton that we seek there [in *Areopagitica*] more than anything else." Alluding to *Paradise Lost*, Lowell writes, "We listen to him as Adam to the angel, and the voice lingers not only in the ear but in life." Likewise, in the flourishing ending to his essay on *Areopagitica*, Lowell avows that Milton inspires individuals to work for political improvement: "And it is the breath of this spirit that pours through the 'Areopagitica' as through a trumpet, sounding the charge against whatever is base and recreant, whether in the world about us or in the ambush of our own natures."[53]

This political vision provides yet another part of the answer to "Why Milton?," specifically an elderly blind Milton (he became completely blind in March 1652, at the age of forty-three).[54] As disability studies has demonstrated cogently, literary works often employ characters with disabilities, including those associated with advanced age, to reflect and shape social support systems, whether accommodating or restrictive, the latter often emphasized in satires and tragedies.[55] The specific disability of blindness often plays on the notion of sight and insight, especially in drama. Hugo Tosca notes the interplay in regard to the many blind characters in the plays of Milton's near-contemporary Félix Lope de Vega y Carpio (1562–1635), which move audiences to consider "not only the simple faculty of seeing, but also the capacity to reflect on one's very existence."[56] With the blind, elderly Milton as the focal point, *Milton: A Dramatic Scene* offers a modern ideal of society with gradations of personal and physical abilities, disabilities, and accommodations. The dramatized society in microcosm acts out the playwright's idealized society at large, in this case one in which social progress and personal genius require the plural efforts of like-minded individuals. Milton's lack of physical sight and pecuniary straits are matched by the Duke of York's lack of human empathy and, at the end, the love of a good woman. Indeed even the Duke of York's regal power works to disable him from brawling, much less to do so with someone below his own socioeconomic status, to achieve some revenge on Milton. The diverse aspects of social disability are also represented by the other two main characters: Débora because of her female gender and poverty, and Abraham due to his rank and financial constraints.

Until the antepenultimate scene, the audience is aware of all the dramatic goings-on, informative asides and soliloquies, and literary afterlife of Milton's works. It is only in the penultimate scene that the characters finally possess full knowledge of Davenant's financial and political aid and the Duke of York's false wooing of Débora. In lieu of a pat reconciliation between a would-be Milton's side and a would-be Duke of York's side—an oppositional duality of good guys and bad guys with which this play often toys—the tempered yet positivist message of hope for the present and future lies in an ultimate justice that results in, if not true peace, at least social equilibrium and artistic beauty. The trio of Milton representing the old society and of Débora and Abraham representing the new one cocreate the final stanza, a *décima*, that echoes the breathtaking and also nationally affiliated Shakespearean love sonnet, "If I profane with my unworthiest hand," cocreated by the titular characters of Shakespeare's *Romeo and Juliet*:⁵⁷

Deborah:	My God!
Abraham:	Such pointless horrors!
Milton:	Receive my final saying! . . .
	and pray for me; for praying
	over tombs creates flowers . . .
	and in new and fresh splendors . . .
	that faint spark illuminate,
	like a presence that radiates
	the soul . . . I dream of seeing
	something infinite of a being . . .
	that in the mind germinates! . . .
Deborah:	God of mercy and good,
	don't tear him from my arms' hold,
	or from my heart's shattering mold
	take my orphanhood.
Milton:	Son . . . her livelihood . . .
Abraham:	With God as my witness,
	I swear it! . . .
Milton:	Friend . . . my gratefulness . . .
	Good-bye . . .
Deborah:	Father of my life!
	Cry, hope lost in such strife!
Milton:	Your . . . union . . . I . . . do . . . bless.⁵⁸

The brio of the poetic concert is enhanced by the mimetic quality we can ascertain about the similar hope for a "fit society" (*PL* 8.Argument) for the creators, performers, and audience of the premiere of *Milton: A Dramatic Scene*, brought together at the Apollo Theater on that winter day in 1879. The play's ending signals the success of Milton, Abraham, Débora, and the absent Davenant in creating a household paradise through communal, complementary strengths. Such a moral echoes the social message common to Lowell's use of Milton as a representative of the strength of like-minded but diverse individuals working in community to recognize and remedy social ills.

The ending of *Milton: A Dramatic Scene* also leads us to another important answer for both "Why Milton?" and "Why a staged one-act drama?" The social progressivist view of the play's ending is also resonant with the *alta co-*

media that filled the post-1850 Spanish stage. One of its chief playwrights and a member of the Real Academia Española (Royal Spanish Academy), Manuel Tamayo y Baús (1829–1898), rightly earned the nickname from Gerald Flynn of "Tamayo of the Happy Ending," due to the speedy and deeply moralizing denouements of his plays.[59] As do many works of the *alta comedia*, many of Tamayo y Baús's one- to three-act dramas represent a troubled romantic relationship as a vehicle to comment on contemporary social structures, social pretensions, and socioeconomic dependencies. They often employ characters from high and low classes to call for a return to values that promote social harmony and reduce social fragmentation.[60]

This plot is propelled by the short dramatic form utilized by Tamayo y Baús and many other Spanish playwrights of the period. Using the 1871–72 theater season as an example, Gies summarizes, "Of the total of 267 productions, only six were of four-act plays, thirty-nine of three-act plays, fifteen of two-act plays, and the rest (207) of one-act plays."[61] This formal state of affairs was not welcomed by many conservative Spanish literati, like the Spanish journalist Eduardo de Cortázar, who held five-act plays as a gold standard. To my mind, the nineteenth-century Spanish one-, two-, and three-act plays that proliferated on the Spanish stage are extensions of the presentational and intellectual flexibility that Lope de Vega articulated in terms of the three-act plays that he established in the Spanish Golden Age, and analogous to the flexibility in English meter for long poems that can be traced to Milton's use and justification of "heroic verse without rhyme" in *Paradise Lost* (*PL* "The Verse").[62] The similar plot elements and form of *Milton: A Dramatic Scene* are understandable given that Giner de los Ríos participated in the same congenial circle of Spain's stage as did Tamayo y Baús. For example, the actor who played the titular character in *Milton: A Dramatic Scene*, Antonio Vico, acted in the 1870 premiere of Tamayo y Baús's *Los hombres de bien* (Upstanding Men).[63]

Of singular importance to Giner de los Ríos's selection of the English author Milton as protagonist is Tamayo y Baús's *A New Drama*, which features as one of its three main characters Milton's near-contemporary Shakespeare. Tamayo y Baús's three-act drama premiered on May 4, 1867, just about a decade before *Milton: A Dramatic Scene* and at the nearby Zarzuela Theater.[64] Before *A New Drama*, Spanish translations of two nineteenth-century French plays that feature Shakespeare as a character graced the Spanish stage. *Shakespeare enamorado* (Shakespeare in Love), staged in 1828, is Ventura de la Vega's Spanish translation of Alexandre Duval's French *Shakespeare amoureux*, staged in France in 1804 and published in 1823.[65] The multiple publications of Vega's translation (in its first decades, in 1823, 1831, 1843) indicate some of the play's popularity. Similarly Enrique Zumel's play *Guillermo Shakespeare* (1853) is "based on Clemence Robert's French novel."[66] While Tamayo y Baús's *New Drama* represents Shakespeare as a mature, reflective man of theater, as seen in the Vega and Zumel translations, its plot is distinct. Well appreciated at home, *A New Drama* appears as one of the *joyas* (jewels) included in the first edition of the often referenced and republished *Autores dramáticos contemporáneos y joyas del teatro español del siglo XIX* (Contemporary Dramatic Authors and Jewels of Nineteenth-Century Spanish Theater; 1881–82).[67] The play also achieved stage success internationally and, significantly, among Lowell's U.S. coterie, specifically Howells. As José Manuel González Herrán notes, the fame of *A New Drama* soon "sobrepas[ó] las fronteras españolas" (extend[ed] beyond Spanish borders) through translations into German, Norwegian, French, and Russian, and "en 1874 se había estrenado en Nueva York una versión inglesa bastante libre, titulada *Yorick*, de Augustin Daly.... Entre 1876 y 1879, Lawrence Barret incluyera en su repertorio una versión diferente" (in 1874 a very free English version of it premiered in New York, titled *Yorick*, by Augustin Daly.... Between 1876 and 1879, Lawrence Barret included in his repertoire a different version), *Yorick's Love* by Howells, staged in New Orleans, Boston, Philadelphia, and San Francisco.[68]

Milton's rise in nineteenth-century Spanish culture, in the form of visual art, literary criticism, and popular staging, is concomitant with Shakespeare's. More specifically, Shakespeare's presence as a dramatic character in French and Spanish drama precedes and is more widespread and sets the stage for Milton's. We can detect some impetus for Giner de los Ríos to do with a dramatic Milton what Tamayo y Baús had done with a dramatic Shakespeare, which is to innovate Western heritage by merging it with Spanish stagecraft for commercial success and, by extension, international cultural prestige for Spain.

Giner de los Ríos and Lowell shared and regularly expressed an unabashed belief in literary authors and their aficionados in the international Republic of Letters as pivotal to societal progress. For example, in the passage from his edition of *Areopagitica* quoted earlier—about Milton's "spirit that pours through the 'Areopagitica' as through a trumpet, sounding the charge against whatever is base and recreant"—Lowell overtly alludes to William Wordsworth's "Scorn Not the Sonnet," which praises a transhistorical, international array of European writers—Englishmen Shakespeare and Edmund Spenser; Italians Francesco Petrarch, Torquato Tasso, and Dante Alighieri;

and Portuguese Luís de Camões—and ends by lionizing Milton's greater use of the verse form, in whose hands "The Thing became a trumpet; whence he blew / Soul-animating strains—alas, too few!"[69] Lowell's poem encourages individuals to act even though long history and large populations may make them feel insignificant, to read and write literature even though doing so may seem trivial and impractical, and to recognize the international solidarity that literature models for international relations. This kind of response has not been superseded, even among sophisticated readers. Wordsworth's and Lowell's reading habits extend, for example, to the Derridean Maurice Blanchot, who effuses, "Kafka wanted only to be a writer, the *Diaries* show us, but the *Diaries* succeed in making us see in Kafka something more than a writer; they foreground someone who has lived rather than someone who has written: from then on, he is the one we look for in his work."[70]

Lowell was wont to share his deep appreciation for Milton the citizen-poet in his written works and conversations. Giner de los Ríos's play and pedagogical manuals demonstrate that he too heard Milton's inspiring strains and thought of Milton as a historical agent during his life and through his textual afterlives. Giner de los Ríos expressed his simpatico, with Lowell, with Milton, in his "first dramatic performance," a vehicle that showcases his appreciation for Lowell, his participation in a vibrant late nineteenth-century Western literary circuit, and his application of his individual talents to rejuvenating the Spanish stage and its dramatic verse.[71]

Spanish Dramaturgy in *Milton*

The full title of Giner de los Ríos's play, *Milton: A Dramatic Scene in One Act and in Verse*, points to the great importance of verse in the play. It is indeed chief among the impressive elements of the play, such as subtle allusions to Milton's works, internal stage directions related to Milton's blindness, and deft mingling of comic and serious scenes. The prosody deserves close attention for three interrelated reasons.

First, it demonstrates as much as possible the artistry of the work. While I use the evaluative principles from New Criticism to help account for the perceived success of this work, I am not bent on offering an aesthetics that can yield unequivocal agreement, something that has heretofore eluded valorous attempts. Yet I do aver that the play's technical acumen is testimony to its likelihood of creating a dynamic and pleasing total performative experience.[72] Second, to attend to the prosody of *Milton: A Dramatic Scene* is to be sensitive to its author's emphasis on cultural aesthetics, logically enough, given that the titular character is central to discussions of poetic art and lived during the century in which criticism "shifted from the practice of commentary on learning to the conscious exercise of 'taste,' 'sensibility,' and 'discrimination.'"[73] The attention that has been given to Milton's choice of blank verse for his English epic has clarified the way prosody interacts with political, spiritual, and generic matters.[74] Due attention to Giner de los Ríos's mixture of rhyme schemes also rewards analysis. Rhyme endured and strengthened on the Spanish stage, while it waned in deference to blank verse and prose on the English stage. Dramatic rhyme is a historically and culturally bound element of Spanish aesthetics, and our appreciation of it as such leads to a firmly grounded appreciation of this specifically Spanish play.[75] Third, the choice and interplay of verse stanzas in *Milton: A Dramatic Scene* contribute intricately to constructing character and propelling action.

Scenes 1 and 2, spoken by three minor characters, the laborers Tom and Edwin and the Duke of York's servant Charles, are entirely in assonant rhyme in even-numbered lines, the *romances* common to Spanish ballads. Tom and Edwin complain to Charles about their unpaid wages from Abraham, the recent arrival of Milton and Débora to the farm, the cost of the upkeep of the two arrivals in light of Abraham's tight financial circumstances, and the presumed death of Milton in a nearby forest. In scene 3, the courtier-poet Davenant makes his only appearance and is the first to speak in consonantal rhyme. In a soliloquy consisting of seven and a half stanzas of the Spanish verse form *quintilla*, Davenant characterizes his secret visit to Abraham's farm as a vaguely defined but "august mission."[76] His poetic speech suggests the validity of his (ambiguous) self-identification as the great English poet of the day. He soliloquizes about aid from or "to one who appears Shakespeare's heir."[77] Reminding us that literary history had not yet been written at the time of Milton's death, Giner de los Ríos makes the most of the ambiguity of the Spanish *al*, which can mean "from" or "to." Is it the Royalist Davenant or the Puritan Milton who is the one "who appears to be Shakespeare's heir"?[78] On the one hand, the historical Davenant was the unofficial English poet laureate before John Dryden and, as Giner de los Ríos notes, "It is believed that Davenant was Shakespeare's illegitimate son."[79] On the other hand, the dramatic Davenant calls Milton the "Homer of Christianity," as he was known especially in Hispanophone biographies.[80] Giner de los Ríos leaves the determination in the balance, as the scene closes abruptly with Davenant saying, "I feel footsteps, someone's coming," but not before he leaves behind a mysterious closed pouch in order to save Milton from yet another "persecution."[81]

Davenant's *quintillas* distinguish him as much from the characters of scenes 1 and 2 as from the characters in the next scene: the dejected Milton and worried Débora of scene 4. Milton's sentences trail off and the stage directions have him speaking "wear[il]y" and "with a weak voice" about the personal, financial, and political calamities that have befallen them. The assonant rhymes in the romances with which Milton speaks manifest his failing strength. Débora corroborates that sense, also in romances, when she laments the rejection of Milton's late-coming masterwork by London publishers:

> [Deborah]:   men
> so impudent to skimp and cut down
> that which is invaluable
> to such commercial dross.[82]

Consonantal rhyme reemerges in scene 5, when Abraham returns from London to tell Milton and Débora that their plan, of faking Milton's death in the forest so that the government authorities will stop searching for him, has worked. The *redondillas*, enveloped consonantal quatrains (*abba, cddc*, etc.), of this scene are appropriately stable for the exposition of the confusing plan. Romances reemerge in scene 6, in which Abraham speaks with only Débora about his failure to secure a publisher for Milton's works before he leaves her alone on stage while he goes to assuage the laborers.

The reintroduction of *quintillas* in scene 7 provides an unexpected shift in the audience's affections and interest. Débora's soliloquy of eight and a half *quintillas*, one stanza longer than Davenant's soliloquy, is an attention-grabbing vehicle that positions her as a candidate for the hero of the play, corroborating the strong casting of this role, as already discussed. As the scene progresses, Débora strengthens her resolve to tell her father the sad fact that her intended choice of husband differs from his of Abraham. Her poetic language, coupled with her brave determination in the face of her subordinate gender and status, positions her as the verbal heir of her rebellious poet-father Milton.[83]

In scenes 8 and 9, the verse signals the pivotal change in Milton's character and the play's tone. Scene 8, in which Débora reveals to her father that her affections have been won by none other than Milton's enemy, the Duke of York, employs *versos pares*, rhymed pairs of lines enclosed by unrhymed pairs of lines. Individual household members complete each other's rhymes in this easy stanza form. In these scenes the aural ease and steadiness of the verse balances the upset in the household's unity.

In scene 9 Milton is alone on stage, the grieving Débora having exited stage right; it is here that Giner de los Ríos provides Milton with a rhyme scheme that marks his renewed strength and that most strongly creates a connection between the Spanish audience and the titular character. As Milton moves from grief to renewed faith in God, he delivers seven stanzas of the complex Spanish verse form of the *décima*, a ten-line stanza of octosyllabic lines with a rhyme scheme of *abbaaccddc*. The first stanza contains a barely acceptable slant rhyme (9.5), implying Milton's slightly weakened poetic powers, but the remaining *décimas* are robust. Speaking nearly twice as many lines in stanzas that are twice as long as Davenant's and Débora's *quintillas*, a reinvigorated Milton implies the answer to the question posed in scene 3 as to the identity of "Shakespeare's heir": the greater poet is Milton, and that greater poet speaks a quintessential Spanish verse form. (Davenant is not included in Giner de los Ríos's *Manual of Literature*.)

The *décima* is commonly used on the Spanish stage "when lofty action is taking place or when some highly significant decision is being made."[84] The specifically Spanish rhyme scheme also positions Milton as a figure in poetic conversation with the Spanish poets of his own seventeenth century, for the *décima*—also known as the *espinel*—is a poetic form that saw its heyday in that century, on the heels of its establishment by the Golden Age poet, playwright, novelist, and musician Vicente Gómez Martínez-Espinel, after whom the verse form was nicknamed. The *décima* was used extensively by Spain's most famous Golden Age dramatists, Lope de Vega, Tirso de Molina, and Calderón. Moreover Milton completes his final *décima*, unlike Davenant and Débora with their unfinished *quintillas*, thus providing the sense of a Milton uniquely in control.

After the Duke of York enters in scene 10 at the end of Milton's show-stopping *décima* soliloquy, the play is entirely in consonantal rhyme. Up to this point consonantal rhyme has been used in private moments between speaker and audience or between household members. But starting in scene 10 it is brought into more mixed interchanges and for defense. The *redondillas* of the scene countervail the tumultuous action, as they do for most of scene 11. The *quintillas* at the end of scene 11 balance the growing narrative tension: the Duke of York is still ignorant of the fact that the man he has been speaking to is blind and is Milton, not Abraham's servant John (the cadaver in the forest); Débora is still ignorant of the fact that the Duke of York has been toying with her affections to get to Milton; and Abraham is still under the mistaken impression that the Duke of York is on his side. The *quintillas* continue into scene 12, when Milton discloses his true identity to the Duke of York and the full import of the duke's machinations are revealed to the incredulous Débora and Abraham. The scene ends with Débora shifting her romantic attentions to Abraham, leading to the catastrophe of the final two scenes of the play.

Scenes 13 and 14 possess the most frantic action and the most complex rhyme schemes: scene 13 with *quintillas* and scene 14 with *décimas*. In the well-populated scene 13, it is apparent that Débora will marry Abraham and that Davenant's pouch contains money and a royal decree—discovered at last—thus eliminating Abraham's financial woes, rendering Milton free from political persecution, and thwarting the Duke of York's conniving. Milton concludes the scene, interrupting the duke with the beginning of a *décima* that triples as an enveloped consonantal quatrain and the beginning of a *quintilla*, with a poetic power that parallels the denotative power he expresses:

> [Duke]: I'm leaving, Milton, but I you assure ... (*To Milton.*)
> Milton: (*Rising with extreme effort, after which he collapses.*)
> Not one more cursed word. Leave
> because your upstart infamy
> corrupts, and your breath impure.
> (*The Duke and his men leave, with the Duke making menacing signs.*)[85]

In scene 14 only Milton, Débora, and Abraham remain on stage. Their lines combine to form two *décimas*, signaling the trio's strong and full union, poetically confirming the play's last words, spoken by a Milton looking forward to his imminent death: "Your ... union ... I ... do ... bless."

Conclusion

The text and context of *Milton: A Dramatic Scene* direct us to a positivist message of earnest work persevering in the face of daunting adversity. Within the play the obstacles to civic and personal liberty are represented in an unthinking lower class overly concerned with individual material needs and ready to give way to violence, especially in the play's opening with the characters of the laborers Tom and Edwin, and in a conniving elite, especially near the play's end with the characters of the Duke of York and his servant Charles. The potential to reach positive social goals, however, lies in a few good individuals of all classes providing the aid that enables the play to end with hope resting in Abraham and Débora's unity. Giner de los Ríos's representation of the farm owner Abraham, court poet Davenant, and daughter Débora as deeply appreciative of Milton's works implies an alliance of correct literary taste with correct social behavior.

While the play's ending is not as grand as the unifying image that Milton uses to end *Paradise Lost*, of Adam and Eve exiting Paradise "hand in hand with wand'ring steps and slow" (12.648) and with the angel Michael and his cohort in the background, it is equally balanced between the stark losses that mark the end of an age and the amazing potentials at the beginning of a new one. The ending of *Milton: A Dramatic Scene* also resonates with Milton's *Mask* and its invitation to audience members, "Mortals," to strive to "Love Virtue, she alone is free, / She can teach ye how to climb / Higher than the sphery chime" (*A Mask* 1018, 1019–21). These textual Miltonic conclusions are cannily related to the political solidarity that Giner de los Ríos and Lowell sought extratextually with England and each other's homelands, a solidarity and social cohesion so often represented on the Spanish stage of the era. Such superimpositions in *Milton: A Dramatic Scene* record the use of a specific version of Milton put to the service of providing a sufficient level of comfort for engaging in discomfiting international affairs. Unlike the Spanish Catholic Inquisition, discussed in chapter 1, which highlighted Milton's political role and suppressed his poetic one, Giner de los Ríos unites and utilizes the two. Unlike the early Spanish translators of Milton's works, discussed in chapter 2, Giner de los Ríos does not display overt signs of representational anxiety but instead blends salient characteristics inherited from Milton's English biographies and European legend with those preferred by Spain's stage tradition.

My aim in this chapter has been to introduce this charming and disarming play to a larger audience than it has had heretofore and to clarify how its internal and external dramas cooperate. Most immediately, *Milton: A Dramatic Scene* is epideictic: a thanks to Lowell as a respected U.S. representative in Spain and a humble invitation for him to remain a Spanish ally at the moment the U.S. was emerging as an international powerhouse and the British Empire drew European and American admiration. Retrospectively, the play is an homage to citizen-writers—Giner de los Ríos, Lowell, and Milton—who act on their convictions to help bring about a "golden" world both in their literary works and in their life's works.[86] That homage is meaningful rather than quixotic because of the very players. Giner de los Ríos and Lowell were two individuals who participated actively and successfully in the formation of modern scholarly groups, like the Free Institute of Teaching and the MLA, and who worked idealistically on behalf of their countries to achieve cooperative personal, national, and international aims. The interactions of national literary aesthetics, biography, and transatlantic politics are in this case meaningful and deeply imbricated.[87] As history tells us, the play did not produce—and indeed could not produce alone—the ultimate unity that it represented. Within twenty years of its 1879 inaugural performance, the U.S. and Spain went to war. Conversely, through his work in cultural and educational reform, Giner de los Ríos helped Spain shed its centuries-long reputation of backwardness, and within just four years, in 1883, Lowell cofounded the MLA and, in 1887 until his death in 1891, served as the second president of an organization that continues to strive to unite disparate nations and languages by engaging critically and globally with literature.

CHAPTER 4

"By Shading Pencil Drawn"
Spanish Illustrations of *Paradise Lost*

This chapter takes its title from the description in *Paradise Lost* of Satan approaching Earth to despoil it. Through Satan's fallen perspective, readers view

> Ascending by degrees magnificent
> Up to the wall of Heaven a structure high,
> At top whereof, but far more rich appeared
> The work as of a kingly palace gate
> With frontispiece of diamond and gold
> Embellished; thick with sparkling orient gems
> The portal shone, inimitable on earth
> By model, or by shading pencil drawn. (PL 3.502–9)

Here, "frontispiece" refers to "the decorated entrance of a building," not the "title-page including illustrations and table of contents," as it came to mean in the early seventeenth century, or any "illustration facing the title-page of a book or division of a book," as is its primary meaning today.[1] The narrator's use of the rich word and commentary about the abilities of the plastic and visual arts are apposite to the topic of this chapter, book illustrations of *Paradise Lost*. We might think of engineered models or pencil drawings as readily apprehensible forms of communication. But Milton suggests otherwise. Artificial and artistic models and shadings may not foster correct apprehension. Rather they may be insufficient in nature or may become idols in practice, their intended and potential truth value contingent on the agents involved, be they the creators or reader-viewers.[2]

Book frontispieces can deceive; they can also fail if their primary function is construed to be faithful representation. Failure is indeed Milton's assessment when he plays the book-art critic in his short Greek epigram "In effigiei eius sculptorem" (Against the Engraver of his Portrait), published under the engraved author portrait of Milton by William Marshall, used as the frontispiece to his *Poems . . . 1645*: "An ignorant hand drew this portrait, you would perhaps say when looking at the original; but since you, my friends, did not recognize the man portrayed, laugh at this abortive likeliness by a rotten artist!"[3] Milton's book-art criticism of another image by Marshall a few years later takes us a bit deeper into understanding the uneasy interplay of the visual and verbal in illustrated books, which is to say books whose visual images illustrate corresponding text. Milton's *Eikonoklastes* (1649) excoriates the frontispiece of *Eikon basilike* (1649), which represents King Charles I of England in prayer.[4] It is not that the "conceited portraiture before his Book" bears little or no resemblance to Charles I but rather that it is "sett there to catch fools and silly gazers" into mistakenly reading the executed king as a martyr, Davidic penitent, or Christ-like figure (*CPW* 3.342). Milton's argument against the image rests on a restricted, albeit viable and useful, definition of a "literary work" along the lines of Gérard Genette and Marie Maclean's definition of "a more or less lengthy sequence of verbal utterances more or less containing meaning."[5] Elizabeth Skerpan-Wheeler calls attention to Milton's failure—or, I would say, rhetorical stance—to recognize that the king's book, like any book, is its "sum total," not just the words of a lone author: in the case of *Eikon basilike*, "Charles's memoranda, John Gauden's editing, Marshall's frontispiece, other illustrations and accretions."[6] As Skerpan-Wheeler argues, *Eikon basilike* and similar works imply and express a distinct definition, in which a book is regarded "as a 'work'—a unified whole under the control of a single author that therefore may be criticized on the grounds of authenticity and accuracy of representation." Thus, *Eikon basilike*'s "authorship is collective rather than individual. . . . Publishers' practices in the mid-seventeenth century confirm that the author, while not dead, was regarded as a fellow participant in publication, rather than its director."[7] This kind of collaborative, multimodal concept of literary works is cannily similar to the concept that the Spanish Catholic Inquisition constructed in its nineteenth-century *Index librorum prohibitorum*. It is a concept that is at the fore in this chapter on illustrations of Spanish editions of *Paradise Lost*.

The Milton of *Eikonoklastes* is in agreement with Skerpan-Wheeler and Joseph Wittreich that illustrations are interpretations by artists and publishers and that they can have a profound impact on subsequent interpretations by reader-viewers.[8] Guglielmo Cavallo and Roger Chartier's considerations of illustrated books affirm Milton's keen attentiveness to the force of the image of Charles I in a book more than two hundred pages long:

> Often used to accompany a printed text, images set up a protocol for reading that was intended either to present the same message as the one formulated in the written text, using a different sign language but an identical grammar, or else to present, in a language specific to the image, what logical discourse was powerless to express. In either case (and the two indicate quite different functional relationships between the text and the image), when the illustrations were given the task of guiding interpretation, they might instead bear an "other" reading, detached from the letter of the text and capable of creating a space of its own.[9]

Milton's critiques of frontispieces in *Paradise Lost* and *Eikonoklastes* alert readers to image-makers, in the case of the latter, to the artists, engravers, publishers, and readers whose ideas of verisimilitude diverge from his.[10]

A number of Milton's readers have played book-art critics and have provided valuable interpretive direction especially with British and French illustrations, such as those by William Blake, John Martin, and Gustave Doré. Wendy Furman-Adams has explored the illustrations of Milton's works by well-known and lesser-known artists. She and others have amply demonstrated that illustrations of Milton's works are major tools in constructing those works' very canonicity and in both reflecting and affecting interpretation. This is certainly the case with Milton among Spaniards. The Spanish woman of letters Emilia Pardo Bazán concludes her long discussion of Milton's marriage to Mary Powell, in the chapter "Milton" in *Los poetas épicos Cristianos* (The Christian Epic Poets; c. 1880), by noting, "A la reconciliación de marido y mujer no tardó en seguir el nacimiento de una niña, la primera de esas famosas hijas de Milton que tanto han dado que hacer á pintores y poetas" (It was not long after the reconciliation of the man and wife that a girl was born, the first of those famous daughters of Milton who have so busied painters and poets).[11] She is referring to the many "blind Milton dictating" illustrations by an international cadre of visual artists that depict Milton's daughters acting as amanuenses to their blind father.[12]

In this chapter, I play the book-art critic and attend primarily to three sets of Spanish illustrations of *Paradise Lost*: those by John Baptiste de Medina in the first fully illustrated English edition of the poem (1688), those by Doré in the first illustrated Spanish prose and verse translations of 1873 and 1883, and the almost completely ignored yet brilliant sketches by the modernist Gregorio Prieto in a deluxe volume of 1972. While other Spanish illustrations of *Paradise Lost* and Milton's other works deserve attention, these key sets provide both historical breadth and creative depth. Further, they reflect the active agency of Spaniards in the visual reception and production of Milton's epic.

Medina and the First Illustrated English Edition of *Paradise Lost*

Nearly two decades before the Spanish Catholic Inquisition's 1707 Marín Index proscribes Milton's works within Spanish territories, Jacob Tonson's illustrated edition of *Paradise Lost* (London, 1688) records the interaction of an artist of mixed Spanish heritage with Milton's masterwork. By 1688 John Baptiste de Medina (1659–1710) was residing in London, well outside of Spanish territories and the purview of the Spanish Catholic Inquisition.

In the 1688 Tonson *Paradise Lost*, the identities of the illustrators and engravers appear discreetly at the bottom of most of the edition's engravings, with some illustrations absent of any identifiers. The art-historical detective work of scholars has led to the current consensus that, of the twelve copperplate engravings, Medina illustrated those for books 3, 5, 6, 7, 9, 10, and 11 that bear his name, as well as for book 8; Bernard Lens "designed the illustration for Book IV," the one that bears his name; and Henry Aldrich "probably designed the illustration for Book I and certainly for Books II and XII."[13] The nationalities of this set of visual artists alone demonstrate the transcultural nature of this *English* edition of *Paradise Lost*: Flemish Spanish Medina, known for his portraits of primarily Whig Scots; the Dutch Lens (1659–1725), known for his engravings; and Aldrich (1648–1710), the English theologian and musician.

In her foundational interdisciplinary study *Milton and English Art* (1970), Marcia Pointon defines "English art" based on its intended primary audience and the location of publication rather than on the native homeland of the visual artists. Early on in her study, she concedes the utility of a hermetic, national notion despite decided transculturalism: "The history of Milton illustrations during the period 1688–1720 is pre-eminently an account of foreign artists who settled in England."[14] Defining national domains by the location of the consumers rather than producers of commodities provides her informative study with an easy-to-follow governing organization, even though it counters the common practice of defining commodities by their point of origin or the artists' heritage or homeland; for example, Oriental rug, Spanish cubism, American fast-food chains. So what counts as *Spanish* art in this study of illustrated Spanish editions of *Paradise Lost*: visual art made or published only in Spain? visual art accompanying only verbal texts translated into Spanish? created by English or Spanish natives or citizens? commissioned by English, Spanish, or even other national presses? These questions do not have uniform answers for the three showcased sets of illustrations. Indeed their variety nuances our understanding of the affiliation and alterity, the Ours and Others, that reside fluidly within them.

Medina is defined variously as Flemish, Scottish, Spanish, and hyphenated variants of these. The unhyphenated attribution of "Scottish" in his brief biography by the National Galleries of Scotland is a charming indicator of Scotland's warm claim on the artist. Though "born in Brussels, the son of a Spanish army captain," he moved to Scotland in 1688, was "knighted in 1706 by the last Scottish parliament before the Act of Union," and spent the remainder of his life there.[15] "Spanish" has a double claim on Medina through parentage and birthplace, given that Brussels was an erstwhile territory of Spain and the birthplace of the Habsburg King Charles V (1500–1558), ruler of the Burgundian Territories, King Charles I of Spain, king of Naples and Sicily, archduke of Austria, German king, and Holy Roman emperor.

The cosmopolitanism of Medina and the visual arts world is reflected even in his signatures and engraved attributions. The artist attributions engraved in the 1688 Tonson edition are "JB. de Medina" and "Medina," usages that minimize the Spanish practice of utilizing the first name, paternal surname, and maternal surname. Three of his original signatures elsewhere—on his portraits of Sir William Bruce and of James Ogilvy, 1st earl of Seafield, and on a letter of December 8, 1709—reflect his, rather than an engraver's, practice of both Spanish and English surname use.[16] Code-switching, or shifting between discursive and cultural practices, between British and Spanish in this case, however, cannot be fully established. Many other Spanish visual artists of the period used only their paternal surnames rather than their paternal and maternal surnames; thus the absence of a second surname does not necessarily code as non-Spanish.[17]

The pliable nature of national and geopolitical identities applied to artists of all kinds adheres regularly both before and after the seventeenth century.

For example, the artist and architect Gian Lorenzo Bernini (1598–1680) is regularly referred to as Italian, given that he was born in Naples, which is in present-day Italy but which in his lifetime was variously under Spanish rule. Similarly Joseph Rudyard Kipling (1865–1936) is referred to as British or English rather than Indian, despite his having been born in Bombay (Mumbai), India which during his lifetime was under British rule. With national identifications come connotations and associations, as is clear from the critical reception of Medina's role in the 1688 Tonson *Paradise Lost*. Helen Gardner is balanced in her assessment of Medina's agency, that he "was not without talent, and he was either a careful reader of the poem himself, or was carefully directed by someone else."[18] Taking one side is C. H. Collins-Baker, who regards Medina as "having set the subjects to be illustrated," rather than requiring direction.[19] Taking the other side is Mary Ravenhall, who conceives of Medina's non-British and perhaps specifically Spanish heritage as constituting an alterity that required collaboration with the English Francis Atterbury: "Since Medina . . . was a recent immigrant of Spanish extraction and Flemish training, Tonson must have recognized the need for an advisor to aid in the selection of scenes for illustration. All the evidence presently available points to Atterbury as the man who filled the role."[20] While conceding that we know little about Medina, she bases her hypothesis of Medina's possible need for direction on his cultural, educational, and linguistic alterity, given that he was "a newcomer to England, presumably unfamiliar with Milton's poem, which had not yet been translated into any language but German."[21] However, Medina's specific alterity would not render him less qualified but potentially more qualified, for as Pointon notes, "Flemish and French book illustration in the first half of the seventeenth century was certainly of a superior quality in general to that executed in England."[22] Flemish painting flourished in the seventeenth century with Peter Paul Rubens, Anthony Van Dyck, and other artists well appreciated in England and throughout Europe.[23]

While Medina's national identities are variously noted and interpreted, curiously the confessional or denominational overtones often associated with those identities have been ignored: they are absent in critical discussions of his visual interpretations, or what Wittreich calls "nonverbal criticism."[24] The religious ecumenism of book illustrations of Milton's epic and their criticisms contrasts sharply with the religionational schisms that are at the forefront of Spanish access to Milton's works and early translations of his epic.[25] It was only when I reviewed Medina's familiar illustrations within the context of Milton among Spaniards that they became sufficiently defamiliarized for me to see "with other eyes," to use Wendy Furman and Virginia Tufte's useful term.

In chapter 2, I demonstrate the ways in which Spanish translators of *Paradise Lost* insert Catholic and Spanish literary-cultural elements into the representations of the table(s) and "transubstantiation" of book 5 and of the Virgin Mary in book 12. Here I align those same passages and figures with Medina's illustration of book 5. Furman and Tufte observe the critical unease with the ritual elements of this illustration "in the face of Milton's highly Reformed Protestantism" in regard to the foregrounded and largest depiction of Eve, rife with elements from Catholic visual representations of religious women (see Figure 3).[26] They note that, in contrast to depictions of Eve as "merely open and pious," "Medina's Eve wears an expression far more ardent, even somewhat beseeching; and her arms cross her breasts in a gesture simultaneously evocative of a penitent Magdalene" and "Virgin Annunciate."[27] The visual allusion to the Virgin Mary countermands the low level of Mariology in *Paradise Lost*. Conversely, it coordinates with the vibrant Hispano-Catholic tradition of Mariology, as discussed in chapter 2.

The table scene in this same illustration similarly coordinates with Hispano-Catholic tradition. The translator Juan Escóiquiz sidesteps Milton's pointed term "transubstantiate" (*PL* 5.438) by not using the readily available Spanish verb *transubstanciar* but rather by having the angel Raphael conclude pre-dinner pleasantries with a call to mealtime prayer. Escóiquiz correlatively eliminates Milton's Eucharistic commentary created through his translation of "table(s)" in book 5. Milton's original describes the table at which Raphael, Adam, and Eve "sit and taste, till this meridian heat / Be over": "this table. Raised of grassy turf / Their table was, and mossy seats had round" (*PL* 5.369–70, 391–92). Medina depicts the table at which the divine (Raphael) and earthly (Adam and Eve) mingle as "a natural formation . . . a lamina of a slaty rock."[28] Medina's table, slightly raised with its shaded left-most edge hiding Adam's left foot (see Figure 4), contrasts sharply with Blake's and other visual artists' renderings of high tables for the same scene. Medina's table deters ready apprehension of Milton's Eucharistic commentary in the original, very much in accordance with Escóiquiz's erasure of it in his verbal translation.

Whatever the nature of Medina's collaboration with the other agents of the 1688 Tonson *Paradise Lost* and whatever his religious proclivities, he cre-

Figure 3 (opposite page). John Baptiste de Medina's illustration of book 5 of the 1688 Tonson *Paradise Lost*. (Courtesy of the British National Library)

Figure 4. Detail of the table scene in John Baptiste de Medina's illustration of book 5 of the 1688 Tonson *Paradise Lost*. (Courtesy of the British National Library)

ated elements in great accord with Hispano-Catholic tradition in a work that has contributed greatly to Milton's canonicity in English literature and world literature. Worth emphasizing is that the critical literature on this important illustrated edition reflects the perceived insignificance of intermingled national and religious identities of the illustrators, identities that are so strongly documented in the series of Spanish Catholic indexes of proscribed texts and authors and in Spanish translations of *Paradise Lost*.

Doré and the First Illustrated Spanish Editions of *Paradise Lost*

In the nineteenth century, illustrated editions of vernacular translations of Milton's epic created another cosmopolitan system in which Spain participated. The fifty plates by Doré became the illustrative lingua franca in the decades following their original 1866 publication. These illustrations, however, cannot easily be designated French, since they were used first in an English-language edition of *Paradise Lost* issued simultaneously in New York, London, and Paris.[29] Further, they were not published in a Francophone edition until the late twentieth century, even though they were used for editions of the epic in Dutch (1875), German (1879), Portuguese (1884), Ancient Greek (1887), Modern Greek (1887), Russian (1899), Finnish (1933), and others, including the Spanish prose translation attributed to Cayetano Rosell of 1873 and an 1883 republication of the mainstay Spanish verse translation by Escóiquiz (orig. 1812).[30]

The 1688 Tonson *Paradise Lost* and the 1866 Doré illustrated deluxe edition by the British printing house of Cassell, Petter, Galpin & Co.

both contain full-page illustrations on unnumbered pages; the numbering on pages with verbal text skips over the pages with illustrations. The 1866 Doré illustrated edition diverges slightly from the full-page format of illustrations facing an entire page of verbal text used in the Tonson edition.[31] Instead each Doré illustration in the 1866 edition is preceded by a nearly blank page with only a brief verbal text with the respective book and line citation. Both the 1688 and 1866 illustrated editions thus maintain a boundary yet establish more of an alliance between visual and verbal art.

The 1873 Doré-illustrated Rosell *El Paraíso perdido* resembles the 1866 *Paradise Lost* more than does the 1883 Doré-illustrated Escóiquiz *El Paraíso perdido*, but both Spanish editions possess some telling divergences.[32] The 1873 Rosell demarcates verbal and visual art, by and large, by assigning consecutive page numbers to the verbal text and none to pages of visual text. However, instead of excerpts of the verbal text on onion paper facing the illustrations, the 1873 Rosell edition includes below the illustrations one line of verbal text all in capitals and with no citation. Further, the 1873 Rosell uses only twelve of the fifty plates, the Escóiquiz forty-five (see Appendix C). This kind of selectivity is not unique to Spanish translations of the epic. For example, the much-acclaimed Finnish translation, *Kadotettu paratiisi* (1933, repr. 1952, 2000) includes only twenty-two of the fifty plates, modifies quotations, and omits citations.[33]

A selectivity distinctive to the 1873 Rosell, however, is its cropping of the Doré illustrations. While its illustrations take up nearly the whole page, they reproduce just over three-quarters of the originals. The diminishment is achieved by removing equal proportions on the left and right, resulting in a roughly 30 percent horizontal reduction, and by removing from the bottom exclusively, resulting in a roughly 15 percent vertical reduction. The latter removes all of Doré's signatures.

A more startling type of selectivity is manifest in the 1883 Escóiquiz, which advertises itself on the ornate title page as an "Edición ilustrada con gran número de viñetas inspiradas en los famosos dibujos de Gustavo Doré" (Illustrated Edition with a Great Number of Vignettes Inspired by the Famous Drawings of Gustave Doré).[34] The illustrations express their nature as "vignette," of a "small size or occupying a small proportion of the space," by the fact that portions of the illustrations are cut into circles, columns, and polygrams and inserted amid verbal text (see Figure 5).[35] The presentational model of the 1883 Escóiquiz is not repeated in any other Doré-illustrated

Figure 5. Plate 20, *PL* 5.12, 13, by Gustave Doré in the 1873 Rosell *El Paraíso perdido* and (opposite page) in the 1883 Escóiquiz *El Paraíso perdido*. (Courtesy of HathiTrust and Purdue University Libraries)

editions of *Paradise Lost* in English, Spanish, or other vernaculars that I have researched. Serendipitously or intentionally, the reading experience of the 1883 Escóiquiz reinforces the verbal text, which expressly truncates passages. Similarly, the publishers (not Escóiquiz, who died in 1820) freely truncate Doré's illustrations.

Another aspect of the 1883 Escóiquiz marks the vignettes as Spanish collaborations with rather than expressions of passive obeisance to the British printing house of Cassell, Petter, Galpin & Co. Rather than containing the signature of "G Doré" that graces the original plates, all the vignettes bear the handwritten word "Escoler," likely the signature of an unidentified engraver or illustrator.[36] Paralleling the verbal interventions by the Spanish translator with Milton's English text, the vignettes signal the visual interventions by Spanish agents (engravers or illustrators) on the imported Doré illustrations.

Other shared elements in the 1873 Rosell and 1883 Escóiquiz illus-

190   EL PARAISO PERDIDO

    Eva. Un vivo encarnado, que teñía
  Su tersa, y blanca tez, una penosa
  Respiracion, y su desordenado
  Cabello, todo anuncia, que ha pasado
  Una noche turbada, y trabajosa.
     Sobre el lecho de rosa,
  Adan en el momento incorporado,
  Contempla aquel objeto de su ardiente

  Amor, siempre á sus ojos delicioso,
  Sea que enajenado, del reposo
  Disfrute, ó que despierta, tiernamente
  Hable con él: la mano suavemente
  Pone sobre la suya cariñoso,
  Y con tono más dulce, que el ligero
  Céfiro, que á las flores enamora,
  Cuando el fulgor del alba las colora,
  La despierta, diciéndola: «¡Oh querida
  »Esposa mia! ¡Hechizo lisonjero
  »De mi alma! Mitad cara de mi vida!
  »¡Eva! ¡Tú, de quien sola una mirada,
  »Hace ver la existencia
  »De un Dios criador, y su beneficencia!

trated editions indicate an active engagement rather than passive replication of the French-British-U.S. verbal and visual texts they appropriated. In the 1866 original, Plate 22 (*PL* 5.468–470) steers clear of any Eucharistic commentary in the scene of Raphael and the Edenic couple sitting down to eat, by not depicting a table. The reduction of the background in Plate 22 for the vignette in the 1883 Escóiquiz results, in turn, in a reduction of reader-viewers' potential awareness of the missing tables. Further, Plate 22 is not among the twelve Doré illustrations in the 1873 Rosell edition, and both Spanish editions reposition illustrations in ways that demonstrate an appreciation of Milton's verbal text and Doré's visual text. This is the case with the nine illustrations that the 1866 Doré-illustrated *Paradise Lost* originally places outside of the books they illustrate. For example, Plate 6 (*PL* 2.1–2) resides between book 1 and book 2, facing the end of book 1, since it is on the recto side of the page. Both the 1873 Rosell and the 1883 Escóiquiz place this illustration at the beginning of book 2, close to the cited text.

Other repositionings of illustrations closer to corresponding text can be derived from Appendix C, which contains page numbers for the start of each book in the illustrated Rosell and Escóiquiz editions. In the 1873 Rosell, Plate 9 (*PL* 2.949, 950) is the first in the edition; the illustration surprises not only because of the delay of any visual text until its appearance, just past page 52, but also by its position on the verso side of the unnumbered page. Below Plate 9 is the excerpt, in all capitals, "Y con cabeza, manos, alas y pies, nada, se submerge" (and with head, hands, wings and feet, he swims, he submerges himself), which corresponds to the same text on the recto page it faces, page 53. In the 1883 Escóiquiz, the effect of the repositioning of Plate 20 (Figure 5) is particularly effective. The round vignette of Adam gazing at Eve is preceded by the verbal text "[Adán] contempla aquel objeto de su ardiente" ([Adam] contemplates the object of his ardent) and is followed by "Amor, siempre á sus ojos deliciosos" (Love, always pleasing to his eyes).[37] Reader-viewers are thus held between adjective and noun in the very Adamic suspension described. The 1873 Rosell shows similar care in its placement of Plate 20, on the verso side so that it faces page 105, which opens book 5 and thus faces the same textual excerpt. By contrast, the repositionings of the illustrations in the c. 1885 illustrated *Paradise Lost* published by Heritage Press reflect clearly the pragmatic aim of saving paper by printing illustrations on both sides of the page and of saving composition time by clustering pages with illustrations, resulting in some instances of moving illustrations out of the books that contain their corresponding text (see Appendix C).

The twelve plates (9, 12–15, 20, 33–36, 48–49) in the 1873 Rosell redirect interpretations to be derived from the fifty Doré illustrations toward danger and separation, as the first two and last two illustrations selected for that edition clearly reflect. The first illustration is Plate 9 (*PL* 2.949,

950), the image of a foregrounded Satan clinging to a ledge as he journeys desperately from Hell through Chaos to the universe to tempt humankind. It is followed by Plate 12 (*PL* 3.739–41), the dark image of Satan as he approaches a light, star-studded, and still unfallen universe. Satan's isolation and attendant dangers are at the fore in these plates, unmitigated by his impressive public persona depicted in other early plates. The penultimate image is Plate 38 (*PL* 9.182, 183), an ancient urban landscape strewn with humans grieving their impending deaths as the Noachian Flood overcomes the Earth. The last illustration of the 1873 Rosell is Plate 49 (*PL* 12.236–38), of a foregrounded Moses, stern and strong, holding up the tablets of the Ten Commandments as he returns from Mount Sinai to the Israelites, who had turned to idolatry. The absence of Plate 50 (*PL* 12.645) in the 1873 Rosell exemplifies the power of illustrations to affect interpretation of verbal text. In the original 1866 edition and the 1883 Escóiquiz, Plate 50 resides right before the last page of the epic. It depicts a foregrounded Eve, lamenting and holding the hand of Adam, who has his back toward her and the audience as he looks to the archangel Michael in the right background, in a moment before they depart "hand in hand with wand'ring steps and slow / Through Eden" (*PL* 12.648–49). This last image captures the poised ending of Milton's verbal text of a more distanced but still proximal communion of human and divine, in contrast to Plate 49, which emphasizes stern deific instruction to an obstinate humankind.

The use of the Doré illustrations in these two late nineteenth-century Spanish editions indicates the participation of Spain in making Milton's simultaneously English and Spanish verbal art and Doré's simultaneously English and French visual art into world art, as well as in actively attempting to secure Spain's position in that system. As such, these editions mirror Spanish efforts at the end of nineteenth century to integrate Spain into the Western and world cultural communities through the arts, in line with the cluster of Spanish plays featuring Milton as a dramatic character in the 1870s and 1880s, as discussed in chapter 3.

These two illustrated Spanish editions of *Paradise Lost* also display simultaneously cosmopolitan and distinctively Spanish aspects in a feature common to modern books, the author portrait.[38] The 1873 Rosell includes no author portrait in the opening paratext, and in lieu of an author portrait per se the 1883 Escóiquiz includes an engraving based on "The Blind Milton Dictating *Paradise Lost* to His Daughters" (1878), the renowned painting by Hungary's Mihály Munkácsy. Both these Spanish editions reposition the traditional site of author portraits from the opening paratext to the book

Figure 6. Book covers of the 1873 Rosell *El Paraíso perdido* and 1883 Escóiquiz *El Paraíso perdido*. (Courtesy of University of Texas at Austin Libraries and Purdue University Libraries)

covers (Figure 6). The image on the sturdy brown cover of the 1873 Rosell is stamped and gilded; the image on the pine-green cover of the 1883 Escóiquiz is stamped and raised. The visual artists who created the book covers are anonymous. Both covers draw attention to the original creator of the verbal text, Milton, and prepare audiences for visual text. The 1883 Escóiquiz is more playful, with the coin-like orbs doubling as fruit set amid stamped tree branches and serpent's scales in allusion to Satan at the Tree of Knowledge of Good and Evil. While Pardo Bazán's nearly coeval *Christian Epic Poets* (c. 1880) would leave her Spanish readers unenthusiastic about reading Milton's epic but willing to do so for cultural refinement, the publishers of these two editions did what they could to draw would-be readers' interest and pocketbooks.

Prieto's Inspired Line Sketches of *Paradise Lost*

In the years surrounding the tercentenary of Milton's death in 1974, cultural and educational institutions the world over sponsored exhibitions and published scholarship and commemorative editions of his works.[39] Two Spanish contributions most germane to this chapter are a set of seventeen black-and-white sketches by the Manchegan Gregorio Prieto Muñoz (1897–1992) for an exclusive edition of selections of *Paradise Lost* published in 1972, *Milton | El Paraíso perdido*, and a set of ten illustrations absent of poetic text by his Catalonian friend Salvador Dalí (1904–1989) for an exclusive edition published in 1974, *Paradis perdu. Quatrième chant*.[40] The latter set can be classified as Spanish based on Dalí's heritage or French based on the text's language and publisher. The Prieto-illustrated *Milton | El Paraíso perdido*, however, is decidedly Spanish, since it is illustrated by a Spaniard, uses Spanish text, is accompanied by a preface by a Spanish writer, and was published in Madrid. Moreover it boldly translates English-language, internationally esteemed poetic lines into Spanish yet universal sketch lines and merges early modern English verbal art with modern Spanish visual art, creatively instantiating modernity's sense of fragmentation that produces delight rather than anxiety.[41]

The resonances between Giner de los Ríos's play *Milton: A Dramatic Scene in One Act and in Verse* (1879) and Prieto's *Milton | El Paraíso perdido*, published nearly a century later, are significant: both works have been generally ignored at home and abroad, despite strong reception of the artists' other works; both were created by individuals who achieved national fame for life's work committed to strengthening Spain's national culture; both pay tribute to the culture of a purported Other; and both are in genres, drama and visual art, that are much more social and impermanent (performances and gallery showings) than are written texts. The first characteristic, of disregard, is curious: by all accounts Prieto's set of tercentenary illustrations of *Paradise Lost* should be well-known.[42] Prieto was a member of Spain's Generación del 1927, which included such international luminaries as Rafael Alberti Merello, Dalí, Federico García Lorca, and Pablos Picasso.[43] Furthermore, *Milton | El Paraíso perdido* includes a prologue by the Spanish poet Vicente Aleixandre, awarded the 1977 Nobel Prize in Literature just a few years after the edition's 1972 publication. Finally, Prieto's sketches include selections taken from a whole set of multimedia works that were the showcase exhibition held from February to March 1974 at Spain's National Library in Madrid.[44]

Prieto's critically underexamined illustrations provide us with a critical tabula rasa, in sharp contrast to the Medina and Doré illustrations. Indeed

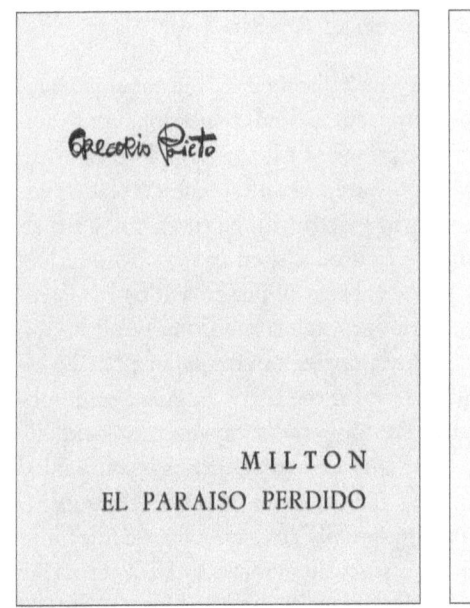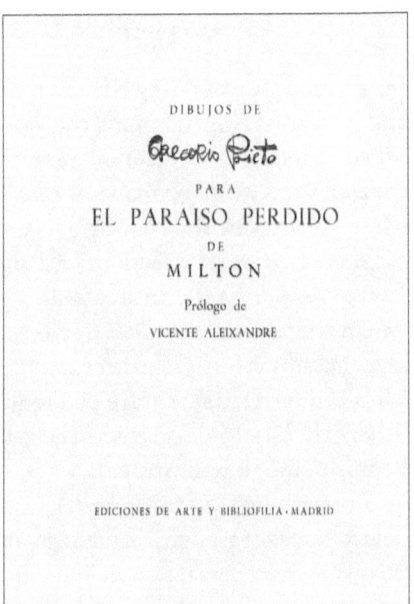

Figures 7. Cover and title page of *Milton | El Paraíso perdido* (1972). (Courtesy of Harvard University Libraries)

James Treadwell felt compelled to caution against the power of the critical heritage of some of the more famous illustrations of *Paradise Lost* to confound careful close readings: "Just as the poem forces artists to revise the relation of image to text, so by unravelling that revision it becomes possible for us in turn to reconsider the criteria by which we examine the illustrative process."[45] In "unravelling" the intratextual conversation between Milton's verbal text and Prieto's visual text, we find it intertwining in another unexpected intertextual conversation, one that includes a set of arresting poems by Lorca.

From the very beginning, readers' encounters with *Milton | El Paraíso perdido* perplex the usual hierarchy of illustrated editions. Readers whose encounter begins with electronic library catalogues find that WorldCat lists Prieto rather than Milton as the first author of the work. Similarly the book cover positions the title with Milton's name on the lower right, visually on par with or subordinate to Prieto's handwritten signature at the upper left. Then, while the first title page positions the title "EL PARAISO PERDIDO" after Milton's surname, the title on the second title page is "DIBUJOS (Drawings) DE | Gregorio Prieto | DE | MILTON | Prólogo de | VICENTE ALEIX-

ANDRE" (see Figure 7). Certainly the placement and distinct writing prioritize Prieto, but the dark purple ink used only for the names Gregorio Prieto, Milton, and Vicente Aleixandre on the title page merge these artists' identities—a merging similar to the one I claim later in this chapter among Prieto, Milton, and Lorca. On the second title page, Milton is inserted between two Spaniards: the creator of the visual text, Prieto, and Prieto's Generación del 1927 compadre, Aleixandre. As it turns out, Aleixandre's prologue somewhat surprisingly contains more words (1,115) than the entirety of Milton's text (1,007) in the volume. *Milton | El Paraíso perdido* includes only short (Hispanophone) excerpts of the epic. It establishes at least a loose relationship between verbal and visual text, and perhaps even a subordinate role of verbal to visual in ways that extend beyond its minimal use of the epic's words. One subtle mechanism is the absence of attribution of the Spanish translation, which is the Escóiquiz. A more overt form of the subordination of verbal to visual is the deviation from the verbal text's sequencing.

A brief review of the original edition of *Paradise Lost* and some of its most famous illustrated editions highlights the labyrinthine nature and creativity of the Prieto edition, as well as its participation in a transnational Western artistic circuit. The original edition of *Paradise Lost* of 1667 is stark, containing no illustrations, focusing all attention on the verbal text. The first illustration to be included is an author portrait by the English engraver William Dolle after a painting by the English artist William Faithorne in an English edition of 1674. The first fully illustrated edition, the 1688 Tonson, has an author portrait by the British artist Robert White facing the title page, with the remaining twelve full-page illustrations dictated by the verbal text, placed after each book's "Argument" and before the respective verbal text. Visual art is subordinate to verbal art based on quantity alone: thirteen unnumbered pages of visual text and 331 numbered pages of verbal text. Even the author portrait sustains the importance of verbal text, with John Dryden's laudatory six-line poem at the bottom of the engraving, due both to Dryden's fame and to the layout of the page, the poem taking up about half the space as the portrait.

Something new and important is added to the history of illustrated editions of *Paradise Lost* with the Blake illustrations (1807–22), something that pointedly complicates the notion of an integrated relationship of visual and verbal text.[46] Although created in the first decade of the nineteenth century, the Blake illustrations were not published in a book until the twentieth century. The persistence of the visual text united with only excerpts of the verbal text beneath them, rather than within the whole of the epic, amplifies Blake's influence on reader-viewers and by extension interpretations of the full verbal text if or when reader-viewers return to it in a separate edition. Further, when the Blake illustrations are included in, for example, the deluxe edition of 1970 by Heritage Press, the frontispiece is not a portrait of Milton but rather the illustration for book 12, "The Expulsion from Eden."[47]

A less bound relationship between visual and verbal text also occurs half a century later with the 1866 English *Paradise Lost*, in which the Doré illustrations first appear. The fifty illustrations adhere to the verbal text's chronology, except in one case: the opening illustration is not a portrait of Milton but rather Plate 24 (*PL* 6.207–9). This displacement of the illustration of the War in Heaven gears readers toward consideration of nonterrestrial domains, in contrast to Prieto's earthy choices. The displacement is also part of a trajectory in subsequent Doré illustrated editions of *Paradise Lost*. As Appendix C demonstrates, in the deluxe editions published by Cassell, et al., in 1866 and in 1885, the Doré illustrations are repositioned and, in some cases, relabeled. While Prieto's reordering is much more extreme, there is a precedent of active agency.

In all three illustrated editions, the proportion of visual to verbal art is much greater than the first illustrated edition, the 1688 Tonson, but visual art still remains subordinate to verbal art, with fifty pages of visual text and just over three hundred pages of verbal text. The subordination of visual to verbal, however, did not persist with this set. What we might call art suppliers responded to audience interest and increased the division between Doré's visual art and Milton's verbal art. From the nineteenth century onward, a number of gallery showings of the Doré illustrations of *Paradise Lost* subordinated Milton's verbal art to Doré's visual art, with Milton's epic replaced by the verbal placards accompanying the gallery artwork. Further prioritizing the visual text are an Anglophone paperback from the late twentieth century that includes all fifty Doré illustrations completely absent of Milton's text and a nearly coeval Hispanophone paperback that places a Spanish summary of the verbal text on verso pages facing all the Doré illustrations on recto pages.[48] The presentational modes of these sets of illustrations and those of the over 190 illustrators of Milton and his works create the artistic space for the Prieto-illustrated volume.[49]

The 1972 *Milton | El Paraíso perdido* contains Prieto's full-page sketches on recto pages facing verso pages that contain six to eighteen lines of Escóiquiz's Spanish translation. No verbal text exists on the recto except for Prieto's handwritten signature in all sketches. Moreover the verbal text no longer governs the organization of the visual text. Table 1 summarizes the

Table 1. Description of the Seventeen Sketches in *Milton | El Paraíso perdido* (1972)

Book and line numbers from *Paradise Lost* with brief description and beginning of the selection	Sketch number and brief descriptive title
None	I, House
7.430–34, the creation of fowl "so steers the prudent crane / Her annual voyage"	1, Bird and Rose
1.128–33, Beelzebub's first response to Satan "O Prince, O chief of the many thronéd Powers"	2, Multiple Faces
8.465–75, Eve's creation "and took / From thence a rib, with cordial spirits"	3, Adam's Back, Eve's Profile
8.470–78, Eve's creation "Under his forming hands a creature grew"	4, Eve's Upper Torso and Head
8.253–56, Adam's first awakening "As new waked from soundest sleep/ Soft on a"	5, Adam, Upper Torso and Head
8.295–99, God's first approach to Adam "one came, methought, of shape divine"	6, Female Figure amid Flowers
1.1–5, first invocation "Of man's first disobedience and the fruit"	7, Adam Grasping a Tree
9.896–99, Adam's first response to seeing fallen Eve "O fairest of Creation, last and best"	8, Eve at Adam's Feet
4.313–20, Narrator's description of couple's purity "Then was not guilty shame, dishonest shame"	9, Eve and Adam Reclining
8.266–71, Adam's initial moments of life "With fragrance and with joy my heart o'erflowed"	10, Adam Walking and Lying Down
7.501–2, Creation of the world "earth in her rich attire / Consummate lovely"	11, Couple in Glade with Flying Angel
7.131–35, Raphael's transition from War to Creation "after Lucifer from heaven / (So call him)"	12, Two Profiles
4.762–63, Adam and Eve at their bower "Her love his golden shafts employs, here lights"	13, Adam and Eve amid Eyes
4.708, Adam and Eve arriving at their bower "Here in close recess with flowers, garlands"	14, Eve and Bower
4.689–700, Adam and Eve conversing "Thus talking hand in hand alone"	15, Adam and Eve Entwined
4.477–88, Eve's description of first seeing Adam "Till I espied thee, fair indeed and tall"	16, Adam and Eve in a Natural Setting

unsequencing of the chronology of Milton's original poem. *Milton | El Paraíso perdido* subverts the basic conventions of illustrated editions. It does not follow the epic's chronology; it unevenly depicts some books, two illustrations of book 1, five of book 4, three of book 7, five of book 8, and one of book 9; and it completely disregards others, books 2, 3, 5, 6, 10, 11, and 12.

It is worth noting that similar reorganization occurs in other literary works illustrated by Prieto, a keyhole view of which provides us with a sense of the active assertions of agency in the twentieth-century publishing world. In the preface to *The Sonnets of William Shakespeare with Twenty-Eight Drawings by Gregorio Prieto* (1948), the editor, the Irish typographer Seán Jennett (1912–1981), notes that, while the edition "is based, like others, on the quarto printed in 1609 by G. Eld for T.T.," there are "many differences" that he feels "bound to explain." "In my opinion," he avers, the 1609 edition's "order is corrupt," therefore,

> I have adopted the order suggested by Sir Denys Bray, and based upon a scheme of rhyme linkages that connects all the sonnets in a continuous chain. I am not convinced this is the true order. Sir Denys Bray's theory is plausible, however, and his re-arrangement, while it raises obvious objections, is in general the best I have seen, regarded from the point of view of the reader who is looking for poetry and not for scholarly casuistry or antiquarian research. It is this kind of reader that I have had constantly in view.

Resistant to "any idea of what might have been the practice of the period" and determining with his "printer's eye" that the quarto is "a shoddy piece of typesetting," Jennett "amended the punctuation to bring it into line with modern practice."[50] We are reminded of the active if unexplained agency by "Escoler" with the vignettes of the Doré plates in the 1883 Escóiquiz *El Paraíso perdido*. The vignettes modernize the content through the replacement of the Doré signatures with those of his latter-day adaptor Escoler and the formatting and methodologies per typesetting innovations. This is to say that purposeful agency and collaboration are hallmarks of these Prieto-illustrated works, as much as the 1883 Escóiquiz.

Gotthold Ephraim Lessing's highly influential *Laocoön* (1766), about the ways that visual art communicates in contrast to verbal art, is helpful in assessing the active agency of unsequencing in *Milton | El Paraíso perdido*. Lessing asserts that visual art is synchronic, immediately apprehensible, while poetry is diachronic, unfolding its meaning chronologically. He articulates a still dominant way of distinguishing the sister arts. Such an approach, however, does not work well with illustrated books and modern works, much less modern illustrated books. Given that, in illustrated books, visual text tends to appear sequentially along with verbal text, readers of illustrated editions generally anticipate a diachronic nature for sets of visual texts, as is the case with the Tonson, Blake, Martin, and Doré illustrated editions of *Paradise Lost*.

Milton | El Paraíso perdido unfolds its meaning distinctly. "Sketch 2, Multiple Faces" and "Sketch 7, Adam Grasping a Tree," are the only illustrations for book 1 but do not come first sequentially, as one might expect. They urge audiences to question the emphasis in other illustrated editions on Satan and hellfire for book 1. Sketch 7, illustrating book 1's invocation, reminds us that, after all, the book and the epic start with "a man and a tree"—to revise the famous opening of Virgil's *Aeneid*, "Of arms and the man." Sketch 7 depicts the invocation's emphasis on human-deific relationships: to "justify the ways of God to men" (*PL* 1.26), with Satan and the rebel angels important only insofar as they inform that human-deific relationship (see Figure 8). Sketch 7 emphasizes the human will in direct engagement with, ambiguously, the Tree of Knowledge or the Tree of Life, removing the mediation of an external force of evil; indeed, it is absent of any Satanic snakes. Moreover it represents the ecological unity of humankind and the Earth in two ways:[51] first, by interposing rather than superimposing Adam and natural elements—the tree, the bird, the grass—so that neither dominates or interrupts the other; second, by depicting hands as constituting the tree's branches. This latter artistic touch inscribes Milton's characterization of humans as stewards of nature.

The upset chronology of *Milton | El Paraíso perdido* also influences the interaction among the various visual and verbal texts. For example, audiences are propelled to read Sketch 7 diachronically but not sequentially, in conversation with "Sketch 3, Adam's Back, Eve's Profile" (see Figure 1 in Chapter 1). The resemblance of Adam's posture in both sketches collapses the two respective verbal texts: Milton's creation of the epic through the muse (*PL* 1.1–12) and God's creation of Eve through Adam (*PL* 8.465–77). The epic's creation from book 1 in Sketch 7 is complicated by the fact that it is subsequent to Eve's creation from book 8 in Sketch 3. Similarly the placement of Sketch 2 right before Sketch 3 and before the sequence of sketches focusing on Adam and Eve can move audiences to consider the painful bond between the fallen compatriots Satan and Beelzebub, represented in Sketch 2, in conjunction with the bond of the innocent human couple in Sketch 3.

A generous interpretation of the reordering is to see it is as a clever visual

Figure 8. Gregorio Prieto's "Sketch 7, Adam Grasping a Tree," in *Milton | El Paraíso perdido* (1972). (Fundación Gregorio Prieto; image courtesy of Harvard University Libraries)

employment of the verbal epic structure, with flashbacks and storytelling confounding a strictly chronological narrative. Milton's epic disrupts the strict chronology of heavenly and earthly events in ways that convert epic conventions of narrative related to chronology into philosophical commentary on deific time. In turn, Prieto's sketches disrupt the strict chronology of Milton's epic to create a pleasurable experience of modernity's disordering of narrative certainties. We can think of a similar treatment of time in *Slaughterhouse Five* (1969) by Kurt Vonnegut, nearly coeval with *Milton | El Paraíso perdido*.

The volume's chronological upsetting energizes our attention to a multiplicity of modes of reading. One of the chief and certainly most enthralling aspects of the sketches is their sparseness. With similarly sparse verbal text, *Milton | El Paraíso perdido* encourages readers to roam their memories and imaginations and thus to enact a version of God the Son's division of Chaos's homely "Matter unformed and void" (*PL* 7.233), parsing the "black tartareous cold infernal dregs / Adverse to life" from "the rest" that will compose a capacious yet orderly world (*PL* 7.238–39, 240). Audiences of the sketches will well appreciate why Prieto was known as the "line poet." The epithet pays tribute both to the genre of sketch he so refined and to his repeated practice of illustrating poetic lines for editions of literary works. Prieto's creative, economical use of the sketch form imitates the Creation that Milton describes in *Paradise Lost*, an interpretation buttressed by the fact that the subsequent (1974) gallery showing of Prieto's work for Madrid's tercentenary commemoration of Milton's death includes other dense visual media, such as collage and watercolor, absent from *Milton | El Paraíso perdido*. In the prologue, Aleixandre asks and answers, "¿Son líneas las que hemos visto? «Poesía en línea» se llama al armonioso conjunto de aquéllos" (Are these [simply] lines that we have witnessed? 'Poetry in lines' is the name for their harmonious unity).[52] Harmonious but in a different key from that to which we may be accustomed.

Elegant interpretations must be argued cautiously, however, because *Milton | El Paraíso perdido* possesses either basic mistakes or confusing elements that do not lead to or reflect "validity in interpretation."[53] Most of Sketches 1–16 correspond easily with their adjoining verbal text, but roughly a quarter of them do not; then there is the matter of the frontispiece, "Sketch I, Cottage." Below the sketch are the words "Cottage Halfont, casa natal de Milton en St. Giles" (Cottage Halfont, Milton's Birthplace in St. Giles). The spelling of "Halfont" may or may not be a mistake, given Spanish translational variety with "ch" sounds. The designation of the place, however, is certainly mistaken. Chalfont Cottage is not Milton's birthplace but rather the mature Milton's home from 1665 to 1666 to escape the plague. Milton was born at the Spread Eagle on Bread Street, Cheapside, London. We might ascribe the error to an editorial assistant and to the lack of attention paid to the front-matter, where this illustration resides. Doing so, however, might be as misguided as the English printer Richard Bentley's response in the eighteenth century in correcting what he considered errors in Milton's epic, or it might be as actively engaged as Jennett's choices with the mid-twentieth-century illustrated *Sonnets of William Shakespeare* just discussed.[54] In any case, the Halfont error was repeated in the gallery showing of 1974.

Other instances are much more consequential, as two examples demonstrate. First, difficulties arise with "Sketch 6, Female Figure amid Flowers," which faces the passage from book 8, "one came, methought, of shape divine" (*PL* 8.295–99). The chief image of the illustration is a female figure amid flowers and trees, with her feet in a pond, upon which floats a swan and next to which is the profile of what appears to be Adam's face. Oddly, the verbal text is Adam's description to Raphael of God's "shape divine" shortly after his creation, before the first woman was created. Since none of the other sketches depicts God, we cannot corroborate an intentional depiction of God as female, which would certainly counter Milton's representation of God the Father and God the Son as male. Equally valid interpretations are that Prieto was either confused or playing with the feminine nouns and adjectives of "desconocida / Persona, de hermosísima figura" (unknown / Person of beautiful figure), all grammatically feminine, to describe God, or that he erred and believed these lines to refer to Eve approaching Adam, as described shortly after these lines.

Another dilemma arises with "Sketch 9, Adam and Eve Reclining," depicting a grove, absent of animals and insects and containing two angels in the upper bower and two human figures within it. The Miltonic lines they refer to are "earth in her rich attire / Consummate lovely smiled" (*PL* 7.501–2), which end the archangel Raphael's description of the creation of animals and insects, right before the creation of humankind. During the Creation, Milton would have all the angels remain in Heaven, witnessing the astounding event; humans were not yet created.

We should of course keep in mind that many illustrators of *Paradise Lost* deviate from strict adherence to Milton's text. There are Aldrich's illustration of book 12 of Adam and Eve naked as they depart from Eden in the 1688 Tonson edition and Blake's illustration of the same scene with the couple covered with leaves. Following Genesis, Milton has the pair covered in the animal skins that God had provided them in book 10. Readers are left to assess whether the many representational divergences between visual and verbal texts in *Milton | El Paraíso perdido* are based on artistic license, carelessness, ignorance of Milton's life and *Paradise Lost*, or some other cause. In reaching such active assessments, we encounter interpretive gems, such as "Sketch 15, Adam and Eve Entwined," which accompanies the description of the Edenic couple as they make their way to their bower, where they will end their day in prayer, then lovemaking: "Thus talking hand in hand alone they passed" (*PL* 4.689–700; see Figure 9). As discussed in chapter 2, Escóiquiz, other translators, and critics censure this scene based on the criterion of taste, although the matter of Edenic human sex also extends to religion. This sketch blithely eschews the troubled topic. Instead, through its subdued surrealistic sketch lines, Sketch 15 represents the couple's joyous physical communion. Prieto pays visual homage to Escóiquiz's verbal text on the verso side, "Con el laurel el mirto se hermenaba" (With the laurel the myrtle united itself), by having both the leaves of the plants and the Edenic couple entwined.

The sketch also interacts gorgeously with Milton's verbal text. In *Paradise Lost*, the "roof / Of thickest covert" of the couple's "blissful bower" is made of evergreens, laurel trees, and myrtle bushes, as well as undefined flora, "what higher grew / Of firm and fragrant leaf" (*PL* 4.690–95). Prieto renders the trees' leaves, fruits, and flowers rather freely, not with botanical precision. In setting the couple amid trees rather than in the "Mosaic" of flowers underneath, Sketch 15 recalls a memorable image from earlier in book 4 of the pervasive integration of the Edenic couple with Edenic flora. In their first appearance in *Paradise Lost*, Adam is described as having "hyacinthine locks . . . Clust'ring," Eve "wanton ringlets wav[ing] / As the vine curls her tendrils" (*PL* 4.301–2, 306–7). The visual movement of Prieto's upward-tending flora is compounded by the stars and the moon at the upper left. The reflective and inherent beauty of the moon is a motif endemic in Prieto's illustrations and Milton's epic; it also makes a cameo, along with the sun, in the *décima* poem to be discussed shortly.

Thus, despite the intratextual dilemmas described, the sketches are powerful. Those that easily correspond with their respective verbal text capture the thrill of Milton's epic; those that do not jarringly move readers to recognize the incompatibility of some visual art to verbal art, no matter how beautiful. The same cannot be said of Aleixandre's prologue in relation to the ensuing illustrations. When Aleixandre calls "Sketch 7, Adam Grasping a Tree," "el primer cuadro de la serie" (the first illustration of the series), we are left wondering if he wrote his prologue before the edition was completed

Figure 9. Gregorio Prieto's "Sketch 15, Adam and Eve Entwined," in *Milton | El Paraíso perdido* (1972). (Fundación Gregorio Prieto; image courtesy of Harvard University Libraries)

and resequenced. Perhaps the edition had originally been designed to follow the chronological order of the epic, in which case Sketch 7 indeed would have been first. The hypothesis of a different sequencing helps to account for Aleixandre's commentaries on Sketches 3, 4, 8, and 12. I call attention to only the first two because their associations with the verbal text expand to another set of verbal texts that will be discussed shortly. Aleixandre relates "Sketch 3, Adam's Back, Eve's Profile," not to the description of Eve's creation accompanying it but rather to Adam's creation described in book 8: "Adán nace de la tierra. Nace como nace el árbol. Adán era la tierra, o la tierra era también Adán, como era todo, el todo" (Adam is born from the earth. He is born as is the tree. Adam was the earth, or the earth was Adam too, as he was all, all). Aleixandre also asserts of Sketch 3, "El triunfo de la mujer, señalado como el opulento instante de la creación, se contempla en el dichoso cántico, que eso es el cuadro siguiente de la Eva completa" (The triumph of the woman, signaled as the opulent instance of creation, is contemplated in the blessed hymn, which is the sketch that follows it, of a fully formed Eve). The sketch that follows, "Sketch 4, Eve's Upper Torso and Head" is of Eve, but the details that he refers to, such as her "vientre" (stomach), do not appear. His description seems better suited to "Sketch 8, Eve at Adam's Feet."[55]

The power and frustration attendant on visual art for illustrated books arises also intertextually, in relation to the reappearance of some of the sketches in the 1974 gallery exhibition, two years after the book's publication. That exhibition further destabilizes the relationship between Milton's verbal text and Prieto's visual text. The published catalogue of the exhibition, *Milton y Gregorio Prieto* (1974), records a total of forty-one acrylics, collages, paintings, sketches, and watercolors. It reproduces fourteen of the works, of which three are from *Milton | El Paraíso perdido*. Two of the three are accompanied by different texts from those that accompany them in *Milton | El Paraíso perdido*. The only sketch from *Milton | El Paraíso perdido* that retains its verbal text is the sketch of the cottage, with its continued misattribution of "Cottage Halfont, Milton's Birthplace in St. Giles." The verbal text for the second of the sketches, "Sketch 9, Adam and Eve Reclining," is no longer *Paradise Lost* 4.313–20, part of Milton's panegyric to wedded sexual union. Instead it is a continuation of the verbal text from the gallery sketch preceding it in *Milton y Gregorio Prieto*, which does not appear in *Milton | El Paraíso perdido*. The text of that gallery illustration is as follows:

Tiernamente me hieres con tu flecha gozosamente enamorada, ya que el beso de amor es unión y equilibrio de eternidad divina y sentido de poder creativo en orden y eternidad.

Pero si no es amor, entonces pecado de perversidad es y se hace pozo profundo, insondable, de maldita serpiente, que manipula un Paraíso y se pierde.

(Tenderly you wound me with your arrow so pleasurably enamored, now that the kiss of love is union and equilibrium of divine eternity, and felt as the creative power of order and eternity.

But if it is not love, then it is the sin of perversity and turns itself into a profound cesspit, unfathomable, of a damned serpent, that manipulates a Paradise and is lost.)

We may concede that this verbal text refers lightly to the married union extolled in the excerpt from *Paradise Lost* in *Milton | El Paraíso perdido*. But our concession is thwarted when the gallery text continues:

Leonardo da Vinci, en perfecto dibujo anatómico, así los describe en plasticidad lineal, ya que solo sexo sin amor, Paraíso Perdido es.

Pero Miguel, Santo Arcángel Celestial, lo salva, lo encuentra y no se pierde, y en consecuencia Milton escribe el «Paraíso Reconquistado», donde tranquilos y reposados viven hombre y mujer en clarividente y sorprendente armonía.

(Leonardo da Vinci, in perfect anatomic illustration, describes it just so in plastic lines, now only sex without love is Paradise Lost.

But Michael, Blessed Celestial Archangel, saves it, he finds it and it is not lost and consequently Milton writes *Paradise Regained*, where man and woman live tranquil and reposed in lucid and surprising harmony.)

Jarringly, Michael plays a less salvific role in *Paradise Lost* than the gallery text suggests, and *Paradise Regained* centers on the chaste Jesus. Finally, for the last of the three sketches, "Sketch 3, Adam's Back, Eve's Profile," the excerpt from *Paradise Lost* (8.465–75) describing Eve's creation is replaced by part of Aleixandre's prologue to *Milton | El Paraíso perdido*.

It is not only the subsequent history of some of the illustrations of *Milton | El Paraíso perdido* that destabilizes the relationship between Milton's verbal text and Prieto's visual texts; the preceding history does too.[56] Aleixandre's prologue explains that the drawings are not "ilustrativos de" (illustrative of) but rather "inspirados por" (inspired by) Milton's poems. "Inspired by" indicates a large spectrum of the relationship of visual and verbal texts; it is the same phrasing used in the 1883 illustrated Escóiquiz *Paraíso perdido* with Doré illustrations. The lack of correspondence between the visual and verbal texts here, however, hints at the possibility that the illustrations were not "inspired by" or, as the gallery catalogue would have it, "preliminary studies for" Milton's text in ways we may traditionally conceive of such terms. Indeed, upon reading, reviewing, and re-reviewing the unusual catalogue, I sensed that Milton's verbal text was being used, simply put, as a convenient catalyst for a visual feast, a late occasion for these two still-living members of Spain's Generación del 1927—the heyday for which was nearly half a century before—to develop their modernist and postmodernist theories and practices. In the "Nota preliminar" (Preliminary Note) to a nearly coeval publication by Prieto, *Lorca y la Generación del 27*, José Ruiz-Castillo Basala describes the commemorative nature of that work: "Con motivo de celebrarse el primer cincuentenario de la Generación de 1927, todos los medios de comunicación y, naturalmente, los editores se vienen ocupando de la gloriosa pléyada de los poetas que la integran" (With the motivation of celebrating the first fiftieth anniversary of the Generation of 1927, all means of communication and, naturally, all the editors have seized upon the matter of the glorious band of the poets that make up the group).[57] My hunch proved valid.

It turns out that five of the illustrations in *Milton | El Paraíso perdido* and two in the catalogue *Milton y Gregorio Prieto* had been published a few years earlier, among roughly two hundred sketches, paintings, and multimedia illustrations by Prieto and his fellow Spaniard Lorca in *Lorca en color* (1969). That work is devoid of any verbal reference to Milton or *Paradise Lost*, even though it makes direct verbal mention of many artists; among Anglophone writers, Percy Bysshe Shelley, John Keats, Shakespeare, Ian Gibson, and Walt Whitman.[58] Thus the only way in which at least these two visual texts in *Lorca en color* can be thought of as "preliminary studies" for *Milton | El Paraíso perdido* is if we think of all of an artist's previous works as preliminary to future works, and perhaps we should. Moreover if we treat visual texts like verbal texts, as the trajectory of this history of Spanish illustrations of *Paradise Lost* warrants, we readily note two strong visual allusions to *Paradise Lost* in the colorful collage that opens *Lorca en color* (see book cover and Figure 10). One of the twelve crowned figures in the collage, near the bottom left is the William Dolle engraving of Milton from the 1674 English edition of *Paradise Lost*, the first edition of the epic

Figure 10. Opening collage of *Lorca en color* (1969) by Gregorio Prieto. (Fundación Gregorio Prieto; image by Kristin Leaman, courtesy of Indiana University Libraries)

to include an author portrait.[59] Another crowned figure, at the middle right edge, is Satan from "Satan Rousing the Rebel Angels" in the Butts set of Blake's illustrations of *Paradise Lost*.

So with these clues, what then can we make of the five recycled illustrations in *Milton | El Paraíso perdido*? How far should we go in trying to theorize our way out of the conundrum? This case must be treated very differently from, for example, the reuse of illustrations from woodcuts in the medieval period, when such commodities were expensive and therefore often recycled. Electronic splicing, reuse, and modifications of visual images in today's digital age are moving us to apprehend more readily the medieval period's conceptualization of the fluid author and artist before copyright. Can artists plagiarize themselves, or can they render themselves exempt? Many visual art critics have raised questions about self-plagiarism in regard to many visual artists. For example, Joanna Richardson writes of Doré's illustrations of *Paradise Lost*, "All too often, Doré seems to plagiarise himself," in relation not to exact duplication of previous work but rather to "playing with a limited number of formulae."[60] Prieto presses the issue of plagiarism and recycling even with the little verbal text he authored. For example, his text for the section "Pintar con palabras" (Paint with Words) in *Lorca en color* is repeated word for word in the section "Federico García Lorca como pintor" (Federico Garcia Lorca as Painter) in yet another book, *Lorca y la Generación del 27*.[61] While the latter book acknowledges that it is a synthesis of essays, it does not cite the original publications, leaving knowledge and access to the interrelationships haphazard.

In any event, the silently recycled sketches in *Milton | El Paraíso perdido* work brilliantly when we consider this recycling as visual allusion and allow that allusion to inform our reception in ways that poetic allusions do. One of the sketches in *Lorca en color* is "Sketch 10, Adam Walking and Lying Down" (Figure 11). In *Milton | El Paraíso perdido*, the illustration accompanies the passage in *Paradise Lost* in which Adam describes his initial moments of life to the archangel Raphael:

With fragrance and with joy my heart o'erflowed.
Myself I then perused, and limb by limb
Surveyed, and sometimes went, and sometimes ran
With supple joints, as lively vigour led:
But who I was, or where, or from what cause,
Knew not. (*PL* 8.266–71)

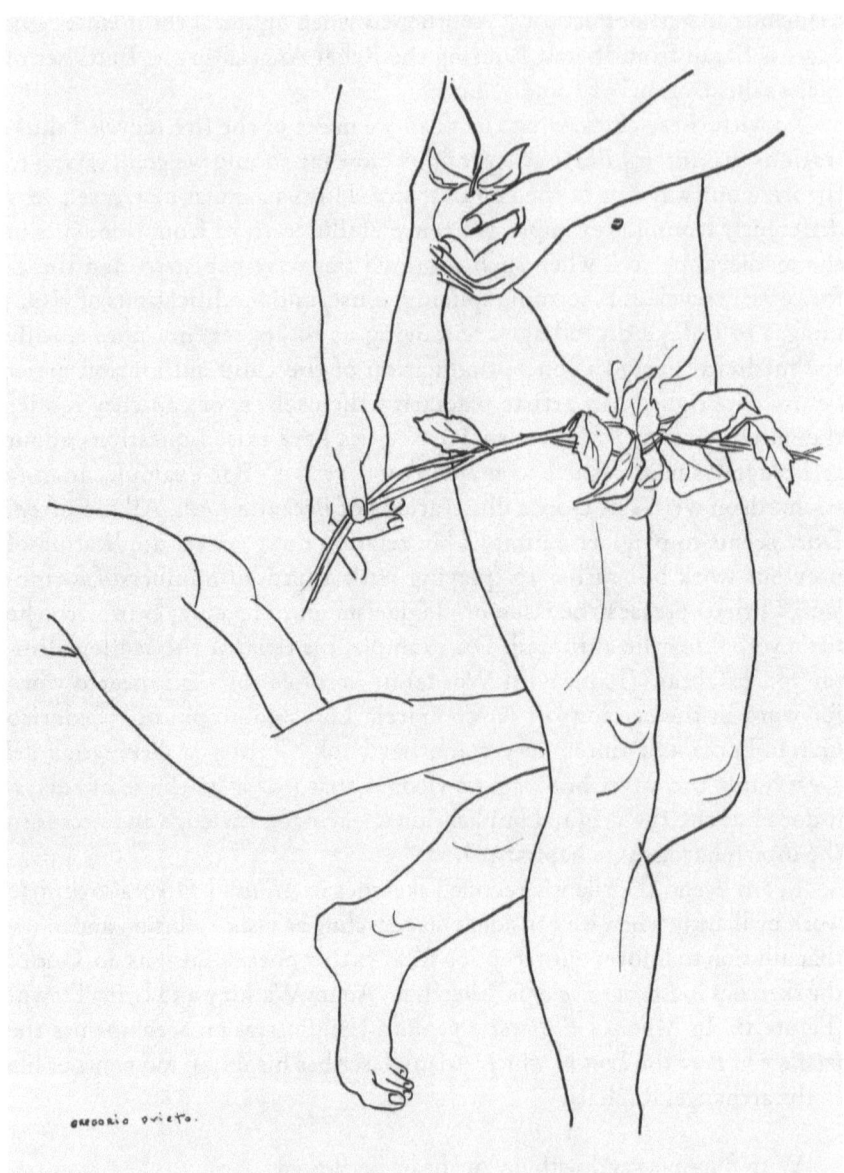

Figure 11. Gregorio Prieto's "Sketch 10, Adam Walking and Lying Down," in *Milton | El Paraíso perdido* (1972). (Courtesy of Harvard University Libraries)

Alongside this verbal text, the illustration moves us to peruse Adam's limbs and read Prieto's illustrated Adams sequentially. Prieto's prone Adam guides us back to the moments preceding the excerpt where Adam is supine—"As new waked from soundest sleep / Soft on the flow'ry herb I found me laid / In balmy sweat" (PL 8.253–55)—then to the upright Adam from the excerpt. In *Lorca en color*, the accompanying quotation is "Adán sueña en la fiebre de la arcilla" (Adam dreams in the fever of the clay) from Lorca's powerful sonnet "Adán."[62] Coupled with only Milton's text, Sketch 10 represents two diachronic, sequential instances of Adam's creation: his supine awakening to life, followed by his willful and joyful arising. In the sestet of Lorca's poem, the illustration represents two synchronic Adams: "Adán" and "otro Adán oscuro" (another dark Adam; 12). Prieto's conjunction of these two otherwise disparate visions of Adam by Milton and Lorca enacts the very multiplicity that time and perspective produce, the awakening to existence that art represents.

Prieto's creation of a palimpsest of visions is even more complex in "Sketch 4, Eve's Upper Torso and Head" (see Figures 12 and 13). With Sketch 10, the referents in the accompanying texts are both Adam, in one way or another. With Sketch 4, the verbal texts by Milton and Lorca refer to two distinct figures. In *Milton | El Paraíso perdido*, the accompanying text is Adam's description of Eve's creation:

Under his forming hands a creature grew,
Manlike, but different sex, so lovely fair,
That what seemed fair in all the world, seemed now
Mean, or in her summed up, in her contained
And in her looks, which from that time infused
Sweetness into my heart, unfelt before,
And into all things from her air inspired
The spirit of love and amorous delight. (PL 8.470–77)

In *Lorca en color*, the sketch is linked to a poetic "Norma" from Lorca's "Dos Normas" (Two norms/Normas).[63] *Norma* is an ingenious pun in Spanish on a common female name and the feminine noun for "common" or "norm," a pun all the more undecipherable because the uppercase "N" at the beginning of lines 1 and 11 can be controlled by either its placement at the beginning of a sentence or its function as a proper noun.

Lorca's verbal doubling is paralleled by Prieto's visual doubling. Lorca includes the visual text of sketches of a moon at the start of the poem's first

Figure 12. Gregorio Prieto's "Sketch 4, Eve's Upper Torso and Head," and adjoining text in *Milton | El Paraíso perdido* (1972). (Fundación Gregorio Prieto; image courtesy by Kristin Leaman, courtesy of Harvard University Libraries)

stanza, which starts with the word "Norma," and of a sun at the start of the second stanza, which also starts with the word "Norma." Prieto replaces Lorca's two sketches with Sketch 4, with Eve's orb-like breast drawing the greatest attention in one of the most minimalist sketches in *Milton | El Paraíso perdido*; no longer Lorca's "Norma de seno y cadera" (Norma of breast and hip; 11) but Prieto's Eve of breast. Both Milton's and Lorca's poetic passages emphasize the bodies of the female figures, the former setting up the archangel Raphael's warning to Adam to avoid attending too much to "An outside" (*PL* 8.568). In "Dos Normas," Lorca's second *décima* fantastically represents the conflation of the first female with all women, since the female figure is a mythic *norm, la norma*, of all women.[64] The tree, as at once "antigua y recién nacida" (ancient and recently born; 13), sets up the unfulfilled quest of Lorca's speaker for a "pura / locura de brisa y trino" (pure / madness of breeze and trill; 19–20) in Norma's "locura" (madness; 18). In a sense, Prieto's illustration visually revises Lorca's poem so that it becomes a fulfilled quest through

Figure 13. Gregorio Prieto's "Norma de pecho" and adjoining text in *Lorca en color* (1969). (Fundación Gregorio Prieto; image by Kristin Leaman, courtesy of Indiana University Libraries)

its unity of Lorca's two sketches in his single sketch of the original norm/ Norma.

This visual multiplicity parallels yet another spectral multiplicity. Lorca's texts often exist in multiple versions because he left many poems unpublished, either intentionally in response to censorship or unintentionally due to his early, unanticipated death, and because of the intentional and unintentional modifications by editors, publishers, and transcribers. What *Lorca en color* renders as "pecho" (chest), other versions render as "seno" (breast). As the verbal descriptor of the sketch's visual centerpiece, the modification accrues more attention to the originary site of the fulfillment of human hunger and of female nurturing, creativity, and beauty.⁶⁵ It alerts audiences to their own active co-creation of the Norma or the Eve of the poems. And perhaps Prieto felt completely authorized to do so with his friend Lorca or any other true artist. Such is the implication in the anecdote with which Prieto ends his *Garcia Lorca as a Painter* (1946), from decades earlier: "I remember that one day as we were sitting in the cool shade of the poplars in the Residencia he [Lorca] said to me: 'You know, Gregorio, the poetry of your painting and the painting of my poetry spring from the same source.'"⁶⁶ Such too is the implication of Lorca's longtime friend and art critic of the magazine *L'Amic de les Arts*, the Barcelonan Sebastian Gasch, whom Prieto quotes in the opening paratext, all in capital letters, of *Lorca en color*:

> Mi reencuentro con Gregorio Prieto ha resucitado en mi mente fatigada el recuerdo fresco y vivo de Federico García Lorca y, a través de mi entrañable Gregorio—o mejor, en él—, he hallado la misma sinceridad, la misma autenticidad, la misma exuberante cordialidad y el inconmensurable talento de Federico.
>
> (My reunion with Gregorio Prieto has resuscitated in my fatigued mind the fresh and vivid memory of Federico García Lorca and, through my dear Gregorio—or better said, in him—I have found the same sincerity, the same authenticity, the same exuberant cordiality and the incommensurate talent of Federico.)⁶⁷

No niceties about personal authorship and individualism. Indeed *Lorca en color* does not include any identifiers to its more than two hundred illustrations. Thus any visual allusions to *Paradise Lost*, as in the opening collage (Figure 10), are as attributable to Lorca as to Prieto. Audiences new to Lorca's and Prieto's single-artist illustrations may be moved to ascribe the opening collage to Prieto upon reaching the section of *Lorca en color* titled "Dibujos de Federico" (Federico's Drawings), full of illustrations in Lorca's signature single-artist style, which is quite distinct from the collage.⁶⁸ Audiences familiar with Lorca's famously flexible style in collaborative works, however, would not. Ultimate authorship is left open, to be ascribed to some "same source," much like the Muse, Spirit, and other artistic sources to which Milton refers in *Paradise Lost* and other poetic works.

This triangulation of Prieto, Lorca, and Milton centered on the single creative source that informs artistic work quadrangulates when reader-viewers are made aware of and choose to participate in the creative process, one that is, rightly considered, a network, an "All in All" (PL 3.341). This is the active process that Richard Macksey rightly derives from Genette's *Paratexts*: "The invitation (and challenge) is to *read*, with vigilance as well as knowledge, and, as [Laurence] Sterne also reminds us, to become through this reading a collaborator in the on-going literary construction."[69] My argument is that Prieto was such a collaborative reader-viewer and that he sought to generate and include collaborative reader-viewers, past, present, and future. Alongside "Dos Normas," Prieto's sketch re-creates the chest/breast of Lorca's Norma and Milton's Eve with paper and pencil, printers, publishers, and so on, and his reader-viewers are left to acknowledge how much they co-create Norma's "hip"—and perhaps Eve's too—which Prieto generously leaves us to do by absenting it visually.

Conclusion

Genette defines paratexts as fungible thresholds—one might even say "frontispieces," to recall the quotation that opens this chapter—that "change continually, depending on period, culture, genre, author, work, and edition, with varying degrees of pressure."[70] While Genette expressly excludes illustrations from his long study, the unique nature of illustrations and shifts in codes since *Paratexts* was first published leaves the relationship of verbal and visual paratexts and texts not simply worth exploring but exigent. In this chapter's exploration of the illustrations in *Milton | El Paraíso perdido* we find further validation of Macksey's assessment about paratexts, that the "signs of authorship are repeatedly undone."[71] The bracing view that we are left with urges us to question our assumptions about how much we allow the relationship of verbal and visual art in illustrated editions to determine or inform our interpretations of both, and how much we allow the relationship of any Spanish elements and Milton's works to do so as well. My response to the first is a recognition that, while Spanish illustrations are not high in number, they are deep in meaning: Medina's participation in the 1688 illustrated *Paradise Lost* thwarts (still not uncommon) assumptions about the uniformly antagonistic nature of early modern Anglo-Hispanic encounters; the careful manipulations of the Doré illustrations in Spanish editions of *El Paraíso perdido* at the end of the nineteenth century reflect active participation in Western cultural circuits rather than ignorance or passive replication of it; and the promiscuous history of Prieto's brilliant if little-known Spanish sketches in the exclusive Spanish edition and elsewhere demonstrates the playful, fluid relationship of art writ large. My response to the second is more visceral and appropriately open-ended. The sets of visual texts discussed in this chapter have prompted me to rethink what Milton's works mean, to acknowledge what they have meant to others, and to participate in reshaping what they can mean.

EPILOGUE

Juan Milton, el Inglés

I conclude by revisiting the concept and practice of Ours and Others mapped out in the introduction, explored in each of the four main chapters, and now warranting discussion at the end of the four interdisciplinary studies of Spanish institutional censorship, translation, staged drama, and visual art related to Milton's works and legend. I aim to elucidate some of the ways in which the series of powerful engagements with Milton among Spaniards weave together, or, to use the terms of the introduction, to highlight the affiliations of the elements that have been presented separately. Equally important, this epilogue provides me with the opportunity to enact the Spanish academic sensibility I have attempted to instill less overtly throughout *Milton among Spaniards*, or, again to us the terms of the introduction, to enfold a Spanish critical sensibility into this English critical study. Such a concluding enactment fulfills my commitment to give both of the cultures under study their due, and it puts to service the plural term "Criticisms" that John Phillips uses in his English translation of *Don Quixote* and that English-Spanish comparative literature specialists will find apposite to describe the two certainly related but distinct sets of features of English and Spanish reception and academic criticism with which they will no doubt be familiar. The differences between the two are subtle but powerful; they include topics, presentational modes, linguistic and therefore rhetorical strategies, and personae that predominate in each.[1]

My elucidation and enactment takes up Miguel de Unamuno's invitation to do so in his use of Milton and Don Quixote at the end of his collection of philosophic essays, *Del sentimiento trágico de la vida* (The Tragic Sense of Life).² At the end of the penultimate chapter, "El problema práctico" (The Practical Problem), Unamuno keys in on the irreplaceability of each person, each thing, and each encounter of each person and each thing (including books), an ultimately tragic sense that requires passion to recognize and inhabit.³ He singles out the "gran inquietador puritan Juan Milton, el secuaz de Cromwell y cantor de Satanás" (great Puritan disturber of spiritual peace, John Milton, Cromwell's agitator and the singer of Satan) as the epitome of writers able to assert a passionate agency with the "armas . . . de la paciencia y la resignación" (weapons . . . of patience and resignation).⁴ He cites Milton for having heard and articulated the voice of Patience in his "estupendo soneto" (stupendous sonnet), "When I consider."⁵ (This is but one instance of Milton's minor works, neglected perforce in the preceding chapters, operating among Spaniards.) Then, in the concluding chapter, "Don Quijote en la tragicomedia europea contemporánea" (Don Quixote in Contemporary European Tragicomedy), Unamuno articulates his own passionate agency in terms of the intimate affiliations of Quixote and "yo" (I)—at once Unamuno himself and anyone who takes up the subject and object positions that he invites them/us to do—requisite for engaging in the process of what he admits to be his own contradictory philosophy.⁶ The indeterminate nature of that philosophy should be welcomed by Miltonists, sharp observers of ambivalences in early modern discursive practices.

Unamuno concludes his collection of philosophical "ensayos" (essays), which he offers tentatively, as a Quixotic "ensueño," "por temor también—¿por qué no confesarlo?—a la Inquisición, pero a la de hoy" (dream/reverie, for fear also—why not confess it?—of the Inquisition, but of the modern one).⁷ The self-protection he establishes in offering his conclusion as a dream or reverie highlights the tentative nature that adheres more strongly in the contemporary Spanish word *ensayos* than in the contemporary English word "essays," in the sense of sallies or rehearsals, as much as of "composition[s] of moderate length on any particular subject."⁸ Unamuno is not referring to two distinct fearsome institutional entities centralized in Rome and Spain but rather updating the overlapping meaning of "Inquisition" to refer to the diffuse censorial mechanisms that uphold their prescribed values and, as a result, can exclude others' and ours. The varying affiliating and differentiating nature of those values is signaled by the ending of the full title of Unamuno's collection, often suppressed in its English translations: *en los hombres y en los pueblos* (of Humans and in Villages). In the text he clearly defines those villages as Spanish. Like the most famous protagonist created by the Golden Age Miguel and self-representation constructed by his *tocayo* (name twin, in reference to someone who shares the same first name) philosopher Miguel, I found myself with *Milton among Spaniards* reading obscure and well-known works and uncovering in them correspondences that others had not, given those agents' differing agendas or given that they had not read the "rimero" (pile) of disparate English and Spanish books together.[9] I also discovered in the passions of the agents of those texts my own scholarly passion, representative no doubt of the passion that some of the most fortunate literary critics experience and that they manifest in their "Criticisms" but, in the main, leave unrecorded. I leave this record.

At the start of this study, I describe Prieto's "Sketch 3, Adam's Back, Eve's Profile," in *Milton | El Paraíso perdido* as emblematic of the dual aspects of affiliation and alterity, or Ours and Others, inherent in the representations of Milton among Spaniards (Figure 1). Here, I put the delicate lines of the sketch to work one more time, as emblematic of the fact that the texts and topics of this book's four main chapters, while discussed in some depth, provide only a sketch or a partial answer to this study's governing question: What does a Spanish Milton—or, better stated, what do Spanish Miltons—look like?

The Miltons among Spaniards are by no means synonymous with the composite Milton recorded in major Milton criticism, constructed primarily by British, American (U.S. and Canadian), French, and to a lesser degree German audiences and "Criticisms." At times, Spanish Miltons are in general accord with that composite Milton and are in such accord very intentionally, their creators being aware of the reputation of Spanish cultural isolation and seeking to showcase Spanish participation in general Western cultural systems. Such is my claim in chapter 4 regarding one of the first illustrated editions of *El Paraíso perdido* (1883), based on the 1812 Escóiquiz translation, with its use of visual paratexts that won acclaim and were reprinted across nineteenth-century Europe and America: the engraving based on Munkácsy's painting "The Blind Milton Dictating Paradise Lost to His Daughters" (1878) and the illustrations by Doré throughout the work. At times, however, Spanish Miltons are noticeably distinct, as Prieto's portrait of Milton illustrates (see Figure 14).

By empirical standards, Prieto's portrait does not accurately reflect Milton's facial features, captured in the portrait, circa 1629, at the National Portrait Gallery in London. Neither does it overtly domesticate the English Milton for Spanish audiences in the revisionary mode that is common with

Figure 14. Portrait of John Milton by Gregorio Prieto in *Milton y Gregorio Prieto* (1974) and by an unknown artist, c. 1629. (Fundación Gregorio Prieto; image courtesy of National Library of Spain / National Portrait Gallery, London)

many world authors and as is done, for example, in the author portraits on the book covers of the 1873 Cayetano Rosell and 1883 Escóiquiz *El Paraíso perdido* illustrated editions (Figure 6).[10] Unlike William Marshall, whose author portrait for *Poems . . . 1645* Milton derided in his Greek epigram "In effigiei eius sculptorem" (Against the Engraver of his Portrait), Prieto was certainly capable of a more accurate rendering, as his many portraits of famous figures amply demonstrate. Moreover Prieto had access to accurate depictions of Milton through his extended travels in England and elsewhere. As discussed in chapter 4, Prieto included the William Dolle engraving of Milton in the opening collage (Figure 10) of his deluxe book *Lorca en color* (1969). Thus we are called to think about intentionality, a subcategory of agency that I am emphasizing in this epilogue.

In her discussion of the genre of illustrations of "the blind Milton dictating," Anna Zsófia Kovác cautions that many artists are not "driven by historical accuracy." Indeed some of the illustrations of Milton reproduced in her article are as unrecognizable as Prieto's author portrait or as Blake's better known depiction of a naked, muscular, short- and curly haired Milton. Kovác chooses to argue for artistic choice rather than artistic error or incompetency: "Artists did not really attempt to have Milton's own features set in the character they wished to mold; rather they sought to depict a face that corresponded with the effect and state of mind they projected into the figure."[11]

What is the "effect" of Prieto's rendering of Milton? One hypothesis is that Prieto playfully used his or one of his friends' facial features, a strategy practiced by Raffaello Sanzio da Urbino in his *School of Athens* (1509–11) and by Michelangelo Merisi da Caravaggio in many of his works, most poignantly of himself in *The Taking of Christ* (c. 1602). While Prieto's Milton bears no resemblance to Prieto, to any of the main members of Prieto's personal circles, or to famous Spanish figures of the day whom I investigated, Prieto's immediate audience may have been well aware of the identity of the individual in this visual allusion. Whatever the case, we must acknowledge that, alarmingly, Prieto's author portrait leaves uninformed audiences misled about Milton's facial features, as much as does another of Prieto's sketches referencing Milton's biography, that of "Halfont Cottage, Milton's Birthplace."

Milton's younger contemporary John Dryden brings in the matter of visual translation to illustrate a point about verbal translation that still applies to audience expectations about author portraits: "When a painter copies from the life, I suppose he has no privilege to alter features and lineaments, under pretense that his picture will look better: perhaps the face which he has drawn would be more exact, if the eyes or nose were altered; but 'tis his business to make it resemble the original."[12] Prieto's style in Milton's portrait, a sufficiently standard depiction of a human face, provides none of the signs that his fellow artists utilized in order to signal to audiences their departure from the artist's "business." The portraits by Prieto's contemporary and friend Pablo Picasso are so distanced from empirical representations of facial forms that there is no sense of betrayal. Conversely, the audiences of Prieto's portrait could be hoodwinked or feel betrayed.

We are thus led to construct other hypotheses. If we credit Prieto with keen knowledge of the issues of verbal-to-visual and international translation, we can interpret his author portrait as reinforcing the new Milton he sought to create in his sketches in *Milton | El Paraíso perdido*, his gallery exhibition of 1974, and scattered throughout other publications. If we ascribe to Prieto a deep appreciation of the differences between the products of the two Johns/Juans—John Milton's original English epic and Juan Escóiquiz's Spanish verbal translation of it, used in *Milton | El Paraíso perdido*—we can interpret the portrait as commenting ironically on the limited resemblance between the two. If we approach the author portrait without the benefit of previous exposure to Prieto's *Lorca en color* or other contextualization, we might charge Prieto with insouciance and, in turn, (mis)judge this case as yet another instance of Spanish cultural isolation or a paucity of Anglo-Hispanic exchange. All of these appropriately tentative interpretive acts focus our attention on Prieto as a human agent engaging within or outside of specific cultural circuits, on our own agency as audiences with varying degrees of relevant knowledge, and on the simultaneous sense of affiliation and alterity that cultural circuits and reading provoke. And these are the very kinds of interpretive acts that *Milton among Spaniards* reflects upon: in the focus on the signs of religious passion evinced by the scholarly branch of the Spanish Catholic Inquisition in chapter 1, which aims to complement the important scholarly studies of the violent passion evinced by the executive branch, and in the exposition in chapter 3 of the internal and external expressions of patriotism and cosmopolitanism in and surrounding Hermenegildo Giner de los Ríos's *Milton: A Dramatic Scene in One Act and in Verse*.

The indeterminacy of these hypotheses is buttressed by the use of the name "MILTON" below Prieto's author portrait, absent of either the Anglophone "John" or Spanish "Juan," as I use in the title of this epilogue. Prieto's use of "Juan" indeed would have been a distinctive sign of affiliation since Milton is regularly referred to in Spanish texts as "Milton" or "John Milton," Englishman. Giner de los Ríos's *Milton: A Dramatic Scene* is a representative case. Its list of "Characters" names the titular character "Milton"; daughter Débora calls Milton "Father"; and the other characters call him "Milton." The one instance of the use of his first name is in one of Milton's soliloquies. In this instance, he calls himself "John," not "Juan," in referring to the name he shares with his *tocayo*, the recently deceased servant whose death he and his allies are reporting as Milton's death so that he can escape political persecution. A major exception to the consistent use of Milton's surname only or of his Anglophone name is the use of his Latin name on the Spanish Catholic Inquisition's lists of proscribed authors and works, which creates an even greater nominative distance. Another telling exception is the use of the name "Juan Milton" by Unamuno.

When we consider the broader context of references to authors in native and foreign languages, it is difficult to draw firm conclusions about the cultural meaning of the retention of "John Milton" among Spaniards. Spanish translations of Shakespeare's works and Spanish plays featuring Shakespeare regularly use both the Anglophone name "William" and the Spanish "Guillermo."[13] We can also observe the domesticating and foreignizing dynamics in English references to the Spaniard Cervantes. In English, the Hispanic "Miguel" is regularly maintained, but Cervantes's second surname, Saavedra, is regularly dropped. The 1687 English translation of *Don Quixote* by Milton's nephew John Phillips does not include any form of Cervantes's name in its opening or closing paratexts. Is this an oversight? If so, one that exhibits the work's lack of editing or that pays testament to Cervantes's popularity? Or is this yet another one of Phillips's playful rhetorical strategies at work? And what do English and Spanish readers mean when referring to the Florentine author of *The Divine Comedy* by his first name only? It may connote intimacy to some; others may (and do) assume it is the author's surname.

All of these nominative facts and queries about world literature authors speak to the varied general reception of a cluster of early modern authors as much as to the varied types of personal agencies exhibited by individual readers, translators, and authors. Addressing the spectrums of affiliation/alterity and agency/passivity is what art calls us to do, and by extension what the chapters in this study have aimed to convey. I turn to Margaret R. Greer to consider the potential for locating our positions on such spectrums. She provides a number of promising models for recognizing my (individual) and our (corporate) agencies in actively creating affiliations and, especially in terms of Anglo-Hispanic relations, in getting "past the age of 'mine' and 'thine,' to shake off the lingering habits of Black Legend thinking and cultural isolationism." Greer is passionate about doing so because she is convinced that "we have much to learn from one another."[14] She calls attention to Barbara Fuchs's updating of the concept of "cultural mimesis" beyond "the first-order imitation among cultures which so fascinated ethnosociologists and historians of the earlier twentieth century" to a focus on aesthetics, culture, and "the deliberate representation of sameness." Fuchs eloquently explains the ways in which recent cultural studies can activate literary studies, since literature as "imitation compromises the narrative of national distinction by emphasizing inconvenient similarities and shared heritages."[15] Chapter 2 touches on instances of cultural mimesis in the inclusion of British and French criticisms and biographies of Milton in Spanish editions of *Paradise Lost*; chapter 3 in the purposeful allusions to the Milton legends circulating at the end of the nineteenth century and attention to the accuracy of costumes recorded in the epilogue to *Milton: A Dramatic Scene*; and chapter 4 in the use of the Munkácsy and Doré illustrations.

With this in mind, I have been struck by how many figures very much like Milton—statesman, poet, and polyglot—emerged in this study, in a kind of cultural-*con*-artistic mimesis, to press Fuchs's insightful concept. I give but a few examples here of the emergence of the Spanish public intellectual according to Milton's model.¹⁶ Escóiquiz followed a trajectory of penning short works leading to longer works, cutting his teeth on English-to-Spanish translation with Edward Young's "Night Thoughts" (orig. 1742–45; trans. 1797) and on the epic genre with his original *México conquistada* (1798). Escóiquiz wrote governmental prose as he advanced from serving as the tutor of the future King Ferdinand VII to respected advisor to the king. It was during his temporary exile in France with the king that Escóiquiz translated the epic of the quintessential "poet of exile" Milton, to invoke Louis Martz's term. Elements of Milton's biography are also to be found with a translator of his prose, the Catalan Josep de Carner. Carner was the first to publish a full Spanish translation of Milton's pamphlet against pre-publication censorship, *Areopagitica* (1644; Spanish 1941). He published poetry from 1904 through the 1920s, then served as vice counsel of Spain to Genoa and elsewhere. The uncanny cultural-*con*-artistic mimesis occurs not just with Milton's translators but also with Giner de los Ríos, who served as a tutor, wrote on pedagogy, and penned his early, charming dramatic piece for a political occasion in which the lives of the staged characters coalesce with those of the actors and audience, as did Milton with his early *Mask Presented at Ludlow-Castle*. Finally, cultural-*con*-artistic mimesis appears like a Dalían clock in a modernist frisson of the Spanish zeitgeist at the end of Francisco Franco Bahamonde's dictatorship (r. 1936–1975), with Prieto "getting as much of his work into print or back into print at the end of his life" as Milton himself did.¹⁷

This assemblage, comparison, and articulation of others' agencies, passions, and affiliations double as my own in some ways. Detachment, paradoxically enough, is generally agreed to be necessary for developing valid "Criticisms," even when—perhaps especially when—investigating the intellectual and affective appeals that texts and topics make. I indeed aimed to "place [myself] in the background" and to convey in each chapter the *simpatico* (a dynamic of affinity) that the texts and their creating and creative agents figured in them:¹⁸ the Spanish Catholic Inquisition's incorporation of Milton as one of the few "Anglus" in its purview; various translators' domestication and personal insertions in rendering *Paradise Lost* into *El Paraíso perdido*; Giner de los Ríos's reaching back to England's Restoration for Milton as the titular character for his first play and Spain's Golden Age for the native *décimas* he puts into his Milton's mouth in a play created for his idol and friend James Russell Lowell; and various Spanish presses' and artists' translations of verbal into visual art and of others' art into their own. Here, however, I forefront the *simpatico* I have had for the most long-lasting comfort, joy, and unexpected spur for dogged research in my creation of *Milton among Spaniards*.

When I expressly embarked on the project of Milton's Hispanic presence nearly a decade ago, I industriously typed into my campus library's electronic catalogue the keywords "Milton" and "Spanish." I was perplexed when I saw the entry for Escóiquiz's 1883 illustrated *El Paraíso perdido* as part of my public university's circulating library. My perplexity increased when I received it in my campus mail and noted its features, so distinct from the English and Spanish literary works with which I was more familiar.

John Hale cites just some of the unanticipated and pervasive effects of multilingualism on Milton in this extended study.[19] His sensitive argumentation moved me to reflect on my own Spanish-English bilingualism as methodology. My multilingualism involved early and regular exposure to a foundational Spanish work that, with Hale's help, I realized provided me with a form of the groundwork that Milton discusses in his tract *Of Education*. My phrasing "expressly embarked" acknowledges the early and sometimes passive steps that contribute to all active critical acts, in my case my youthful reading of my family's Sagrada Biblia (Sacred Bible). The work is of course the ur-text of Milton's masterwork. Equally important as groundwork for this study, my family Bible includes a tripartite series of Roman Catholic approvals, including an imprimatur, and colorful illustrations.[20] These early textual engagements are part of the groundwork in material textuality for chapters 2 and 4 and in cultural contextuality for chapters 1 and 3. In *Of Education*, Milton encourages a recursive learning process and, in that process, a willingness to "procure, as oft as shall be needfull, the helpful experiences of Hunters, fowlers, Fishermen, Shepherds, Gardeners, *Apothecaries*; and in the other sciences, *Architects*, Engineers, Mariners, *Anatomists*," which is to say to listen to and value practitioners with limited formal education (*CPW* 2.393–94). My mother, who had a formal Mexican education through the third grade, provided me with insights into her purchase of that Sagrada Biblia from among the variety available to her in the mid-twentieth-century U.S. and with a purchasing freedom to which she was unaccustomed. Her consumer decision was predominantly based on its authorization and illustrations: recognizing that her education left her an insufficient judge of textual reliability, she sought the authority of what she interpreted not as the Roman Catholic Church but rather the U.S. Catholic Church, given the press location of Chicago; trusting in youthful iconophilia, she hoped the illustrations would attract rather than compel her children to religion and reading. I strive to imitate such methodological awareness, if not aims.

My perplexity about the 1883 Escóiquiz *El Paraíso perdido* turned to fascination when I started reading it. This was a recognizable *Paradise Lost* but not the one I had come to know in my decades-long U.S., Anglophone education and research. I quickly detected Escóiquiz's obvious variances from Milton's original, then in subsequent readings the subtle ones, and I let myself be captivated by the poetic force of the Escóiquiz translation, by its own integrity as a Spanish work and as its own poetic work. Further, the copy evidences that it has been well used: it does not have uncut pages or the smell of unused paper that some of us have encountered in our archival search and recovery work. Indeed the copy has a few erasure marks, and all the pages are soft from being turned—softer now from my use.

No doubt my reading of Spanish philosopher Miguel persuaded me to attend as bravely as possible to the individual and the personal affective responses that translations trigger, even my own.[21] As I regularly mention in the classroom, Milton models the bravery of affective responses by having his Miguel, the archangel Michael, be "also moved" (*PL* 11.453) when he conveys his story to fallen Adam on his last day in Eden. My commitment to such bravery was bolstered by the multiauthor volume *Milton in Translation* (2017). That volume showed me over and over that, in country after country, the translators of Milton's works have been motivated to undertake their translational task for exceedingly affective causes, be it to share a beloved text with others, to move a whole country to political action, or to secure payment to eke out a living, and that readers have responded in like manner. And not just to *Ztracený ráj* (*Paradise Lost*, Czech), *Paradiso riconquistato* (*Paradise Regained*, Italian), and *Tōshi Samuson* (*Samson Agonistes*, Japanese) writ large as artistic commodities that enable readers to enter into world conversations, but also to specific copies that accrue meaning. Milton's definition of books as "not absolutely dead things" is for many not fanciful but rather accurate (*CPW* 2.492). This definition need not lead to mystical fetishizing but is founded and reflects on practicalities, with specific copies sometimes being the only ones available to specific readers and communities of readers, storehouses for notes, heirlooms, and in my case the impetus and storehouse for key research questions and interpretive elements.

My home campus library's copy of the Escóiquiz 1883 illustrated *El Paraíso perdido*, call number 821 M64pS 1883, situated me in my geographical place and historical space at the same time that it enabled me to enter into transhistoric, world conversations. While others might find it hard to understand why a volume well over a century old would be in a U.S. public university's circulating library and unceremoniously sent in a manila envelope through intercampus mail, I hypothesized that my home university of Purdue, founded in 1869, and its main library, established in 1874, acquired this 1883 edition for the circulating collections because it was the most recent and most readily available, and that the book had simply remained on the shelves. (Also in the circulating library is the 1861 *Le Paradis perdu* by François-René, Vicomte de Chateaubriand.) I was right to hypothesize rather than assume.[22] The records regarding the acquisition of the Purdue copy are extinct, again as to be expected from a U.S. public institution, careful with limited funds. But the book carries its own clue: the gift plate with the typewritten name of the donor, Enrique Caracciolo-Trejo. Born in Argentina, Caracciolo-Trejo was a member of the Purdue Spanish faculty from at least the 1980s through 1997 and is now retired in Spain. While I was unsuccessful in tracking him down to ask him my many questions about why he donated this book, he managed to introduce me to a particular network of readers in the 2000s and 2010s.

À la Unamuno *con* the Milton of *Areopagitica*, I have found all library books contain both the potential and the "potency of life in them" (*CPW* 2.492). The potential for potency has been fulfilled not just by my campus colleague of yore but also by my contemporary collaborators, the librarians of the Purdue Archives and Special Collections who have allowed me ready and continued access to my/their/our beloved *El Paraíso perdido* by not recategorizing the book and moving it from the circulating to the noncirculating collection. They learned about this copy's free circulation from my discussions and use of it during my many research visits and teaching workshops there. In contrast, they kindly recategorized a once-circulating Blake-illustrated *Paradise Lost* that I alerted them to, so that it could be saved from further page rips and pen and pencil marginalia. Both of these anecdotes are germane to *Milton among Spaniards*. My experience of the uneven distribution and sharing of power with material books and within institutional and national domains spurred me to ponder the nuanced processes and collaborative nature of power in *inquisitions*, the express topic of chapter 1, and in literary and cultural development, as covered in all chapters.

This is to say that librarians of the past and present worked with scholars, teachers, and many types of readers to make available the Escóiquiz *Paraíso perdido*, the illustrated one, the one that other Hispanophones knew, and, as it happens, an importantly transnational one. One of its transnational features moored me as much as it untethered me: its frontispiece (that word and concept with which I begin chapter 4), "The Blind Milton Dictating Paradise Lost to His Daughters" by the Hungarian Miguel/Michael/Mihály Munkácsy. Even though I had seen this illustration before, *this* illustration in *this* volume combined with a faded color version that one of my doctoral committee members gave me as a graduation gift. That gift is from the U.S., a *Baltimore Sun* newspaper supplement with a 1904 copyright date that hangs, now framed, in my campus office. It is not an exaggeration to say that these two copies were key motivating factors for me to accept an invitation to Hungary for a Milton conference in 2008. I am not by nature a traveler but have become one because of—if I may hide behind a quotation and thus imitate Unamuno (as he quotes, hides behind, yet renders emphatically through his use of the exclamation point in Galileo's famous phrase "Eppur si muove!" [Yet, it moves!])—the power that "moves" as strongly as the Earth whose movement Galileo could not deny, a power that Unamuno finds expressed in the "weapon of patience and of resignation" and, more broadly in *The Tragic Sense of Life*, philology (the love of learning and literature), both subcategories of "the Love that moves the stars."[23] During my trip to Hungary, I stood astonished, silent, when I saw the smaller original painting of "The Blind Milton Dictating" at the Hungarian National Gallery.[24] I returned from that trip with a stronger command of facts about Eastern European and international visual art and with the passion needed to become a book-art critic, and with the at once personal and professional contacts needed for confirmation of facts about it and related matters.

This is to say that, for over two hundred years the Escóiquiz translation writ large has made decided, albeit limited, ambivalent contributions to Milton's reception among Spaniards and Hispanophones worldwide. Those ambivalences are mirrored in my own intimate engagements with it. On the one hand, as I imply in chapter 2 and argue elsewhere, Escóiquiz's *El Paraíso perdido* deserves to be displaced by a still awaited, great Spanish translation of *Paradise Lost*.[25] On the other, the singular Purdue copy of it piqued my great interest in Milton among Spaniards and has served me over and over again for every chapter in this study, whether highlighted, noted in passing, or unstated but contributory to important elements in the chapter's story: its notable absence on the Spanish Catholic Inquisition's list of 1844, as discussed in chapter 1; its engagements with Milton's original and with its at least eighteen successors, per chapter 2; its use by Giner de los Ríos and other Spanish playwrights in the late nineteenth century, featured in chapter 3; and its appearance with the piecemeal versions of Doré's illustrations and later its piecemeal use with Prieto's visual art, as shown and told in chapter 4.

One last thread that merits brief mention is the role of oral Spanish in both interpersonal and staged arenas. I felt deep comfort when I learned about James Russell Lowell's difficulties with his spoken Spanish even though he possessed such considerable knowledge of Spanish language, literature, and culture. As recorded in chapter 3, his relationship with Giner de los Ríos began when the young Spaniard was recruited as his tutor in oral Spanish shortly after he arrived in Madrid to assume his role as U.S. ambassador to Spain. I have regularly struggled in my adulthood with spoken Spanish, as much as I did in my childhood with my other heritage language of English. My *simpatico* with Lowell accounts for my forays into his works and biographies, much more than demanded by this study but resulting unexpectedly in, for example, my knowledge of his birthday and thus my hypothesis about the occasion for the staging of the play *Milton: A Dramatic Scene* on February 19, 1879, only three days before Lowell's sixtieth birthday. It also accounts for my joy in visiting Lowell's institutional home of Harvard to view its copy of Prieto's *Milton | El Paraíso perdido*, since WorldCat indicated that locale as the only site in the U.S. for me to revisit the work, which I had seen for the first time at the National Library of Spain in Madrid, a building that Lowell would have witnessed under construction (1866–92). These pertinent facts are the results not of a primarily utilitarian methodology but of a passion mobilized and well spent.

There is a brilliance to each text and topic of this study that I try to convey throughout. Most stunning to me in my encounters with them all is how they have revised and reinvigorated *my* Milton. Looking from various perspectives at Milton among Spaniards can create something different from what we have had heretofore—not a *Juan Milton* (so rare even among Spaniards) but, I hope, a more capacious *our* Mr. John Milton.[26]

APPENDIX A

Class I and II Entries of English Authors in Volume I of the Spanish Catholic Inquisition's 1707 Marín Index

	Inclusive page numbers for the letter	Total adjusted entries	Total adjusted entries of Anglus and Inglés (as nationality), with names and page numbers
A	All Class I (1–26) Class II (27–66)	389 261 128	7: ALEXANDER FABRICVS (12), ANDR. SADELERVS, ANDR. VVILLETVS, ANTONIVS ANGLVS (18), ANTONIVS GHELVIVS (19), ANTONIVS KOOCHE (20), ANTONIVS SCHORVS (21)
B	All Class I (79–88) Class II (89–114)	309 121 188	7: *1BALDVINVS VVALÆVS (79), *BARTOLDVS SVPERINTENDENS LINCOLNIESNSIS (80), BARTHOLOMÆVS TRAHERON (81), BENTANVS ANGLVS (85), *BRIANVS VVALTONVS, BVLLINGAMVS ANGLVS (87), BENEDICTVS ANGLVS DE CONFELD (93; ALSO BENEDICTO ANGLO DE CANFELD [113])
C	All Class I (153–226) Class II (227–65)	286 232 54	1: CHRISTOPHORVS GODMANNVS (188)
D	All Class I (266–333) Class II (334–41)	125 81 44	0
E	All Class I (372–85) Class II (386–87)	89 84 5	5: EADMVNDVS HALEN (ALEN), EDMVNDVS, EDMVNDVS GRIDALLVS, EDVVARDVS SIEMOVR (372), *ENOC CLAPHAMVS (378)

163

APPENDIX A

	Inclusive page numbers for the letter	Total adjusted entries	Total adjusted entries of Anglus and Inglés (as nationality), with names and page numbers
F	All Class I (394–408) Class II (409–43)	176 91 85	6: *FRANCISCVS BACONVS BARDO DE VERVLAMIO (396, 403), FRANCISCVS BIGOT (396), *FRANCISCVS MAZONIVS (404), FRIGEVILLÆVS GAVTIVS, *FRANCISCO QVARLES, *FVLKO GREVIL (408)
G	All Class I (446–67) Class II (468–80)	334 266 68	15: GEORGIVS BLACVELLVS (449), GEORGIVS CONSTANTINVS (450), GEORGIVS THOMSONVS (456), GVALTERVS MAPVS, *GVILIELMVS AMETIVS, GVILIELMVS ... BARLOVVE (458), GVILIELMVS CAMDENVS (459), GVILIELDVS GRAYE, GVILIELMVS KETHVS, GVILIELMVS TAYLOVS, GVILIELMVS TINDALVS, GVILIELMVS TVRNERVS, *GVILIELMVS VVITAKERVS, GVILIELMVS WVITE, GVILIELMVS VVITINGAMVS (464)
H	All Class I (490–526) Class II (527–42)	278 230 48	4: HENRICVS VIII (494), HENRICVUS SAVILIS (501), HVGO Brougthonus. Seu Brugthonus (521), HVGO Latimerus (526)
I (and J)	All Class I (548–96) Class II (697–762)	1092 890 202	38: IACOBUS IAMES (551), IOACHIMVS FRIZIVS (565), IOANNES ARATRON, IOANNES ASTOC, IOANNES ASSVBARBII (574), IOANNES BOND, IOANNES BRADFORVS (580), *IOANNES BRIDEAVX (581), IOANNES CHECVS (598), IOANNES DIBBEZIVS (602), IOANNES FELDE (614), IOANNES FOXVS (617), IOANNES FRITH (618), IOANNES HOPERVS (641),

	Inclusive page numbers for the letter	Total adjusted entries	Total adjusted entries of Anglus and Inglés (as nationality), with names and page numbers
I (and J) (*cont.*)			IOANNES IOGE (646), IOANNES IVELLVS (647), IOANNES LAMBERT (649), IOANNES MARBEK (653), IOANNES MARDELEY (654), *IOANNES MILTHONIVS, IOANNES NORTON (660), IOANNES OLDVS, IOANNES ONDENCASTEL (662), IOANNES PALMERIVS, IOANNES PARCK HVRSTVS (663), IOANNES PLOVGH, IOANNES POINETTVS (664), IOANNES PVLLANVS, IOANNES PVRVEY, IOANNES RAINALDVS, IOANNES RASTEL (665), IOANNES RICKES, IOANNES ROCHVS (666), *IOANNES SELDENVS (668), IOANNES SKELTONVS (670), IOANNES WICLEPHVS (677), ISAACVS WAACKE (695), IOHAN HOOKER (696)
		3,078	83

APPENDIX B

First Editions of Full Spanish Translations of *Paradise Lost*, Listed Chronologically

Milton, John. *El Paraíso perdido*. Translated by Juan de Escoiquiz. 3 vols. Bourges: Gilles, 1812.
Milton, John. *El Paraíso perdido*. Translated by Benito Ramón de Hermida Maldonado. 2 vols. Madrid: Ibarra, 1814.
Milton, John. *El Paraíso perdido*. Translated by D. Santiago Ángel Saura Mascaró. Barcelona: Libreria de E. Pujal, 1849.
Milton, John. *El Paraíso perdido*. Translated by Dionisio Sanjuán. Barcelona: Casa Editorial la Ilustración, 1868.
Milton, John. *El Paraíso perdido*. Translated by Demetrio San Martín. Barcelona: Jané Hermanos, 1873.
Milton, John. *El Paraíso perdido*. Translated by Cayetano Rosell. Barcelona: Montaner y Simón, 1873–74.[1]
Milton, John. *El Paraíso perdido*. Translated by Enrique Leopoldo de Verneuill. Barcelona: Montaner y Simón, 1873–74.
Milton, John. *El Paraíso perdido*. Translated by M. J. Barroso-Bonzón. Barcelona: Ediciones Ibérica, 1910.
Milton, John. *El Paraíso perdido*. Translated by Juan Matéos. Barcelona: Ibérica, 1914.
Milton, John. *El Paraíso perdido*. Translated by Dionisio Sampión. Madrid: M. Aguilar-Rollán, 1946.
Milton, John. *El Paraíso perdido*. Translated by Antonio Fuster. Barcelona: Editorial Iberia, 1953.
Milton, John. *El Paraíso perdido*. Translated by Pilar Vera. Barcelona: Mateu, 1961.
Milton, John. *El Paraíso perdido*. Translated by Antonio Espina. Madrid: E.M., 1965.
Milton, John. *El Paraíso perdido*. Translated by J. Ribera. Barcelona: Petronio, 1973.
Milton, John. *El Paraíso perdido*. Translated by Esteban Pujals. Madrid: Cátedra, 1986.
Milton, John F. [sic]. *El Paraíso perdido*. Translated by Manuel Álvarez de Toledo. Cádiz: Universidad de Cádiz, 1988.
Milton, John. *El Paraíso perdido*. Translated by Francisco Caudet Yarza. Madrid: A. L. Mateos, 1992.

Milton, John. *El Paraíso perdido*. Translated by Abilio Echeverría Pagola. Barcelona: Planeta, 1993.

Milton, John. *Paraíso perdido*. Translated by Bel Atreides. Barcelona: Galaxia Gutenberg, 2005.

Milton, John. *El Paraíso perdido*. Translated by Enrique López Castellón. Madrid: Abada Editores, 2005.

APPENDIX C

The Doré Illustrations in *Paradise Lost* (1866 and c. 1880–1885) and in *El Paraíso perdido* (1873 Rosell and 1883 Escóiquiz)

	Page number before illustration				
Standard list of illustrations[1]	1866 *Paradise Lost* (Cassell, Petter, Galpin & Co.)[2]	c. 1880–85 *Paradise Lost* (Cassell & Co.)[3]	c. 1880–85 *Paradise Lost* (Heritage)[4]	1873 Rosell *El Paraíso perdido*[5]	1883 Escóiquiz *El Paraíso perdido*[6]
Plate 1, I. 44, 45	2, verso	2, recto	4, recto		17
Plate 2, I. 221, 222	8, recto	8, recto	4, verso		24
Plate 3, I. 331	12, recto, labeled 4	12, recto	12, recto		29
Plate 4, I. 344, 345	12, recto, labeled 3	12, recto	12, verso		31
Plate 5, I. 757–759	24, verso	24, recto	16, recto		49
Plate 6, II. 1, 2	26, verso	26, recto	16, verso		54
Plate 7, II. 628	46, recto	46, recto	32, recto		
Plate 8, II. 648, 649	46, recto	46, recto	32, verso		83
Plate 9, II. 949, 950	56, recto	56, recto	56, recto	52, verso	97
Plate 10, III. 347–349	70, recto	70, recto	56, verso		120

APPENDIX C

Standard list of illustrations	Page number before illustration				
	1866 Paradise Lost (Cassell, Petter, Galpin & Co.)	c. 1880–85 Paradise Lost (Cassell & Co.)	c. 1880–85 Paradise Lost (Heritage)	1873 Rosell El Paraíso perdido	1883 Escoíquiz El Paraíso perdido
Plate 12, III. 739–741	82, recto	82, recto	56, verso	76, recto	137
Plate 13, IV. 73, 74	84, verso, labeled 17	84, recto	88, recto	78, verso	143
Plate 14, IV. 172, 173	88, recto	88, recto	88, verso	82, recto	152
Plate 15, IV. 247	90, recto	90, recto	88, recto	84, recto	
Plate 16, IV. 335, 336	92, verso, labeled 13	92, recto	88, verso		158
Plate 17, IV. 589, 590	100, verso, labeled 16	100, recto	96, recto		169
Plate 18, IV. 798, 799	106, recto, labeled 23	106, recto	96, verso		178
Plate 19, IV. 1014, 1015	114, recto, labeled 22	114, recto	112, recto		186
Plate 20, V. 12, 13	114, recto, labeled 21	114, recto	112, verso	104, verso	190
Plate 21, V. 309, 310	124, recto, labeled 20	124, recto	132, recto		203
Plate 22, V. 468–470	128, recto, labeled 24	128, recto	132, verso		208
Plate 23, VI. 188	148, recto, labeled 30	148, recto	140, recto		235
Plate 24, VI. 207–209	148, recto, labeled 35	opening paratext	opening paratext		238
Plate 25, VI. 327, 328	152, recto, labeled 43	152, recto	140, verso		242
Plate 26, VI. 406	154, recto, labeled 41	154, recto	144, recto		245

APPENDIX C

Standard list of illustrations	Page number before illustration				
	1866 *Paradise Lost* (Cassell, Petter, Galpin & Co.)	c. 1880–85 *Paradise Lost* (Cassell & Co.)	c. 1880–85 *Paradise Lost* (Heritage)	1873 Rosell *El Paraíso perdido*	1883 Escoíquiz *El Paraíso perdido*
Plate 27, VI. 410–412	154, recto, labeled 42	154, recto	144, verso		246
Plate 28, VI. 871	168, recto, labeled 19	168, recto	160, recto		256
Plate 29, VI. 874, 875	168, verso, labeled 18	168, recto	160, verso		257
Plate 30, VII. 298, 299	180, recto, labeled 29	180, recto	168, recto		278
Plate 31, VII. 387–389	182, recto, labeled 26	182, recto	168, verso		286
Plate 32, VII. 415, 416	184, recto, labeled 27	184, recto	168, recto		
Plate 33, VII. 417, 418	184, recto, labeled 28	184, recto	168, verso	162, verso	287
Plate 34, VII. 581, 582	188, recto, labeled 31	188, recto	176, recto	164, recto	
Plate 35, VIII. 652, 653	210, recto, labeled 38	210, recto	176, verso	186, recto	325
Plate 36, IX. 74, 75	212, recto, labeled 25	212, recto	192, recto	188, verso	330
Plate 37, IX. 99, 100	214, recto, labeled 39	214, recto	193, verso		332
Plate 38, IX. 182, 183	216, recto, labeled 45	216, recto	208, recto		336
Plate 39, IX. 434, 435	224, recto, labeled 33	224, recto	208, verso		346
Plate 40, IX. 784, 785	234, recto, labeled 49	234, recto	224, recto		361
Plate 41, IX. 1121–1123	244, recto, labeled 47	244, recto	224, verso		377

APPENDIX C

Standard list of illustrations	Page number before illustration				
	1866 *Paradise Lost* (Cassell, Petter, Galpin & Co.)	c. 1880–85 *Paradise Lost* (Cassell & Co.)	c. 1880–85 *Paradise Lost* (Heritage)	1873 Rosell *El Paraíso perdido*	1883 Escoíquiz *El Paraíso perdido*
Plate 42, X. 99–101	250, recto, labeled 40	250, recto	240, recto		383
Plate 43, X. 439–441	260, recto, labeled 48	260, recto	240, verso		
Plate 44, X. 521–523	opening paratext	262, recto	256, recto		398
Plate 45, X. 610	266, recto, labeled 32	266, recto	256, verso		
Plate 46, XI. 208–210	286, recto	286, recto	292, recto		426
Plate 47, XI. 729	302, recto, labeled 37	302, recto	292, verso		448
Plate 48, XI. 747–749	304, recto, labeled 34	304, recto	300, recto	272, verso	450
Plate 49, XII. 236–238	316, recto, labeled 36	316, recto	300, verso	284, verso	468
Plate 50, XII. 645	328, recto	328, recto	312, verso		482

Notes

Introduction

1. Making the anachronism potentially even greater, *Don Quixote* situates the events as taking place in the recent past. Special thanks to Howard Mancing for his insights on this and related topics.

2. Cervantes, *Don Quixote*, trans. Phillips, 361. For a more denotatively accurate English translation, see Cervantes, *Don Quixote*, trans. Raffel, 429. For discussion of Phillips's translation, see Godwin, *Lives of Edward and John Philips*, 240; Masson, *The Life of Milton*; Shawcross, *The Arms of the Family*; Nardo, "John Phillips's Translation."

3. All quotations from Milton's poetry are from Milton, *The Complete Poems*, ed. Leonard. *Paradise Lost* is cited as *PL*.

4. For a description of the multilingual curriculum, see Darbishire, *The Early Lives*, 60–61. For attitudes toward Romance language training in Milton's England, see Hale, *Milton as Multilingual*; Fletcher, *The Intellectual Development*. This study follows Raymond Williams, who finds an, "if not complete, at least reasonable" definition of culture as "the body of intellectual and imaginative work which has retained its major communicative power" ("The Analysis of Culture," 44).

5. Mancing, *Don Quixote*, 46.

6. For the development of anti-Hispanic representations in English literature, see Maltby, *The Black Legend*. For the development of national stereotyping in Renaissance English drama, see Hoenselaars, *Images of Englishmen*. For the twin sentiments of Hispanophilia and Hispanophobia in relation to intellectual and actual piracy, see Fuchs, *The Poetics of Piracy*.

7. For the threats and penalties of the Spanish Catholic Inquisition, see Kamen, *The Spanish Inquisition*.

8. For the forging of personal voice and national identity, see Colley, *Britons*; Kidd, *British Identities*.

9. An example of national attribution of Martial as a Spaniard is in Martínez Arancón, *Marcial—Quevedo*, in which Martial and Quevedo are referred to as "estos dos grandes poetas españoles" (these two great Spanish poets; back cover). Also representative of national-geographical affiliations is Miguel de Unamuno's descrip-

tion of a "Spanish philosophy" that he traces back to "Seneca, the pagan Stoic of Cordoba.... His accent was a Spanish, Latino-African accent, not Hellenic, and there are echoes of him in Tertullian—Spanish, too, at heart—who... was a kind of Don Quixote in the world of Christian thought in the second century" (*The Tragic Sense*, 313). All English translations of Spanish originals are mine unless otherwise noted. In my transcriptions, I maintain the orthography and punctuation of the Spanish originals.

10. John de Lancey Ferguson's characterization of the international Hispano-U.S. dialogue is true in many ways of the Anglo-Hispanic conversation: "The question as to the source whence the Spaniards gained their knowledge of American literature might be answered in one word—France." Similarly he states regarding Spanish engagements with Milton from the seventeenth to twentieth centuries, "Artistically and intellectually Spain has always been one of the most independent and self-sufficient nations of Europe, and when of recent centuries she has yielded to foreign influence at all, that influence has usually been French" (*American Literature*, 4, 2). Anfòs Par avers a similar trend with Shakespeare, that "todas las representaciones de este período [1772–1836] procedieron de los arreglos franceses de J. F. Ducis" (all the representations from this period [1772–1836] are derived from the French arrangements of J. F. Ducis; *Representaciones Shakespearianas*, 17).

11. Felperin, *Shakespearean Representation*, 6.

12. Paulson, *Don Quixote in England*, xi.

13. Griffin, *English Renaissance Drama*, 195n5.

14. Paulson, *Don Quixote in England*, xi. Paulson's focus is not Milton, yet he initiates a provocative pairing of Milton and Cervantes: "As Milton's *Paradise Lost* (1667) served as a model for the sublime, Cervantes' *Don Quixote* (1605, 1615) served for the comic, an area in which English writers showed much greater competence, occasionally equaling their model" (ix).

15. See Corns, "Milton."

16. Benítez, *Presencia de Milton*, 27, 15.

17. Robertson, *Milton's Fame*, 13.

18. Pegenaute, "La recepción de Milton," 321. See also Benítez, *Presencia de Milton*, 249; Parker, *Milton's Contemporary Reputation*; Thorpe, *Milton Criticism*; Robertson, *Milton's Fame*.

19. The title of this section is from [Milton], *A Manifesto*, 2.466. While the consensus is that the work is of undetermined authorship, it has been variably attributed to Milton and to "England and Wales. Lord Protector (1653–1658: O. Cromwell)" (Worldcat, accessed February 10, 2018).

20. Shawcross, "John Milton and His Spanish and Portuguese Presence," 41; David Gies, email to the author, August 27, 2007.

21. Benítez, *Presencia de Milton*,13. For a similarly cautious definition of Milton's presence versus influence during a historical period, see Gray, *Milton and the Victorians*, esp. 2, 3, 4.

22. Parkinson Zamora, "Eccentric Periodization," 695.

23. Cruz, *Material and Symbolic Circulation*, xviii; Griffin, *English Renaissance Drama*, 17.

24. For the related processes in the Anglo-Italian cultural conversation, see Norbrook, *Poetry and Politics*, esp. 38–39.

25. Griffin, *English Renaissance Drama*, 3. For the habit of constructing early modern Spanish and English cultures' divided heritage despite a shared European heritage, see Greer, "Thine and Mine."

26. All quotations from Milton's prose are from Milton, *The Complete Prose Works*, ed. Wolfe, 2.514 (hereafter *CPW*), unless otherwise noted.

27. Ferguson, *American Literature*, 1.

28. The number of Spanish translations rises by three if we count the Hispanophone translations of *Paradise Lost* that emerged from Latin America: from Mexico, Francisco Granados Maldonado's in 1858 and, from Colombia, Anibal Galindo's in 1868 and Enrique Álvarez Bonilla's in 1896. Global scholarly interest and communication networks in the twenty-first century have enabled us to add the following to the list of complete vernacular translations of *Paradise Lost* published by 1916, the year of Ferguson's study: into Dutch in 1728, Icelandic in 1828, five into Portuguese starting in 1789, Bulgarian in 1898, two into Czech in 1811, two into Hungarian starting in 1796, and Polish in 1791 (Duran, Issa, and Olson, *Milton in Translation*, 167, 215, 262, 298, 309, 330, 349).

29. Islam Issa calls for similar updating for assertions in 2009 and 2010 that only books 1 and 2 of *Paradise Lost* had been translated into Arabic: "By 2002, all twelve books of *Paradise Lost* had been published in Arabic, with Books 1–6 first appearing in 1985" ("Fragmentation," 219).

30. Braider, "Of Monuments and Documents," 160.

31. For language enrollment in U.S. institutions of higher education, see the Modern Language Association's "Language Enrollment Database, 1958–2009," www.mla.org/flsurvey_search, accessed April 10, 2012.

32. Sandra Bermann aptly defines comparative literature "as the transnational and interdisciplinary study of literature" that moves us to self-assess about the disciplines and particular aspects of translation we are integrating into our studies ("Teaching," 8).

33. For the "chameleon" nature of Shakespeare contrasting with Milton's more definable "spirit," see Wittreich, *The Romantics*, 13, 21.

34. Smith, *Is Milton Better*, xv.

35. For the alterity between Spanish and English literatures as well as a mid-twentieth-century intervention to claim their affiliations, see Russell, "English Seventeenth-Century Interpretations."

36. For the development of the concept of literary authorship in the early modern period and in relation to Milton, see Shawcross, *John Milton*. For the manner in which "los autores no escriben libros: escriben textos que luego se convierten en objetos impresos" (authors do not write books: they write texts that are then converted into printed objects), see Chartier, *El mundo*, 111.

37. Greene, *Unrequited Conquests*, 26.

38. Griffin, *English Renaissance Drama*, 21.

39. See Harris, *Globalization*.

40. Roy Flannagan, "'The World All before [Us]': More than Three Hundred Years of Criticism," in Duran, *A Concise Companion*, 48.

41. Cañizares-Esguerra, *Puritan Conquistadores*, 222.

42. Jastrow, "The Mind's Eye," 312.

43. For the parallel developments of technology and world literature, see Puchner, *The Written World*. For the early modern period as prehistory to globalization 1.0, 2.0, and 3.0, see the introductory chapter of Friedman, *The World Is Flat*.

44. Steiner, *After Babel*, 261.

45. An unintended absence in this study is the contributions of Spanish women, due to my minimal findings of such. I do refer to the essays by the Galician novelist, journalist, and critic Emilia Pardo Bazán; the marchioness of Saint Coloma, as editor of the Spanish translation of *Paradise Lost* by her father, Benito Ramón de Hermida, in chapter two; and the actress Antonia Contreras, who played the role of Débora in the play featured in chapter 3. I here note some of the few women members of the Generación del 1927, of which the artist featured in chapter 4, Gregorio Prieto, was a member: Rosa Chacel, Ernestina de Champourcín, Josefina de la Torre, María Teresa León, and Concha Méndez-Cuesta.

46. For other non-Hispanophone Iberian studies related to Milton, see Sims, "Christened Classicism"; Flotats, "Translating Milton"; Hélio J. S. Alves, "Milton in Portuguese," in Duran, Issa, and Olson, *Milton in Translation*, 249–64. I include Portugal in this list because it was a part of Spain during part of Milton's lifetime (1580–1640).

47. For the uses and arguments of *Areopagitica*, see the chapter "*Areopagitica*, Toleration and Free Speech" in Leonard, *The Value of Milton*, 1–21.

1. Heretic Milton, "Of the Devil's Party" per the Spanish Catholic Inquisition

1. Lewalski, *The Life*, 107. See also Campbell and Corns, *John Milton*, 103–27; Forsyth, *John Milton*, 61–64.

2. Milton's name would not have appeared in the earlier "Indices of the seventeenth century," the "1612 [Sandoval y Rojas index] (with an appendix in 1614), 1632 [Zapata Index] and 1640 [Sotomayor Index]" (Kamen, *The Spanish Inquisition*, 116). See also Vílchez Díaz, *Autores*, 6. The 1667 *Index librorum prohibitorum et expurgandorum novissimus* is a reprint of the 1640 index. After the 1707 Marín Index is the 1747 Prado y Cuesta Index, revised in 1782, but not discussed in this study due to its lesser prominence. See Lea, *A History*, 3.495.

3. The indexes are commonly referred to by their year of publication and the name of the main Spanish inquisitor at that time; I use this terminology. The first example is from Diego Sarmiento y Valladeres and Vidal Marín's *Novissimus librorum prohibitorum et expurgandorum*, 1.660 (hereafter 1707 Marín Index). While the paratexts of the Spanish Catholic indexes are primarily in Spanish, the entries are primarily in Latin. The "th" in this entry is not unusual in Spanish Latin and is likely indicative of Span-

ish pronunciation of the "t" preceding "o" sounds. The second example is from Agustín Rubín de Cevallos's *Indice ultimo de los libros prohibidos y mandados expurgar*, 182 (hereafter 1790 Rubín Index). The third example is from Consuelo de Inquisición (Spain), *Indice general de los libros prohibidos y mandados expurgar*, 230 (hereafter 1844 Palacios Index). The "tt" in the entry is not unusual in Spanish Latin and is likely indicative of Spanish pronunciation of the hard "t" sound.

4. As noted in the introduction, I limit this study to Continental Spain, thus ignoring the American branch of the Spanish Catholic Inquisition. For a discussion of the circulation of both the Spanish Catholic Inquisition's and the Roman Catholic Inquisition's indexes in Spanish American and, later, Latin American reader reception, see Duran, "Mexican Miltons."

5. For the interaction of Paolo Sarpi's *History of the Council of Trent* and *Areopagitica*, see Sirluck, "Milton's Critical Use."

6. Stella Revard accurately represents the two Inquisitions rather than eliding them, if only in passing (*Milton*, 83). Paul M. Dowling in "Milton's Use" cites the Roman Catholic Church as the primary example of despicable censorial institutions in *Areopagitica*.

7. Italians composed nearly two-thirds of that Council, with Spaniards a far second. Of course, the Holy Roman Emperor Charles V (r. 1519–1558), also known as King Charles I of Spain (r. 1516–1556), was a strong advocate of the assembly to counter the Protestant Reformation. For the diminution of tolerationist and antischismatic discourses and activities in seventeenth-century Spain and England, see Smith, "Milton and the European Contexts." Milton also partners the two elsewhere in his prose: in *The Reason of Church Government* (1642), when he argues that a prelaty in the fashion of "*Italy* and *Spaine*" promotes "a num and chil stupidity of soul, an unactive blindnesse of minde," and in *The Ready and Easy Way* (1660), when he asks, "What liberty of conscience can we then expect from others far worse principl'd from the cradle, traind up and governd by *Popish* and *Spanish* counsels"? (*CPW* 1.785; *The Complete Works*, ed. Keeble and McDowell, 515).

8. Kamen, *The Spanish Inquisition*, 119.

9. Peréz, *The Spanish Inquisition*, 181. For the slow formation of official forms of censorship, see Lea, *A History*, 3.485; Kamen, *The Spanish Inquisition*, 108; Norbrook, *Poetry and Politics*.

10. For Milton's travels to Florence, see Campbell and Corns, *John Milton*, 109–15, 124.

11. Miller, "The Italian Imprimaturs," 355.

12. For Milton's visit to Galileo, see Forsyth, *John Milton*, 60–61.

13. Seventeenth-century popes include Clement VIII (r. 1592–1605) of Fano, Leo XI (r. 1605) of Florence, Paul V (r. 1605–1621) of Rome, Gregory XV (r. 1621–1623) of Bologna, Urban VIII (r. 1623–1644) of Florence, Innocent X (r. 1644–1655) of Rome, Alexander VII (r. 1655–1667) of Siena, Clement IX (r. 1667–1669) of Tuscany, and Clement X (r. 1670–1676) of Rome.

14. Pope Adrian IV (r. 1154–1159) was the only English pope. The importance and practical consequences of popes' homelands cannot be overstated. See, for example, McDermott, *England*, xi.

15. Milton laments the attraction that France held for English youth in *Of Education*, published the same year as *Areopagitica* (*CPW* 2.414).

16. Miller, "The Italian Imprimaturs," 347, 349.

17. Robertson, *Censorship and Conflict*, 23.

18. For Milton's terminology in *Areopagitica* and his other works, see Loewenstein and Stevens, *Early Modern Nationalism*. Andrew Hadfield avers that "for Milton Catholicism was a variety of customs and conventions rather than simply an institution" and "was also a series of practices that had crept into every aspect of church government under Charles [I], leaving England governed by a very un-English church, which practiced a series of false rituals, promoted superstition instead of reason, and sought to transform an active and engaged congregation into a passive and pliant flock" ("Milton and Catholicism," 191).

19. Leonard, *The Value of Milton*, 5.

20. Milton would have had many ready examples had he chosen to include them: "When Milton was a boy of four, two men were executed for [Arianism] (the last known heretics to be burned in England)" (Hobson, *Milton's Vision*, 106). See also Robertson, *Censorship and Conflict*, 10, 11; Sharpe, *The Personal Rule*, 863.

21. Carr, *Spain*, 77.

22. "Heresy" n. 1.a and "treason" n. 2.a (Oxford University Press, *Oxford English Dictionary Online*, hereafter *OED*).

23. Benítez, *Presencia de Milton*, 32.

24. Redman, *Major French Milton Critics*, 1.

25. French, *Life Records*, 4.329.

26. For Samuel Butler's authorship of this tract, see von Maltzahn, "Samuel Butler's Milton."

27. Parker, *Milton's Contemporary Reputation*, 98; *The Character of the Rump*, 2–3. For heresy charges against Milton in popular discussions in England of the period, see Stoll, *Milton and Monotheism*, 160. Stephen B. Dobranski provides important insights into Milton having been "fined and briefly imprisoned for two of his treasonable books, *Eikonoklastes* (1649) and *Pro Populo Anglicano Defensio* (1651)" in 1660 (*Milton*, 25).

28. Forsyth, *John Milton*, 112. See also Campbell and Corns, *John Milton*, 402n43.

29. Christopher Marlowe's name does not appear where it would have been alphabetically in the 1707 Marín Index in the Class I (1.189, 226) or Class II (1.228, 234) sections; in the 1790 Rubín Index (54); or in the 1844 Palacios Index (216).

30. Kamen, *The Spanish Inquisition*, 108.

31. Vílchez Díaz, *Autores*, 3.

32. Lea, *A History*, 3.536.

33. *Index librorum prohibitorum Innoc XI.P.M.* Milton would have been listed on 207.

34. 1707 Marín Index, 1. For help with this and the next translations from the Latin, I thank John Hale.

35. 1707 Marín Index, 27.

36. *Index Librorum prohibitorum, ac expurgandorum novissimus*, 2.857.

37. 1707 Marín Index, 2.80. The text also appears in the 1844 Palacios Index (213).

For the difficulty of definitively ascribing the Latin *Scriptum Dom. Protectoris reipublicæ Angliæ, Scotiæ, Hiberniæ &c., ex consensu atque sententia concilii sui editum in quo hujus reipublicæ causa contra Hispanos justa esse demonstratur* (London: Henry Hill and John Field, 1655) to Milton, see Fallon, *Milton in Government*, 99. For the process by which the Cromwellian Declaration came to be attributed to Milton in a later season of anti-Spanish agitation, see von Maltzahn, "Acts of Kind Service," 249. For its multilingual dimensions, see Duran, "Not *Either/Or*."

38. Lea suggests human caprice as another reason for the seeming haphazard nature of the lists (*A History*, 3.498). See also Mathews, *A Survey*; Mugglestone, *Lost for Words*.

39. Appendix A includes only authors the Spanish Catholic Inquisition labels as "Anglus" and "Inglés" as nationality, rather than only in the "En Inglés" language section of volume 1 of the 1707 Marín Index. Thus not included are, for example, "*Midletoni Papistomastix, impressus ann.1606. | Militantis &c. Liber ita inscriptus*" (2.78), which appears in the Class III M section, even though it is clearly the *Papisto-Mastix, or The Protestants Religion Defended* by William Middleton (d. 1613) (London: T[homas] P[urfoot] for Arthur Iohnson, 1606); and "Gvilielmvs Tempellvs, Seu, Vvilielmus Cantabriensis, Calvin" (1.464) and "Ioannes Davenantivs, Cantabrigiensis" (1.600), since they are identified as Cantuarians rather than Englishmen. National identifiers are absent from the entries of two of the translators of the King James Version of the Bible, "Franciscvs Dillinghamvs" (1.396), a member of the First Cambridge Company, and "Hadrianvs Saravia" (1.492), a member of the First Westminster Company. For these and other translators of the King James Version of the Bible who appear in the Spanish Catholic indexes, see Duran, "English Bible Translators."

40. Corns, "Milton," 213.

41. 1707 Marín Index, 1.408.

42. 1707 Marín Index, [ii].

43. 1707 Marín Index, [xxii].

44. 1707 Marín Index, [xxii].

45. For Milton's rhetorical strategies in terms of textual corruption, see Hartwell, *Lactantius and Milton*, 7; Lieb, *Theological Milton*, 45.

46. Conklin, *Biblical Criticism*, 35.

47. 1707 Marín Index, [iv]. For a fictional representation-in-small of this process, see Cervantes, *Don Quixote*, trans. Raffel, 29–34.

48. 1707 Marín Index, [vii].

49. 2 Corinthians 3:6.

50. Forsyth, "Sublime Conversations."

51. Blake, *The Marriage of Heaven and Hell*, 65.

52. 1790 Rubín Index, xxxviii. The 1790 Rubín Index contains the same prefatory materials as the 1707 Marín Index as it notifies clearly with its statement, "Asta aquí Advertencias del Expurgatorio antiguo: las que se siguen, se han han [sic] añadido para la inteligencia y uso de este novismimo" (Up to here the Warnings of the old Expurga-

tory Index: the ones that follow have been added for the intelligibility and use of this new one; xxxv).

53. 1790 Rubín Index, xxxviii.

54. For a correlative instance of the cultural importance of name order, we do well to recall the importance of Far Eastern name order of surname followed by first (or given) name and the enduring priority of first names in Icelandic, especially because of the use of patronyms, as evidenced, for example by the use of first names in published lists and in references to native figures in critical works in Icelandic through today. See Crowe, "Cataloging Icelandic Materials." Special thanks to Ástráður Eysteinsson and T. Ross Leasure for advice on this matter.

55. McDowell, *The English Radical Imagination*, 28.

56. 1844 Palacios Index, 6.

57. Purdue University Libraries, www.lib.purdue.edu, accessed June 15, 2008.

58. Harkness, "The Precedence"; Kelley, "First Editions." It was also published in English in 1682 and retitled to call approving attention to Milton: *Miltons Republican Letters*.

59. I use the translation from Campbell and Corns, *John Milton*, 382.

60. For the testimony of Milton's bookseller that Milton had meant to print the work, see von Maltzahn, "Milton and the Restoration *Literae*."

61. Purdue University Libraries, www.lib.purdue.edu, accessed June 15, 2008.

62. Correspondence and subsequent histories indicate the Spanish ambassador to London Alonso de Cárdenas (1640–1655), whom Milton would have known, had a good amount of political sway.

63. For the publication of this Italian translation, see Daniele Borgogni, "'Censur'd to Be Much Inferiour': *Paradise Lost* and *Regained* in Italian," in Duran, Issa, and Olson, *Milton in Translation*, 233n10.

64. Vílchez Díaz, *Autores*, 15.

65. Also extant were Ernst Gottlieb von Berge's German *Das Verlustigte paradeis* of 1682 and Johann Jacob Bodmer's of 1732, William Hogg's Latin *Paraphrasis . . . Paradisum amissum* of 1690, and Nicolas Dupré de Saint-Maur's French *Paradis perdu* of 1727 and Louis Racine's of 1754–55.

66. Milton, *El Paraíso perdido*, trans. Escóiquiz, xiii.

67. For the importance of the word "scandal" in the social contexts of religious censorship, see Keitt, *Inventing the Sacred*, 1–12.

68. Rolli's Italian translation is "Regnar qui è meglio che servir nel Cielo" (Milton, *Del Paradiso perduto*, 11).

69. Milton, *Il Paradiso perduto*, 46; Milton, *El Paraíso perdido*, trans. Escóiquiz, 176.

70. For similar delays in the same period on the Madrid and Barcelona dramatic stages, see Par, *Representaciones Shakespearianas*. Another example of a time lag between decree dates and appearance on the Roman Catholic and Spanish Catholic indexes relates to Andrew Marvell. His name appears on neither the Spanish Catholic Inquisition's 1707 Marín Index (absent on 1.19 and 1.46) nor the 1844 Palacios Index (absent on 218) or on the Roman Catholic Inquisition's index of 1878 (*Index librorum*

prohibitorum justa exemplar romanum; absent on 218), but it appears on the Roman Catholic Index of 1904 with a decree date of 1730: "Marvell, Andrew. An account of | the growth of popery and arbitrary | government in England. *Decr. 28* | *nov. 1730*" (*Index librorum prohibitorum Leonis*, 206).

71. See *CPW* 2.494n26. For particularly accessible accounts of the Spanish Catholic Inquisition, see Rawlings, *The Spanish Inquisition*; Defourneaux, *Inquisición*.

72. Kamen, *The Spanish Inquisition* 96, 104. See also Lea, *A History* 3.480, 504, 548–49. Vílchez Díaz accords with Kamen and characterizes the start of the Spanish Catholic Inquisition as 1502 and the end "ya iniciado en el siglo XIX" (already initiated in the nineteenth century; *Autores*, 3). See also "Capítulo XXIX: Los últimos años de la Inquisición" (The last years of the [Spanish] Inquisition) in Walker, *Historia*, 363–85.

73. Cadalso y Vázquez, *Los eruditos*, 16, 20. See also Benítez, *Presencia de Milton*, 37–38.

74. Benítez, *Presencia de Milton*, 55.

75. Christophe Tournu, "'The French Connection' among Translations of Milton and within Du Bocage's *Paradis terrestre*," in Duran, Issa, and Olson, *Milton in Translation*, 158.

76. Cadalso y Vázquez, *Suplemento*, 52–53.

77. Cervantes, *El ingenioso hidalgo Don Quixote*, n.p.

78. Cervantes, *El ingenioso hidalgo Don Quixote*, 1.i, xliii.

79. Cervantes, *El ingenioso hidalgo Don Quixote*, 1.lxv–lxvi.

80. Cervantes, *El ingenioso hidalgo Don Quixote*, 1.lxxxiv.

81. Martínez y Güertero, "Querellas," 291–310; Pardo Bazán, "Milton," 271.

82. In his widely circulated life of Milton, France's Alphonse de Lamartine represents an elder Milton tormented by the regicide (Redman, *Major French Milton Critics*, 165–68).

83. Martínez y Güertero, "Querellas," 298, 299.

84. Castillo y Soriana, *Núñez de Arce*, 46.

85. Pardo Bazán, "Milton," 5. The work is interspersed with the English original of *Paradise Lost*, Escóiquiz's translation, and her translations.

86. Pardo Bazán, "Milton," 254.

87. Pardo Bazán, "Milton," 277.

88. Pardo Bazán, "Milton," 268, 270.

89. Pardo Bazán, "Milton," 273–74.

90. Pardo Bazán, "Milton," 324.

91. She names "Iconoclasta y Defensa del pueblo *quemados por mano del verdugo*" (burned by the executioner) and lists his "Historia de la Reforma, Observaciones á un contradictor, Razón de ser del gobierno de la Iglesia contra el episcopado, Doctrina y disciplina del divorcio, Tratado de la educación, Areopagitica, Regla de reyes y magistrados, Historia de Inglaterra, Historia de Moscovia, Arte lógica," and "Diccionario ó tesoro de la lengua latina" (Pardo Bazán, "Milton," 303, 294, 304).

92. Pardo Bazán, "Milton," 6.

93. Pardo Bazán, "Milton," 310.

94. Pardo Bazán, "Milton," 249.
95. Pardo Bazán, "Milton," 310.
96. Pardo Bazán, "Milton," 309. She rates Milton a less adept national poet than Shakespeare and on par with the later national poets Byron and Tennyson due to poetic skill and religious sensibilities (311).
97. Pardo Bazán, "Milton," 325.
98. Pardo Bazán, "Milton," 308.
99. Pardo Bazán, "Milton," 330.
100. Dobranski, *Milton*, 25.
101. Norbrook, *Poetry and Politics*, 45.
102. For discussions of the influence of the Roman Catholic Inquisition on Hungarian and Polish translations of Milton's works, see chapters 19 and 20 in Duran, Issa, and Olson, *Milton in Translation*. The Roman Catholic Church also authorized the Portuguese Catholic Inquisition.
103. For the literary independence of Spain, see Warnke, *European Metaphysical Poetry*; Shawcross, "John Milton and His Spanish and Portuguese Presence."

2. "As May Express Them Best"

1. Spanish translations of Milton's other poetry include *El Paraíso recobrado*, trans. Verneuill, and *Sonetos; Sansón Agonista*, trans. Santender. Spanish translations of Milton's sonnets are also to be found in diverse anthologies and the like. For example, "Cromwell, Chief of Men" resides in a Spanish translation of Chateaubriand, *Ensayo sobre la literatura inglesa*, 4.87, and "When I Consider" in Romero, *Síntesis*. Spanish translations of Milton's prose works include *De educación*, trans. Cossio, and four of *Areopagitica*, starting with the one by Carner.
2. On partial translations of *Paradise Lost*, see Robertson, *Milton's Fame*, 13–14; Shawcross, "John Milton and His Spanish and Portuguese Presence"; Pegenaute "La recepción de Milton"; Benítez, *Presencia de Milton*.
3. For a discussion and list of the eighteen original French translations of *Paradise Lost* from 1729 to 2001, see Christophe Tournu, "'The French Connection' among French Translations of Milton and within du Bocage's *Paradis terrestre*," in Duran, Issa, and Olson, *Milton in Translation*, 139–63.
4. Nardo, *Oculto a los ojos mortales*, 15. Mario Murgia echoes this assessment in terms of readers in "Spanish-speaking America" ("Milton in Revolutionary Hispanoamerica," 203–22).
5. The works of non-British writers highly critical of the doctrines and practices of the Catholic Church, like Dante, circulated before this period. For a synopsis of Dante's reception in Spain, see Friederich, *Dante's Fame*, 13–15; González de Amezúa, *Fases*. The National Library of Spain's catalogue includes numerous Hispanophone editions of *La Divina Comedia* and *La Comedia* by Dante. See also Lafarga and Pegenaute, *La Historia de la traducción en España*.
6. Peers, "The Influence," 404.
7. See Dobson and Wells, *The Oxford Companion*, 444–45; González Fernán-

dez de Sevilla, *Shakespeare*; Thomas, *Shakespeare*; Par, *Representaciones Shakespearianas*.

8. Berman, *Towards a Translation Criticism*.

9. Lafarga, "El siglo XVIII," 285. For the reluctance to translate or publish and implicit self-censorship in early published translations of Milton's works, see Benítez, *Presencia de Milton*, 33–34, 40.

10. Holmes, *Translated*, 89.

11. Holmes, *Translated*, 72.

12. Some evidence of the endurance of the Escóiquiz translation is its 1862 reprint in an "édition de luxe" (Peers, "Milton in Spain," 180); its 1883 reissue as an illustrated edition with vignettes of Doré's engravings; quotation in the 1972 limited edition of *Milton | El Paraíso perdido* by the Spanish artist Gregorio Prieto, with an introduction by the Spanish Nobel Prize in Literature laureate of 1977 Vicente Alexandre, as part of the 1974 tercentenary commemoration of Milton's death; and easy availability for order in paperback throughout the first years of the twenty-first century. See the note in Appendix B regarding the ascription of the translator of the Cayetano Rosell translation.

13. I use "literary-cultural" for the "implicaciones estéticas y culturales" (aesthetic and cultural implications) regularly discussed in translation studies in general and Hispanophone ones in particular (Lafarga, "El siglo XVIII," 248).

14. Bing Yan observes a similar aural obstacle in rendering *Paradise Lost* into Chinese in key passages in which Milton links the sibilant "s" sounds (*PL* 8.546–50, 10.517–21) to serpentine sin and by extension epic tradition ("Milton in China 'Yet Once More,'" in Duran, Issa, and Olson, *Milton in Translation*, 445–58).

15. Milton, *El Paraíso perdido*, trans. Escóiquiz, 15; Milton, *El Paraíso perdido*, trans. Álvarez de Toledo, 15. I quote from this edition of the Escóiquiz throughout this chapter because it is much more accessible in material and digital form, a matter I discuss at the end of the chapter. For example, through 2018 the HathiTrust possessed only the first volume of the three-volume original (Bourges: Casa de Gilles, 1812).

16. Milton, *El Paraíso perdido*, trans. Rosell, 97. Antonio Fuster also uses "al mundo y todos nuestros males" (Milton, *El Paraíso perdido*, trans. Fuster, 5).

17. *PL* 1.2 (in this book's invocation), 51, 559, 588, 693, 766; 2.653, 729, 813, 1032 (plural); 3.55 (closing this book's invocation), 179, 214, 215, 253, 268; 4.8; 6.348, 434; 7.24 (in this book's invocation); 8.331; 9.1003; 10.48, 273, 796; 11.54, 273, 366; 12.9, 236, 248, 384.

18. Milton, *El Paraíso perdido*, trans. Escóiquiz, 1.

19. Milton, *El Paraíso perdido*, trans. Álvarez de Toledo, 14.

20. Benítez, *Presencia de Milton*, 55.

21. Virgil, *Aeneid*, 1; Ariosto, *Orlando Furioso*, 1; Spenser, *The Faerie Queene*, 29.

22. Escóiquiz, *México conquistada*, 1.1. Among the relatively early, highly influential French translations, Christophe Tournu cites Nicolas Dupré de Saint-Maur's French prose translation of 1730 (1.3), with the verb "sing" as the second word: "Je chante la désobéïssance du premier homme" ("'The French Connection' among French Translations of Milton and within du Bocage's *Paradis terrestre*," in Duran, Issa, and Olson,

Milton in Translation, 140). An example of a conservative use of the epic invocation in the twenty-first century is the Spanish translation of 2004 by the Latin American Rafael Rutiaga, with the verb "sing" as the first word: "Canta, musa celeste, la primera desobediencia del hombre."

23. Milton, *El Paraíso perdido*, trans. Hermida, 1.1.
24. Milton, *El Paraíso perdido*, trans. Matéos, 15.
25. Lafarga, "El siglo XVIII," 217.
26. Benitéz, *Presencia de Milton*, 63, 61.
27. Milton, *El Paraíso perdido*, trans. Rosell, 97.
28. Milton, *El Paraíso perdido*, trans. Pujals, 210.
29. Milton, *El Paraíso perdido*, trans. Álvarez de Toledo, 102, 219, 265. The denotations and connotations can be traced via the Real Academia Española's *Nuevo Diccionario Histórico del Español*, web.frl.es/DH/, accessed May 2015. James J. Pancrazio notes that Gabriel García Márquez's *Memoria de mis putas tristes* (2004), regularly translated into English into the more subdued *Memories of My Melancholy Whores*, is "una novela cuyo título puede ofender nuestro sentido de la decencia" (a novel whose title can offend our sense of decency; "El triste viejo," 45).
30. Milton, *El Paraíso perdido: Edición bilingüe*, trans. Atreides, 509. For the use of this phrase, see Peratoner, *El ceno*, 84. This phrasing and body part are worth noting here since Eve's breast is emphasized in Gregorio Prieto's sketches of *Paradise Lost*, discussed in chapter 4.
31. Milton, *Complete Poems and Major Prose*, 210. For a discussion of "The Verse" and Milton's prosody, see Wells, "Milton's 'Vulgar Readers'"; for the two in relation to Milton's style, see Leonard, *Faithful Labourers*, 2.251–65. For the political stakes involved in blank verse, see Duran, "Milton among Hispanics."
32. Milton, *Complete Poems*, ed. Leonard, 119.
33. Puttenham, *The Art of English Poesy*, 131.
34. Milton, *El Paraíso perdido*, trans. Castellón, 49.
35. In the preface to his *Paraíso perdido*, Álvarez de Toledo justifies his use of hendecasyllabic meter as being "el mismo metro que la de Milton" (the same meter as Milton's; 12).
36. Johnson, "Life of Milton," 1.183.
37. Andrew Marvell, "On *Paradise Lost*," in Milton, *The Riverside Milton*, 350, 352.
38. Milton, *El Paraíso perdido: Edición bilingüe*, trans. Atreides, 36; Kindle version, 17.
39. Milton, *El Paraíso perdido: Edición bilingüe*, trans. Atreides, 675.
40. See the prefatory "Language and Style," in Milton, *Paradise Lost*, ed. Fowler (1971), 11–21. See "Latin and Milton's Other Languages in the Style of *Paradise Lost*" in Hale, *Milton's Languages*, 105–30.
41. Milton, *El Paraíso perdido*, trans. Pujals, 57. E. Allison Peers and Rubén Benítez share the same assessment.
42. Milton, *El Paraíso perdido*, trans. Hermida, 1.289. The sentence fragment from the Spanish is translated with an eye to accuracy yet denotative meaning.
43. Milton, *El Paraíso perdido*, trans. Escóiquiz, 479, 480.

44. Milton, *El Paraíso perdido*, trans. Castellón, 49–50.
45. Milton, *El Paraíso perdido: Edición bilingüe*, trans. Atreides, 680n34.
46. Angelica Duran, "Paradise Lost in Spanish Translation and as World Literature," in Duran, Issa, and Olson, *Milton in Translation*, 271.
47. Milton, *El Paraíso perdido*, trans. Escóiquiz, 89.
48. Milton, *El Paraíso perdido*, trans. Escóiquiz, xi.
49. Milton, *El Paraíso perdido*, trans. Sanjuán, 40n24; Milton, *El Paraíso perdido*, trans. Castellón, 40. I quote from the 2011 edition.
50. Milton, *El Paraíso perdido*, trans. Álvarez de Toledo, 13.
51. Milton, *El Paraíso perdido*, trans. Pujals, 37n28, 134n26, 409n5.
52. Milton, *El Paraíso perdido*, trans. Escóiquiz, 388.
53. Milton, *El Paraíso perdido: Edición bilingüe*, trans. Atreides, 531.
54. Milton, *El Paraíso perdido*, trans. Escóiquiz, 389.
55. Milton, *El Paraíso perdido*, trans. Rosell, 227; Milton, *El Paraíso perdido*, trans. Sanjuán, 201.
56. Milton, *El Paraíso perdido*, trans. Rosell, 226–27.
57. Milton, *El Paraíso perdido*, trans. Sanjuán, 201.
58. Milton, *El Paraíso perdido*, trans. Rosell, 227, 230, 229, 230.
59. Milton, *El Paraíso perdido*, trans. Álvarez de Toledo, 229, 231, 233.
60. Milton, *El Paraíso perdido*, trans. Álvarez de Toledo, 230, 233.
61. For translational self-censorship and the specter of institutional censorship in eighteenth-century translations of English authors like Daniel Defoe, Jonathan Swift, Samuel Richardson, and Henry Fielding, see Lafarga, "El siglo XVIII," 281–83.
62. Milton, *El Paraíso perdido*, trans. Escóiquiz, xiii.
63. For Hermida's ecumenical attitude toward Milton, see Benítez, *Presencia de Milton*, 60.
64. Milton, *El Paraíso perdido*, trans. Escóiquiz, 28, 495.
65. Johnson, "Life of Milton" 1.184.
66. Milton, *El Paraíso perdido*, trans. Escóiquiz, 497.
67. Milton, *El Paraíso perdido*, trans. Escóiquiz, 508, 509.
68. See Angelica Duran, "*El Paraíso Perdido*."
69. Milton, *El Paraíso perdido*, trans. Sanjuán, 105n13.
70. Schwartz, "Review," 239.
71. Milton, *Paraíso perdido: Edición bilingüe*, trans. Atreides, 11.
72. Milton, *Paradise Lost*, ed. Fowler (1971), 171n3.474–75. Gordon Teskey identifies them as "accoutrements of Roman Catholic devotion and papal arrogance" (Milton, *Paradise Lost*, ed. Teskey, 70n3.490–92). See also Milton, *Paradise Lost: Books III–IV*, 67n3.492.
73. Milton, *El Paraíso perdido*, trans. Hermida, 1.117, 1.279n36.
74. Milton, *El Paraíso perdido*, trans. Escóiquiz, 126.
75. Milton, *El Paraíso perdido*, trans. Escóiquiz, 126, 127.
76. Milton, *El Paraíso perdido*, trans. Rosell, 69.
77. Milton, *El Paraíso perdido*, trans. Rosell, 69; Milton, *El Paraíso perdido*, trans. Sanjuán, 76.

78. Milton, *El Paraíso perdido*, trans. Fuster, 71; Milton, *El Paraíso perdido*, trans. Álvarez de Toledo, 75. *Menor* (Minor) is a common term for Franciscans, or *Ordo fratrum minorum* (Minor Order of Brothers).

79. King, "Milton's Paradise of Fools," 202.

80. Milton, *Paradise Lost*, ed. Verity, 441n3.444–97.B. For Daniel Defoe's theological criticism of *Paradise Lost*, including this section, see McCarthy, "Defoe, Milton, and Heresy."

81. Huntley, "A Justification," 112.

82. Fowler has an extensive note on "transubstantiate" as an "abstract theological term," suggesting "that Adam and Eve were already enjoying Communion with the gods" (Milton, *Paradise Lost*, ed. Fowler (1971), 284n5.438–39). Other editors find that Milton's "use of a theological term may imply a slur on Catholic dogma which holds that Eucharistic bread and wine are changed into *different* substances rather than a different degree of the same substance" (Milton, *Paradise Lost: Books V–VI*, 78n5.438) and comment that transubstantiation was a "loaded term in Milton's day, denoting for Roman Catholics the changing of the bread and wine of the mass into Christ's body and blood. For Milton, true transubstantiation exists in the natural world, in the processes of digestion and in the entire movement of creatures upward on the scale of being toward their Creator" (Milton, *Paradise Lost*, ed. Teskey, 118n5.438). See also Gigante, "Milton's Aesthetics of Eating."

83. Milton, *El Paraíso perdido*, trans. Hermida, 1.208, 284n74.

84. Milton, *El Paraíso perdido*, trans. Escóiquiz, 209.

85. Milton, *El Paraíso perdido*, trans. Rosell, 116; Milton, *El Paraíso perdido*, trans. Sanjuán, 100.

86. Milton, *El Paraíso perdido: Edición bilingüe*, trans. Atreides, 287; Milton, *El Paraíso perdido*, trans. Castellón, 381.

87. Milton, *El Paraíso perdido*, trans. Castellón, 903.

88. King, "Milton's Transubstantiation," 44. For another complex vision of transubstantiation and tables in *Paradise Lost*, see Schwartz, "Real Hunger."

89. Milton, *El Paraíso perdido*, trans. Sanjuán, 167.

90. Milton, *El Paraíso perdido*, trans. Escóiquiz, 216, 209.

91. Milton, *El Paraíso perdido*, trans. Rosell, 187.

92. The title page of the publication advertises that it contains *El Paraíso Perdido por John Milton seguido de El Paraíso Recobrado del mismo autor según el texto de las ediciones mas autorizadas[.] Nueva traducción precedida de la vida del autor por Don Cayetano Rosell* (Paradise Lost by John Milton Followed by Paradise Regained by the Same Author According to the Text of the Most Authorized Texts. New Translation Preceded by the Life of the Author by Don Cayetano Rosell); the second title page (299) introducing *Paradise Regained* specifies that it is "traducido directamente del Inglés por Enrique Leopoldo de Verneuill" (translated directly from the English by Enrique Leopoldo de Verneuill).

93. Milton, *El Paraíso recobrado*, 324, 325, 326, 358.

94. Milton, *Complete Poems*, ed. Leonard, 843n10.313. See also Milton, *Paradise*

Lost, ed. Fowler (1971), 524n10.313; Milton, *Complete Poems and Major Prose*, 414n10.313; Milton, *The Riverside Milton*, 633n18.

95. Milton, *Complete Poems*, ed. Leonard, 844n10.348.
96. Milton, *El Paraíso perdido*, trans. Hermida, 2.142; Milton, *El Paraíso perdido*, trans. Sanjuán, 203.
97. Milton, *El Paraíso perdido: Edición bilingüe*, trans. Atreides, 537.
98. Milton, *El Paraíso perdido*, trans. Rosell, 228, 229.
99. Milton, *El Paraíso perdido*, trans. Rosell, 228. I use the Loeb Classical Library Latin-to-English translation of XV.83 in Marcus Terentius Varo, *On the Latin Language*, 81.
100. Milton, *El Paraíso perdido*, trans. Castellón, 924.
101. Milton, *El Paraíso perdido*, trans. Escóiquiz, 390–91.
102. Milton, *El Paraíso perdido*, trans. Escóiquiz, 456. For Genesis 9:13, 14, 16, the Geneva and King James versions use "bow," not "rainbow"; the Spanish Reina Valera Biblia uses "arco," not "arco iris."
103. Milton, *Milton's Paradise Lost, by Richard Bentley*, [iii].
104. Sakai, "Translation," 26. Correlative to Sakai's comments on contemporary translation of literary works as applicable to other disciplinary domains is Pierre Legrand's use of French translations of Milton's works to illuminate legal translation ("Issues of Translatability," 39). For the "inequívoca voluntad de servicio social" (unequivocal drive for social service) on the part of Spanish translators during the Spanish Enlightenment, see Lafarga, "El siglo XVIII, 214.
105. Milton, *El Paraíso perdido*, trans. Escóiquiz, ix.
106. Milton, *El Paraíso perdido*, trans. Hermida, 1.x, xii, ix, xiv.
107. For Jungmann and Djilas, see, respectively, Šárka Tobrmanová, "Jungmann's Translation of *Paradise Lost* in the Vanguard of Modern Czech Culture," and Marjan Strojan, "Milton in Serbian/Montenegrin: *Paradise Lost* from behind Bars," in Duran, Issa, and Olson, *Milton in Translation*, 309–27, 366–79. For Granados, see Duran, "Mexican Miltons."
108. Milton, *El Paraíso perdido*, trans. Sanjuán, title page; Milton, *El Paraíso perdido*, trans. Rosell, 1.
109. Milton, *El Paraíso perdido*, trans. Escóiquiz, v, vii, vi; Milton, *El Paraíso perdido*, trans. Sanjuán, 6, 11. The "Biografía" was first introduced in the Escóiquiz translation in 1862, as far as I have been able to determine.
110. For example, in 2016 the search engine for the electronic catalogue of the first library of the Americas, the Biblioteca Palafoxiana in Puebla, Mexico, biblioteca.colmex.mx/palafoxiana/, was not set up for fuzzy searches: "Shakespeare" as a keyword did not produce the library's holding of, for example, an 1809 "William Shakspeares [sic] selected plays, from the last edition of Johnson and Steevens." Cataloguers had accurately transcribed the title page's variant spelling of Shakespeare's name and lack of possessive apostrophe.
111. Milton had no middle name, and his mother's maiden name was Jeffrey.
112. Milton, *El Paraíso perdido: Edición bilingüe*, trans. Atreides, 61. A note on the

linguistic matters of this passage is warranted. Milton creates an acoustic web within the passage through the many "h" sounds, from "hail horrors, hail" to the final word in the passage, "Hell" (PL 1.250–70), and an acoustic argument for Satan's fixity on his present place, the also aspirant "here" (PL 1.258, 260, 261), constructed by the higher repetition of "Hell" (six times, PL 1.251, 255 [twice], 262, 263, 270) than "Heav'n" (four times, PL 1.255 [twice], 263, 270). Serendipitously, *Infierno* (Hell) and *Cielo* (Heaven) are assonant rhymes and thus create for Spanish readers the aural unity produced for English readers by the "h" alliterations. Rosell reduces the use of *infierno* and *cielo* by one each, including in the blasphemous line (Milton, *El Paraíso perdido*, trans. Rosell, 12). Álvarez de Toledo reduces Milton's poetic strategy converting the chiasmic "make a Heav'n of Hell, a Hell of Heav'n" (PL 1.255) into "Del Cielo hace un Infierno y viceversa" (Makes a Heaven of Hell and vice versa), then replacing the place-names with "here" and "there" in the blasphemous line: "Mejor aquí reinar que allí servir" (Better to reign here than serve there; Milton, *Paraíso perdido*, trans. Álvarez de Toledo, 21). See also Milton, *El Paraíso perdido*, trans. Matéos, 34; Milton, *El Paraíso perdido*, trans. Sanjuán, 7; Milton, *El Paraíso perdido*, trans. Fuster, 11.

113. Milton, *El Paraíso perdido*, trans. Escóiquiz, x.

114. Milton, *El Paraíso perdido*, trans. Escóiquiz, 495.

115. Addison, *Criticisms*, 3. Addison states that humankind's "enemies are the fallen angels, the Messiah their friend, and the Almighty their protector" (5).

116. "Enemy" is repeatedly used in the Argument to book 5 and the Argument to book 9 but is used only once, and powerfully, as quoted, in the text itself.

117. Milton, *The Complete Poetry and Essential Prose*, 407n4.741–43.

118. Milton, *Complete Poems*, ed. Leonard, 770n4.744–9. See also the close reading of this and related passages in Karen Edwards, "Gender, Sex, and Marriage in Paradise," in Duran, *A Concise Companion*, 144–60.

119. Milton, *El Paraíso perdido*, trans. Escóiquiz, 176, 177.

120. Obach, *The Catholic Church*, 100, 109; Thomas Ryba, University of Notre Dame theologian in residence, email to author, October 5, 2015.

121. Milton, *El Paraíso perdido*, trans. Escóiquiz, 324.

122. Milton, *El Paraíso perdido*, trans. Hermida 2.63.

123. Milton, *El Paraíso perdido*, trans. Sanjuán, 193.

124. See Flood, "Marian Controversies."

125. Luke 1:28, 31.

126. Milton, *El Paraíso perdido*, trans. Escóiquiz, 206.

127. Milton, *El Paraíso perdido*, trans. Hermida, 1.205–6.

128. Milton, *El Paraíso perdido*, trans. Escóiquiz, 473.

129. Milton, *El Paraíso perdido*, trans. Escóiquiz, 418; Milton, *Paradis perdu*, trans. Delille, 2.206–9.

130. Milton, *El Paraíso perdido*, trans. Rosell, 249–50.

131. Milton, *El Paraíso perdido*, trans. Pujals, 442n43.

132. Milton, *Complete Poems*, ed. Leonard, 854n10.1,086–1,104.

133. Milton, *El Paraíso perdido*, trans. Castellón, 927.

134. Luke 15:18–19, 21. The Geneva, King James Version, and Reina-Valera render the exact repetition. In the second instance, the father interrupts the son before he can complete his planned speech of penitence with "Make me as one of thy hired servants."

135. For example, the Fowler edition cites the same chapters from Isaiah and Psalms but not the Jeremiah or the New Testament passages (Milton, *Paradise Lost*, ed. Fowler (1971), 562n10.1090).

136. Milton, *El Paraíso perdido*, trans. Hermida, 2.10, 262.

137. Milton, *Paradise Lost*, ed. Fowler, 367n7.176–79; Milton, *Complete Poems*, ed. Leonard, 805n7.176.

138. Milton, *El Paraíso perdido*, trans. Castellón, 907. Sanjuán suggests that the attribution of artillery to Satan is Milton's invention (Milton, *El Paraíso perdido*, trans. Sanjuán, 123n3).

139. Milton, *El Paraíso perdido*, trans. Sanjuán, 143n7. For a brief history of the Catholic Church's interventions with the calendar, see "Reform of the Calendar," *New Advent Catholic Encyclopedia*, www.newadvent.org/cathen/03168a.htm, accessed February 1, 2018.

140. Milton, *Paradise Lost*, ed. Fowler (1971), 378n7.374–5; Milton, *Complete Poems*, ed. Leonard, 808n7.374–75.

141. Milton, *El Paraíso perdido*, trans. Castellón, 938n12.700.

142. Milton, *Paradise Lost*, ed. Fowler (1971), 635n.12.528–30; Milton, *Complete Poems*, ed. Leonard, 872n12.529–30.

143. Milton, *El Paraíso perdido*, trans. Castellón, 723, 926, 869, 938.

144. Milton, *Complete Poems*, ed. Leonard, 848n10.616–17.

145. Martin Puchner's intertwining of the history of the book and reflections on his own research history in his sweeping *The Written World* is a model for my much briefer excursus.

146. Nardo, *Oculto a los ojos mortales*, 9–11.

147. Info Galaxia Gutenberg, email to author, July 20, 2016.

148. I am one of the "numerosas personas de dentro y fuera de España" (numerous persons inside and outside of Spain) who contacted the translator Bel Atreides asking him how to get a hold of the book, as he records in "Prólogo a la edición en Kindle 2017" (3). In the 2010s my campus librarians advised me that the Atreides edition could be purchased for a dear US$1,000. Even the active University of Texas at Austin libraries were unable to provide me with the Atreides translation within my two-month fellowship at its Harry T. Ransom Center in spring 2016, although they were able to locate one in Spain from a partner institution and graciously offered to cover the cost of its transatlantic journey.

149. Bel Atreides, email to author, July 20, 2016.

150. For such active intervention, see Damrosch, *What Is World Literature?*

3. "To the Well-Trod Stage Anon"

1. Per the translator I. G. Burnham, Victor Hugo's "*Cromwell* has never appeared on stage" (Hugo, *Oliver Cromwell*, 419). Benítez, however, refers to "La primera rep-

resentación en España del *Cromwell* de Victor Hugo, en citado beneficio de la actriz Concepción Samaniego" (The first performance in Spain of Victor Hugo's *Cromwell*, with the actress Concepción Samaniego; *Presencia de Milton*, 179). Walter Scott Hasting records that the "unfinished," unpublished, "complete text of *Cromwell* is to be found in the Chantilly collection of Balzac drama" (*The Drama*, 20, 15n3). For a discussion of Milton's influence and character in Hugo's *Cromwell*, see Blythe, "Milton, Cromwell," 255–82. For the influence and nature of the French reception of Milton, see Brinkley, "Milton"; Redman, *Major French Milton Critics*; Tournu, *Milton in France*. For indicators of French influence in the Spanish reception of Shakespeare, see the entry on "Spain" in Dobson and Wells, *The Oxford Companion*, 444–45.

2. Also related is the two-canto poem created for public oral delivery in 1799: Reinos and Lista, *La inocencia perdida*.

3. This chapter does not directly address either the Anglo-Protestant and Hispano-Catholic divides so prominent in the censorial indexes and translations discussed in chapters 1 and 2 or the generalized Christianity that is present in muted form within the play's text and context. Among the many indicators of a Spanish participation in an ecumenical community of Western European Christians, especially in relation to James Russell Lowell, is the three-page obituary for Lowell in the *Boletín* of the Institución Libre de Enseñanza (Free Institute of Teaching), which cites Lowell's works and activities as displaying a "cristianismo transcendental . . . humanista y social, sin formas externas" (transcendental Christianity . . . humanistic and social, without external forms"] (Institucíon Libre de Enseñanza, "James Russell Lowell," 242).

4. Gies, *The Theatre*, 2.

5. See Marcus, "Justice," and "The Earl."

6. Universidad Complutense de Madrid, *Veinticuatro diarios*, 2.325–26.

7. Par, *Representaciones Shakespearianas*, 2.325–26.

8. Milton, *El Paraíso perdido*, trans. Pujals, 2.325–26. *Milton's Paradise* also receives mention in *La ilustración española y americana* (The Spanish and American Enlightenment) 2 (January 1884): 26.

9. Giner de los Ríos, *Manual*, 3.311.

10. Johnson, "Life of Milton," 1.153.

11. Barton, "'Ill Fare the Hands.'"

12. Edward Jones cites "Nov 9 or 10," 1674, as Milton's death-day ("Select Chronology," in Duran, *A Concise Companion*, 234). For anecdotes about the mutual political interventions by Davenant and Milton, see Johnson, "Life of Milton," 1.127–30; Darbishire, *The Early Lives*, 31; Parker, *Milton*, 2.1017.

13. Scene 6, lines 37–38, in Giner de los Ríos, *Milton: A Dramatic Scene*, 247.

14. Milton, *El Paraíso perdido*, trans. Escóiquiz, vii.

15. Pardo Bazán, "Milton," 289. For details about the contract for *Paradise Lost* between Samuel Simmons and Milton, see Lewalski, *The Life*, 453–56; MacLennan, "John Milton's Contract."

16. Giner de los Ríos, *Historia*, 308.

17. For Milton legends circulating in the nineteenth century, see part 1 of Nardo, *George Eliot's Dialogue*.

18. Milton, *El Paraíso perdido*, trans. Sanjuán, xiv. For the "obscure story," see also Johnson, "Life of Milton," 1.131–32.

19. Scene 9, line 42, in Giner de los Ríos, *Milton: A Dramatic Scene*, 265.

20. Shawcross, *The Arms of the Family*. See especially "Christopher Milton, Royalist and Brother," 13–46.

21. Robert T. Fallon, "A Reading of His Left Hand," in Duran, *A Concise Companion*, 9.

22. For Deborah and Abraham's marriage and Milton's knowledge of it, see Campbell, "Milton in Madras."

23. Symmons, *The Life*, 509; French, *Life Records*, 4.390.

24. Pardo Bazán, "Milton," 295. Redman indicates that Chateaubriand conveyed the anecdote of the duke of York's visiting Milton and that Alphonse de Lamartine conveyed the variant of Charles II making the visit, during which the king offered "Milton his old position" (*Major French Milton Critics*, 158). Lamartine's life of Milton circulated widely in Europe and the Americas.

25. Pardo Bazán, "Milton," 294. See chapter 1 for the inclusion of *Defence of the English People* on the Spanish Catholic Inquisition's list of heretical authors and works. Lamartine also includes this story, which is absent of any reference to a servant's body being used as a stand-in for Milton's (Redman, *Major French Milton Critics*, 158).

26. Giner de los Ríos, *Milton: A Dramatic Scene*, 290n71.

27. Masson, *The Life of Milton*, 6.753.

28. Giner de los Ríos, *Milton: A Dramatic Scene*, 287.

29. There had been talk about Lowell's possible appointment in London even before his invitation to become U.S. ambassador to Austria or Spain. President Rutherford Hayes nominated him to the post, which he began in March 1880 (Greenslet, *James Russell Lowell*, 184, 191; Scudder, *James Russell Lowell*, 255, 258). The delay to March was due to the illness of his wife, Fanny.

30. Lawes and Milton, *A Maske*, title page, ii–iii, 35, n.p.

31. Milton, *Poems of Mr. John Milton both English and Latin*, 67, 69–72, 74.

32. Giner de los Ríos, *Milton: A Dramatic Scene*, 223.

33. López Ruiz, *Historia*, 17, 24; Gies, *The Theatre*, 322. For Shakespearean performances at the Apollo and Vico's presence on the Spanish stage, see Par, *Representaciones Shakespearianas*, 2.41, 55, 57, 64, 220.

34. Par, *Representaciones Shakespearianas*, 2.41, 48, 128.

35. Works consulted include Lowell, *Impressions of Spain*; Hermegildo Giner de los Ríos, handwritten note to Lowell, August 6, 1879, Harvard Houghton Library, bMS Am 1484, 128; Lowell, *New Letters*; Lowell, *More New Letters*; and the U.S. government documents webpage, www.us.gov, accessed July 20, 2014. Lawrence H. Klibbe notes, "I have been able to locate only three letters from Hermenegildo Giner de los Ríos to Lowell," dated August 7, 1880, August 14, [?], and May 20, 1880 ("James Russell Lowell's Residence").

36. For the low state of Lowell studies at the beginning of the twenty-first century, see Rapple, "James Russell Lowell."

37. Pujals's conjecture is worth noting here: "Siempre me he inclinado a creer que el decreto parlamentario de 1642, prohibiendo las representaciones dramáticas, privó a Inglaterra de tener en Milton el Calderón inglés" (I have always been inclined to think that the Parliamentarian decree of 1642 prohibiting dramatic representations deprived England from having in Milton the English Calderon; "Estructura," 210).

38. Gies comments, "The new dramas also had to compete with the still popular translations of French plays and the ever-present 'refundaciones' of Golden Age drama," central to which were Calderón's plays (*The Theatre*, 13).

39. Gies, *The Theatre*, 27.

40. Klibbe, "James Russell Lowell's Residence," 110; Gayangos de Riaño, "Mr. Lowell," 292.

41. Klibbe, "James Russell Lowell's Residence," 116; Scudder, *James Russell Lowell*, 222–42; Greenslet *James Russell Lowell*, 190.

42. Klibbe, "James Russell Lowell's Residence," 113; Armitage, "Some New Letters."

43. For an extended version of these roles, see Smith, *Is Milton Better*.

44. Harvard University, "Official: From the Records of the Corporation," 205; Brown, *The Life*, 256.

45. McGlinchee, *James Russell Lowell*, 100.

46. Klibbe, "James Russell Lowell's Residence," 129; Lowell, *The Works*, 7.37–38. See the similar assessment by Unamuno in the introduction. For the respected position that Hartzenbusch held in late nineteenth-century Spain, see his biography in the oft referenced and republished Cánovas del Castillo, *Autores*, 404–28. Further research into the literary milieu of late nineteenth- and early twentieth-century Spain in relation to Milton studies is warranted by Hartzenbusch's having penned a prologue to the Spanish verse translation of Dante's *Divine Comedy* (1872) with illustrations by Doré. The Cayetano Rosell edition with the prose translation of *Paradise Lost* (1873) also contains illustrations by Doré. As discussed in chapter 2, the Rosell *El Paraíso perdido* remains the most used Spanish prose translation of the epic through today.

47. Klibbe, "James Russell Lowell's Residence," 145; Lowell, *The Works*, 16.64. See also Brown, *The Life*, 254.

48. For the "Orientalization of Spain . . . promoted most by the French" that influenced U.S. reception of Spain, see DeGuzmán, *Spain's Long Shadow*, xv, 80. Gayatri Chakravorty Spivak notes that while Edward Said's "path-breaking book *Orientalism* (1978) ostensibly wrote about the Middle East being constructed as the 'Orient' by French intellectuals of the eighteenth and nineteenth centuries, it was the Spanish and British empires that formed the main fields of colonial discourse studies" ("Postcolonial Theory").

49. Lowell, *A Fable*, 59, 70–71.

50. Brown, *The Life*, 89. For evaluations of early U.S. drama, see the introductory section and "Beginnings: Colonial to Civil War" in Watt and Richardson, *American*

Drama, 1–18, and the early chapters of Richardson, *American Drama*, 1–152. Special thanks to Thomas Adler for helping me to refine my understanding of early U.S. drama.

51. Giner de los Ríos, *Manual*, 3.360, 361.

52. For Lowell's work as public intellectual and social reformer, see the encomium by Hart, "James Russell Lowell." Decades earlier, Lowell mentions poets only from the U.K., including Milton, in his recommendation to an aspiring poet in the U.S.: "Read Shakespeare, Spenser, Milton, Wordsworth, Burns, Coleridge, Byron, Keats & Shelley—they will tell you better than I whether you are a poet or not" (Autograph letter signed ["J. R. Lowell"] to A. M. Ide Jr., Cambridge, MA, June 13, 1843, cited with gratitude to the Grolier Club, New York, for access to this letter.)

53. Lowell, *Latest Literary Essays*, 108, 109, 110. For similar inspiration found in Milton the man as articulated elsewhere in Lowell's New England milieu, including Ralph Waldo Emerson, see Anglen, *The New England Milton*, 64–66, 109–49.

54. Jones, "Select Chronology," 230.

55. See especially Mitchell and Snyder, *Narrative Prosthesis*.

56. Tosca, "El tema," 390. Lope de Vega's references and allusions to Polyphemus are sufficiently numerous to have merited the book-length study by Osuna, *Polifemo*.

57. Act 1, scene 5, lines 93–106 of Shakespeare, *Romeo and Juliet*, 1066.

58. Giner de los Ríos, *Milton: A Dramatic Scene*, 285, 287.

59. Flynn, *Manuel Tamayo y Baús*, 632.

60. Flynn, *Manuel Tamayo y Baús*, 30. Gies notes of the Generation of 1850 that the works of this new generation of playwrights share many of the goals of the *alta comedia* and are "characterized by an interest in the economic realities of their day, strong moral posturing, a concentration on middle- and upper-middle-class characters, a predominately urban environment, and an attempt to convey refined emotion and sentimentality to their audiences as opposed to the intense emotionalism which characterized Romantic drama" (*The Theatre*, 261). The social/socialist drama at the end of the century focused on underdogs, like Milton (see 309–31).

61. Gies, *The Theatre*, 37.

62. See Lope de Vega, *Arte nuevo*.

63. Amancio Labandeira, introduction to Tamayo y Baus, *Un drama nuevo*, ed. Labandeira, 26n71.

64. Tamayo y Baus, *Un drama nuevo*, ed. Escudero, 150. For the stagings of *Shakespeare enamorado* in Barcelona and Madrid, see Par, *Representaciones Shakespearianas*; and Dobson and Wells, *The Oxford Companion*, 444. See also Sumillera, "Manuel Tamayo y Baus's *Un Drama Nuevo*."

65. Duval, *Shakespeare enamorado*.

66. Dobson and Wells, *The Oxford Companion*, 444.

67. González Valdés and de Novo y Colson, *Autores*.

68. González Herrán, "*Un Drama Nuevo*," 76. Mark Twain praised a performance of the play in a personal letter to Howells of March 11, 1880. The play's status has obtained: Gies lists it as one of the three examples of "selected masterpieces, plays which have been

read and studied in university classrooms and which have been said to have had a major impact on the direction of theatrical activity in the last [nineteenth] century" (*The Theatre*, 1).

69. William Wordsworth, "Scorn Not the Sonnet," in *The Sonnets*, 54.

70. Blanchot, *The Work of Fire*, 1.

71. Giner de los Ríos, *Milton: A Dramatic Scene*, 223.

72. A costume performance by undergraduate students in 2006 and a dramatic reading by graduate students in 2015 of the English translation of the play at my home institution of Purdue University proved captivating for even resistant and initially uninterested audiences.

73. Williams, *Marxism and Literature*, 49.

74. See Weinfield, *The Blank-Verse Tradition*. For Jorge Luis Borges's argument about the correlation between blank verse and liberty, see Duran, "Milton among Hispanics."

75. For rhyme on the Spanish stage of this period, see Gies, *The Theatre*, 4–5. For Giner de los Ríos's definition of aesthetics, see his *Teoría de la literatura y de las artes*.

76. Scene 3, line 32, in Giner de los Ríos, *Milton: A Dramatic Scene*, 233. Quintillas are five-line stanzas of octosyllabic lines in one of four rhyme schemes: *ababa, abbab, abaab,* or *aabba*. In Spanish drama, the *quintilla* "is commonly used when feeling and emotion, rather than action, are expressed" (Sturgis E. Leavitt, introduction to Calderón de la Barca, "*La vida es un sueño*," 17).

77. Scene 3, line 34, in Giner de los Ríos, *Milton: A Dramatic Scene*, 233.

78. Gordon Campbell refers to a similar ambiguity that Milton makes in the four lines of Greek verse beneath the engraved author portrait by William Marshall for the frontispiece of Milton's *Poems . . . 1645*, discussed in chapter 4: is the engraving "of a worthless artist" or "by a worthless artist"? ("Milton and the Languages," 17). See also Mabbett, "Item 58."

79. Giner de los Ríos, *Milton: A Dramatic Scene*, 288n32. For the designation of Davenant as unofficial British poet laureate, see Edmond, *Rare Sir William Davenant*.

80. Scene 3, line 7, in Giner de los Ríos, *Milton: A Dramatic Scene*, 233. Giner de los Ríos perpetuates this moniker in his section on Milton in his *Manual* (3.309). For many of the biographical and poetic links between Milton and Homer, see "Homer" in Martindale, *John Milton*, 53–106. Also worth noting are instances of the subtle alliances between Homer and Milton, as in the quotation of John Phillip's English translation of *Don Quixote* in the opening pages of the introductory chapter of this book: "*Du Bartas,* and *Paradise lost*" substitute for the original's Homer and the verse of the *Iliad*.

81. Scene 3, lines 36, 21, in Giner de los Ríos, *Milton: A Dramatic Scene*, 233.

82. Scene 6, lines 31–33, in Giner de los Ríos, *Milton: A Dramatic Scene*, 247.

83. For a representation of another Débora opting for obedience to her role as dutiful daughter over personal desire, see Echeverría and Santivañes's *El Paraíso de Milton*.

84. Calderón de la Barca, "*La vida es un sueño*," 17.

85. Scene 13, lines 29–32, in Giner de los Ríos, *Milton: A Dramatic Scene*, 285.

The lines allude to Milton's *Paradise Lost*, verbally through the use of hyperbaton and denotatively in the representation of pure locales expelling impurity, as in God the Father's justification for expelling fallen Adam and Eve from Eden (*PL* 11.46–57).

86. Philip Sidney contrasts the worlds of nature and of literary art: "her world is brazen, the poets only deliver a golden" (*A Defence*, 24). See also the epigraph about the "Golden Age" from Cervantes's *Don Quixote* in the introduction to this book.

87. For the benefits of being alert to such intersections, see especially Stephen M. Fallon, who states, "To read as I do with intention in mind is not to restrict oneself either to the explicitly stated intentions or even to consciously intended meanings of an author. Even those skeptical of imposed biographical intentionalism allow for intentions discernible *within* texts. Texts, as Paul de Man has argued, can exhibit 'structural intentionality,' an aim decipherable in the text as opposed to applied to the text a priori. This structural intentionality and operative mind may or may not be identical to the conscious intention of the historical author" (*Milton's Peculiar Grace*, 12). See also "Form and Intent in the American New Criticism" in de Man, *Blindness and Insight*, 20–35.

4. "By Shading Pencil Drawn"

1. "Frontispiece," n.1, 3, 4, *OED*. Milton combines multiple definitions in his use in *Areopagitica* in sarcastically imagining extending book censorship, as his editor Ernest Sirluck notes: "The Windows also, and the *Balcone*'s must be thought on, there are shrewd books, with dangerous Frontispices set on sale; who shall prohibit them, shall twenty licencers?" (*CPW* 2.524).

2. Taking my lead from the translator Enrique López Castellón, discussed in chapter 2 (see n143), I note that those who have stood in the same museums and palaces as did Milton during his Italian travels of 1638–39 are keenly aware of the ability of pencil shadings in particular to deceive.

3. I use the title and translation from Hale, "Milton's Greek Epigram." Like Hale, John Leonard calls attention to the ambiguity of the last line, which he translates "*of a rotten artist*" (Milton, *Complete Poems*, ed. Leonard, 602, emphasis mine). In the 1673 *Poems*, the visual text is absent and the epigram appears between *Philosophus ad regem* and *Ad Salsillum*, an example of the untethering of verbal and visual texts, to be discussed later in this chapter.

4. Of "some 35 editions in England and 25 in Ireland and abroad in 1649 alone," some contain only the Marshall engraving and others a handful of illustrations (Gardner-Flint, "The King's Book").

5. Genette and Maclean, "Introduction," 261.

6. Skerpan-Wheeler, "Authorship and Authority,"109. See also Sharpe, "'So Hard a Text'?"

7. Skerpan-Wheeler, "Authorship and Authority," 109, 111.

8. Wittreich, "Illustrators," 56.

9. Cavallo and Chartier, introduction, 35.

10. For the relationship of book illustrations and extratextual illustrations of writ-

ten works, see Horsfall, "The Origins." For the sake of brevity and focus, this chapter does not address illustrations in juvenile literature, adaptations, and editions with only author-portraits, single frontispieces, or ornaments. See, for example, *El Paraíso perdido* adapted as a juvenile edition by Manuel Vallve and as a graphic novel by Pablo Auladell.

11. Pardo Bazán, "Milton," 283; see also 299–300.

12. For images and discussion of major illustrations of the genre, see Kovács, "Milton Dictating"; Duran, "John Milton and Disability Studies."

13. Furman and Tufte, "'With Other Eyes,'" 145. See also Gardner, "Milton's First Illustrator," 27; Ravehall "Francis Atterbury" and "Sources and Meaning in Dr. Aldrich's"; Boorsch, "The 1688 *Paradise Lost* and Dr. Aldrich."

14. Pointon, *Milton and English Art*, 1.

15. National Galleries of Scotland, "Sir John Baptiste de Medina," https://www.nationalgalleries.org/art-and-artists/artists/sir-john-baptiste-de-medina, accessed October 30, 2018. Up to the early eighteenth century, Brussels was part of the Habsburg Empire. Wai Chee Dimock refers to "the Flemish Scottish painter John Baptiste de Medina" (Dimock, "Editor's Column," 11).

16. I am grateful to the Scottish National Portrait Gallery for access to the portraits and the National Library of Scotland for access to the letter. The attributions in the 1688 Tonson edition are as follows: books 3 and 6, "Medina inven."; book 5, "JB. de Medina Inu."; book 7, "Medina delin."; books 9 and 10, "JB. de Medina Inven."; book 11, "Medina Invent." The full surname of Medina's father is "Medina de Caustanais" (Lee, *Dictionary of National Biography*, 37.203). The surname of Medina's mother remains unknown, but it may begin with "F" (Scottish National Portrait Gallery, emails to the author, October 2015).

17. For a related case in literature, we have a number of examples of Miguel de Cervantes Saavedra using his full surname in his signatures. For a related case in painting, see the discussion and images of Rembrandt's signatures at Jean-Marie Clarke, *Rembrandt Signature Files*, http://www.rembrandt-signature-file.com/, including his use of "F" and "Fecit" (Latin, "he made," used not uncommonly) when writing part or all of his name. See also Jean-Marie Clarke, "Give Me an F," 2013, http://www.rembrandt-signature-file.com/remp_texte/remp028.pdf. Many thanks to Sarah Jeffcott at the National Museum of Scotland for consulting with the senior curator and to Jeffrey C. Smith (University of Texas at Austin) in determining the unlikelihood that the "F" ending in some of Medina's signatures is an equal initial that could stand for "Fecit."

18. Gardner, "Milton's First Illustrator," 27.

19. Collins-Baker, "Some Illustrations," 3.

20. Ravenhall, "Francis Atterbury," 34.

21. Ravenhall, "Francis Atterbury," 33.

22. Pointon, *Milton and English Art*, 1.

23. The publisher Jacob Tonson took five years of "careful preparation" to produce *Paradise Lost*, the "first of fifteen" important subscription editions that he would publish. Kathleen M. Lynch concludes her biography of Tonson noting of his most famous portrait, "In his hand he holds conspicuously a handsomely bound copy of the

fourth edition of *Paradise Lost*" (*Jacob Tonson*, 104, 177). Ellis K. Waterhouse implies high praise for Medina by aligning him with Godfrey Kneller, who painted Tonson's portrait: "Kneller's equivalent in Scotland was undoubtedly John Baptist Medina" (*Painting in Britain*, 150).

24. Wittreich, "Illustrators," 56.

25. See for example, Ravenhall, "Sources and Meaning"; Suzanne Boorsch, "The 1688 *Paradise Lost*"; Wittreich, "Milton's 'First' Illustrator"; Sullivan, "Illustration as Interpretation."

26. Furman and Tufte, "'With Other Eyes,'" 141.

27. Furman and Tufte, "'With Other Eyes,'" 148. Mary Groom's and Carlotta Petrina's illustrations of Milton's Eve from the 1930s are among others that subsume but veer from the Catholic visual tradition (171).

28. *OED* table I.5.a., I.1.a.

29. Milton, *Paradise Lost* (1866).

30. The biographer Dan Malan notes that, among the more than ten thousand engravings and four thousand editions with Doré's illustrations, "to date there has not been a single French edition" of *Paradise Lost* with them (*Gustave Doré*, 79).

31. Illustrated editions of *Paradise Lost* moved away from distinct demarcation of visual and verbal art certainly by the time of the 1937 publication of Mary Groom's illustrations. Even the Groom illustrated edition, however, is less free in the shapes and placement of visual art than the 1883 illustrated *El Paraíso perdido*.

32. See Appendix B for the attribution of the translator of the Rosell edition.

33. Per David Robertson (email to the author, January 21, 2016), the plates included in the three issues of the Finnish translation of *Paradise Lost* are 1–2, 4–6, 8–9, 12, 14, 16, 18, 20–23, 27, 29–31, 36, 39, and 48. For discussion of this Finnish translation, see David Robertson, "Traces of the Birth of the State of Finland in Jylhä's Translation of *Paradise Lost*," in Duran, Issa, and Olson, *Milton in Translation*, 199–214.

34. Milton, *El Paraíso perdido*, trans. Escóiquiz, title page.

35. *OED* vignette 1a.

36. I extend my thanks to Jeffrey Chipps Smith for helping me decipher the signature and for his aid in trying to determine the identity of this still unidentified artist or engraver, absent on the standard electronic research tool, Blouinartinfo, and other standard material resources.

37. Milton, *El Paraíso perdido*, trans. Escóiquiz, 190.

38. A similarly cosmopolitan move is to be found with the dashing portrait of Milton, *Giovanni Milton*, engraved by the Dutch Gerard van der Gucht in an Italophone *Del Paradiso perduto*, held at the Scottish National Portrait Gallery.

39. Further work is to be done regarding the fact that the 1970s was an important period for Spain as it began a massive transformation at the end of Franco's dictatorship (r. 1936–1975).

40. Milton, *Paradis perdu*, trans. Messian. Special thanks to Joseph Wittreich for alerting me to the variant spelling of translator Messian's surname, Messiaen. Special thanks to the curators at the Dalí Museum in St. Petersburg, Florida, for making its

copy available to me. In *Dalí and His Books*, Oliveras, Fornes, and Dalí record "405" copies (68), while Field's *Official Catalog of the Graphic Works of Salvador Dalí* records "430 plus proofs" (97).

41. My readings of *Milton: El Paraíso perdido* are indebted to Starn, "The 2006 Josephine Waters Bennett Lecture."

42. Through the first decade of the twenty-first century, the only Anglophone critical work that I have found making even passing mention of Prieto is John Shawcross, "'Shedding Sweet Influence': The Legacy of John Milton's Works," in Duran, *A Concise Companion to Milton*, 28. The neglect of the Prieto illustrations cannot be attributed only to their being published originally in exclusive editions, since the Blake illustrations were also originally exclusive. By contrast, in "'Consider First,'" Wendy Furman notes the logic of the obscurity of Mary Groom's illustrations of *Paradise Lost* in an edition of only two hundred copies and given that she is a little known British wood engraver. Further, neglect differs from the negative reviews that Henry Fuseli received for his "Milton Gallery," exhibited "in London in 1799 and again in 1800" (Furman-Adams and Tufte, "The Choreography of Passion," 213).

43. Prieto's national fame in Spain continues into the twenty-first century, as demonstrated by the fact that many of his pieces are regularly displayed as part of the home collection of the Prado Museum in Madrid and by the existence of the Gregorio Prieto Foundation's museum in Valdepeñas.

44. The exhibition is documented in Prieto and Biblioteca Nacional, *Milton y Gregorio Prieto*.

45. Treadwell, "Blake, John Martin," 363.

46. William Blake's illustrations are reproduced and described in Milton, *Paradise Lost*, ed. Masson; Milton, *Paradise Lost*, ed. Hofer and Winterich; *Milton and Blake, Thirteen Watercolor Drawings*; British Library, "William Blake's Illustrations for *Paradise Lost*," https://www.bl.uk/collection-items/william-blakes-illustrations-for-paradise-lost-1808, accessed October 30, 2018. Special thanks to the late John Shawcross for helping me decipher the history of these illustrations.

47. Milton, *Paradise Lost*, ed. Hofer and Winterich, n.p.

48. Doré, *Doré's Illustrations*; Doré, *Ilustraciones*. While not advertised in the opening paratext, catalogue descriptions, or an index (it has none), the Spanish volume includes a twenty-four-page summary version of *Paradise Regained* with no illustrations, followed by seventy-six pages with thirty-eight Doré plates on recto pages illustrating Coleridge's *Rime of the Ancient Mariner*, a Spanish version of which is on verso pages. My base text is that of the Universidad Nacional Autónoma de México, consulted January 2017.

49. Furman-Adams and Tufte, "Illustrations," 160.

50. Jennett, preface, 7, 8, 9. My base text is copy No. 117 (6) at the Harry T. Ransom Center at the University of Texas at Austin, which I cite with gratitude.

51. For a distinct ecological perspective of the illustrations of *Paradise Lost* by Carlotta Petrina, see Furman-Adams, "The Fate of Place."

52. Prieto and Milton, *Milton: El Paraíso perdido*, n.p. Subsequent references to this work are without citation or notes given that the work lacks pagination.

53. For some strategies for forming valid interpretations, see a work of criticism nearly coeval with *Milton: El Paraíso perdido*, Hirsch, *Validity in Interpretation*.

54. Milton, *Milton's Paradise Lost, by Richard Bentley*, [ii].

55. The same dilemma occurs in the next paragraph, which refers to "Sketch 12, Two Profiles," rather than "Sketch 5, Adam's Upper Torso and Head" or "Sketch 9, Adam and Eve Reclining," as "the next illustration."

56. Prieto's illustrations for Prieto and Shakespeare, *Shakespeares Sonnets* and *The Sonnets of William Shakespeare* warrant investigation into another kind of overlap. It is worth mentioning that Aleixandre opens his preface to *Milton: El Paraíso perdido* by indicating Prieto's greater *simpatico* with Shakespeare.

57. Prieto, *Lorca y la Generación del 27*, 7 and front cover flap.

58. Prieto and Lorca, *Lorca en color*, 65, 66, 119, 144, 160, 162, 194.

59. The engraving is based on the portrait of Milton by William Faithorne, published in Milton's *History of Britain* (1670) and now at the National Portrait Gallery, London.

60. Richardson, *Gustave Doré*, 77. Two other illustrations in *Milton y Gregorio Prieto* are strikingly similar to illustrations in *Lorca en color* and are akin to the multiple treatments of similar visual scenes and tropes that other visual artists demonstrate, as in the case of "Fuseli's fascination with *Paradise Lost*" (Furman-Adams and Tufte, "The Choreography of Passion," 213).

61. Prieto and Lorca, *Lorca en color*, 115–21; Prieto, *Lorca y la Generación del 27*, 17–28. The primary difference is that the latter quotes larger sections of highlighted poems.

62. For the English translation by Christopher Maurer, see Federico García Lorca, "Adam," in *Selected Verse*, 345, 347. The Spanish original of "Adán" is here reproduced, with gratitude to the Heirs of Federico García Lorca:

> Árbol de sangre moja la mañana
> por donde gime la recién parida.
> Su voz deja cristales en la herida
> y un gráfico de hueso en la ventana.
> Mientras la luz que viene fija y gana
> blancas metas de fábula que olvida
> el tumulto de venas en la huida
> hacia el turbio frescor de la manzana.
> Adán sueña en la fiebre de la arcilla
> un niño que se acerca galopando
> por el doble latir de su mejilla.
> Pero otro Adán oscuro está soñando
> neutra luna de piedra sin semilla
> donde el niño de luz se irá *quemando*. (346, 348)

This poem's early publication history is endemic of the promiscuous circulation of the works of the Generación del 1927. As Maurer records, "*Adán / Adam*. Ms. Dated 'December 1, 1929. New York.' Published in *Héroe* (Madrid) in 1932, in *Poesía* (Buenos Aires) in 1933 (with the dedication 'For Pablo Neruda, surrounded by phantasms'), and again in the chapbook *Primeras canciones*, 1936" (385).

63. For the English translation by Maurer, see Federico García Lorca, "Two Norms," in *Selected Verse*, 347, 349. The Spanish original of "Dos Normas" is here reproduced, with gratitude to the Heirs of Federico García Lorca:

[Sketch of a moon]
Norma de ayer encontrada
sobre mi noche presente.
Resplandor adolescente
que se opone a la nevada.
No pueden darte posada
mis dos niñas de sigilo,
morenas de luna en vilo
con el corazón abierto;
pero mi amor busca el huerto
donde no muere tu estilo.
[Sketch of a sun]
Norma de seno y cadera
baja la rama tendida,
antigua y recién nacida
virtud de la primavera.
Ya mi desnudo quisiera
ser dalia de tu destino,
abeja, rumor o vino
de tu número y locura;
pero mi amor busca pura
locura de brisa y trino. (348, 350)

64. Future work on the deployment of *décimas* by Lorca here and Giner de los Ríos in his play *Milton*, as discussed in chapter 3, will no doubt prove fruitful.

65. Furman and Tufte note that, in the "spirit of innocent, sensuous joy," the artist Mary Groom "also has some visual fun with her text—sexy visual fun at that"—with Eve's breasts at the table scene of book 5 ("'Consider First,'" 170).

66. Prieto, *García Lorca as a Painter*, 16.
67. Prieto and Lorca, *Lorca en color*, 7.
68. Prieto and Lorca, *Lorca en color*, 127–50.
69. Richard Macksey, "Foreword," in Genette, *Paratexts*, xxi.
70. Genette, *Paratexts* 2, 3.
71. Macksey, "Foreword," xii.

Epilogue

1. Faye Halpern and Peter J. Rabinowitz, for example, note that "academic writing puts strictures on autobiographical revelation, strictures that have weakened in recent years but that still hold some sway," an observation discussed in the excellent essays in the "Theories and Methodologies: Reading over Time" section of the *PMLA* they have edited (631).

2. Gordon Campbell avers, "Unamuno was, of course, an admirer of Milton: his own copy of *Paradise Lost* was heavily annotated, and Unamuno's *Abel Sánchez* is on one level a contemporary version of *Paradise Lost*" (epilogue in Duran, Issa, and Olson, *Milton in Translation*, 494). For some of Unamuno's many allusions to Milton, see García Blanco, "Poetas Ingleses"; Cannon, "The Miltonic Rhythm."

3. Unamuno, *The Tragic Sense*, 260–96; Unamuno, *Del sentimiento trágico*, 221–47.

4. Unamuno, *The Tragic Sense*, 284. Flitch's English translation—mysteriously, alarmingly—omits translating "Juan Milton" into "John Milton" and instead uses only his surname (Unamuno, *Del sentimiento trágico*, 239); it also omits the original's direct mention of Cromwell: "Milton, the great fighter, the great Puritan disturber of spiritual peace, the singer of Satan." This translational divergence is worth noting because this English translation resides quite extensively in U.S. libraries and is the base text of the Project Gutenberg Etext, www.gutenberg.org/files/14636/14636-h/14636-h.htm.

5. Unamuno, *The Tragic Sense*, 284–85; Unamuno, *Del sentimiento trágico*, 239.

6. Unamuno, *The Tragic Sense*, 248–49.

7. Unamuno, *Del sentimiento trágico*, 251. See also Unamuno, *The Tragic Sense*, 302.

8. "Essay" II.n.8, *OED*. For the older meaning of "essay," see I.1.a "A trial, testing, proof; experiment."

9. Cervantes, *Don Quixote*, vol. 1, ed. Clemencín, 110. This is the process articulated by many careful readers, for example, Miguel/Mikhail Bakhtin as the "point of contact" ("The Discourse of the Novel," 272). The Chicana writer Sandra Cisneros deftly represents the cultural importance of *tocayo/a* through the name of the protagonist Esperanza [Hope] in her novella *The House on Mango Street* and discusses it in her memoir *A House of My Own*. Significations in the works of the Argentine Jorge Luis Borges and the Mexican Octavio Paz are also enhanced by the recognition of this linguistic and cultural element. My valuation accounts for my recognition of the intimacy of the use of first names as the organizing principle in the earlier editions of the Spanish Catholic Inquisition's *Index librorum prohibitorum* and of the import of the shift to using surnames as the organizing principle in the 1844 edition of the indexes, discussed in chapter 1.

10. For the domestication of Spanish verbal texts for early modern English audiences, see Russell, "English Seventeenth-Century Interpretations."

11. Kovács, "Milton Dictating to His Daughters."

12. Dryden, "Ovid," 154.

13. Manuel Tamayo y Baus's three-act *A New Drama* lists the main character as "Shakespeare" (*Un drama nuevo*, ed. Labandeira, 69). Shakespeare is an imposing, elder character in *A New Drama* and thus regularly addressed as simply "Shakespeare"

(72, 83, 100, 109, 115, 116, 120, 122, 123, 125, 132, 136, 144). But when his first name is used, it is "Guillermo" (77, 79, 91, 101, 102, 107, 120, 134). The first use of "Guillermo" inspires the endnote "Es la primera vez que Yorick tutea a Shakespeare llamándole por su nombre (William)" (This is the first time that [the character] Yorick uses the informal address with Shakespeare calling him by his [first] name [William]; 147). Popular on the nineteenth-century Spanish stage, the Spanish translation of *Shakespeare in Love: Comedy in One Act, Written in French*, lists him in the Personae as "Shakespeare" (Duval, *Shakespeare enamorado*, n.p.). Characters refer to him as "Shakespeare" (4, 8, 10, 11, 13, 19, 20) and "Guillermo" (8).

14. Greer, "Thine and Mine," 223, 219.

15. Fuchs, *Mimesis and Empire*, 3, 4.

16. I am here echoing the title of Kevin Pask's astute study, *The Emergence of the English Author*, which marks Milton as diverging from a specifically Virgilian model.

17. Roy Flannagan, "'The World All before [Us]': More than Three Hundred Years of Criticism," in Duran, *A Concise Companion*, 44.

18. Strunk and White, *The Elements of Style*, 70.

19. Hale, *Milton as Multilingual*.

20. *Sagrada Biblia*, title page recto and verso.

21. For a discussion of many affective aspects of and in literature, see "Special Topic: Emotions," *PMLA* 130, no. 5 (2015).

22. I also hypothesized about John de Lancey Ferguson's assumption that the 1883 Escóiquiz illustrated edition was that translation's first publication, as mentioned in the introduction. Ferguson's *American Literature in Spain* is based on his 1916 dissertation at Columbia University: I was unable to determine which edition or editions Columbia possessed in the first decades of the twentieth century, and of course Ferguson might have used a non-library copy. His comment was made in passing and thus he does not record which copies he had available to him, and the Columbia University Library catalogue did not list any material copies of *El Paraíso perdido* in January 2014 and March 2016.

23. Unamuno, *The Tragic Sense*, 302–3; Unamuno, *Del sentimiento trágico*, 252. Dante, "Paradiso 33," *Digital Dante*, digitaldante.columbia.edu/dante/divine-comedy/paradiso/paradiso-33/, accessed November 8, 2018.

24. The first and larger original resides in the New York Public Library. I thank Miklós Petí for confirming the authenticity of the painting hanging in the National Hungarian Gallery per my email request in March 2016.

25. Angelica Duran, "*Paradise Lost* in Spanish Translation and as World Literature," in Duran, Issa, and Olson, *Milton in Translation*, 265–78.

26. Milton's *Poems* (1645) designates him "Mr. John Milton," as do his *Areopagitica; A Speech of Mr. John Milton* (1644) and *Poems, &c. . . . Mr. John Milton* (1673).

Appendix B

1. Further study is needed to determine the translator of this *Paraíso perdido*, which circulates under Cayetano Rosell's name as translator. Enrique Leopoldo de

Verneuill is attributed as the translator of the Spanish *Paradise Regained* that is published under the same cover as the Rosell Spanish *Paradise Lost*, and some catalogues ascribe the translation of *Paradise Lost* also to Verneuill.

Appendix C

1. I retain the Roman numerals for books, all digits in number spans, and space between the numerals and digits used in these editions in this appendix, to reflect their visual experience, but use contemporary citation formats throughout the rest of the book.

2. The base text is the Newberry Library's folio PR3560 1866, 42.5 cm x 30 cm. It does not have a "List of Illustrations." The opening paratextual plate has "44" at the left bottom of the illustration. Corresponding text is printed centered on the onion-skin page that separates the illustrations' pages from the verbal text's pages. I have included plate numbers only when out of order; other illustrations have the same plate numbers as in the leftmost column of the table. I include data on the mislabeling of some illustrations, inconsistent with their actual position in the edition and with the order of the corresponding cited text. The first page numbers of each book are as follows: book I, p. 1; book 2, p. 27; book 3, p. 60; book 4, p. 83; book 5, p. 115; book 6, p. 143; book 7, p. 171; book 8, p. 191; book 9, p. 211; book 10, p. 247; book 11, p. 247; book 12, p. 309.

3. The base texts are the Harry T. Ransom Center's PR 3560 A1 1885 and HathiTrust copy. Below the bottom left of the illustrations are page numbers rather than plate numbers, except for an error on the last plate, which has "p. 50" rather than "p. 322"; corresponding text is printed centered below the illustration.

4. The base text is the Purdue Archives & Special Collections-Heritage Press 821 M64p8. No plate or page numbers are on the illustration pages. The first page numbers of each book are as follows: book 1, p. 1; book 2, p. 25; book 3, p. 57; book 4, p. 80; book 5, p. 111; book 6, p. 138; book 7, p. 165; book 8, p. 184; book 9, p. 204; book 10, p. 240; book 11, p. 273; book 12, p. 300.

5. The base text is the University of Texas at Austin Perry-Casteñada Library's 821 M642 PTR. The first page numbers of each book are as follows: book 1, p. 5; book 2, p. 29; book 3, p. 57; book 4, p. 77; book 5, p. 105; book 6, p. 130; book 7, p. 153; book 8, p. 170; book 9, p. 187; book 10, p. 220; book 11, p. 251; book 12, p. 278.

6. The base text is the Purdue University Libraries' 821 M64pS 1883. The first page numbers of each book are as follows: book 1, p. 15; book 2, p. 53; book 3, p. 103; book 4, p. 139; book 5, p. 189; book 6, p. 227; book 7, p. 269; book 8, p. 299; book 9, p. 327; book 10, p. 379; book 11, p. 419; book 12, p. 457.

Bibliography

Addison, Joseph. *Criticisms on* Paradise Lost. Edited by Albert Cook. Boston: Ginn, 1892.
Anglen, K. P. *The New England Milton: Literary Reception and Cultural Authority in the Early Republic*. University Park: Pennsylvania State University Press, 1993.
Armitage, W. H. "Some New Letters of James Russell Lowell." *Notes and Queries* 255 (1950): 207–8.
Ariosto, Lodovico. *Orlando Furioso*. Edited by Pietro Micheli. Milan: F. Vallardi, [1922].
Auladell, Pablo. *El Paraíso perdido*. Madrid: Sexto Piso, 2015.
Bakhtin, M. M. "The Discourse of the Novel." In *Four Essays by M. M. Bakhtin*, edited by Michael Holquist. Austin: University of Texas Press, 1981.
Barton, Carol. "'Ill Fare the Hands That Heaved the Stones': John Milton, a Preliminary Thanatography." *Milton Studies* 43 (2004): 198–260.
Benítez, Rubén. *Presencia de Milton en la literatura española* [Milton's Presence in Spanish Literature], *1750–1850*. Palencia: Cálamo, 2010.
Berman, Antoine. *Towards a Translation Criticism: John Donne*. Translated by Françoise Massardier-Kenney. Kent, OH: Kent State University Press, 2009.
Bermann, Sandra. "Teaching in—and about—Translation." In *Profession 2010*, edited by Rosemary Feal. New York: Modern Language Association of America, 2010.
Blake, William. *The Marriage of Heaven and Hell*. Oxford: Bodleian Library, 2011.
Blanchot, Maurice. *The Work of Fire*. Translated by Charlotte Mandell. Stanford, CA: Stanford University Press, 1995.
Blythe, John. "Milton, Cromwell, and Napolean in Chateaubriand and Hugo." In *To Repair the Ruins*, edited by Mary Fenton and Louis Schwartz. Pittsburgh, PA: Duquesne University Press, 2012.
Boorsch, Suzanne. "The 1688 *Paradise Lost* and Dr. Aldrich." *Metropolitan Museum Journal* 6 (1972): 133–50.
Braga, Francisco Joaquim da Costa. *Milton: Cómedia em um acto*. Lisbon[?]: Camaroteiro do Theatro das Variedades Dramáticas, 1867.
Braider, Christopher. "Of Monuments and Documents: Comparative Literature and the Visual Arts in Early Modern Studies, or the Art of Historical Tact." In *Compar-*

ative Literature in an Age of Globalization, edited by Haun Saussy. Baltimore: Johns Hopkins University Press, 2006.

Brinkley, Florence. "Milton in French Literature of the Nineteenth Century." *University of Toronto Quarterly* 27 (1957–58): 243–55.

Brown, E. E. *The Life of James Russell Lowell*. Boston: D. Lothrop, [1887].

Cadalso y Vázquez, José de. *Los eruditos a la violeta, ó, curso completo de todas las ciencias dividido en siete lecciones para los siete dias della semana, con el Suplemento de este* [The Sciolists, or, a Complete Course of All Knowledge Divided into Seven Lessons for the Seven Days of the Week, with a Supplement for It]. 1772. Madrid: Isidoro de Hernandez Pacheco, 1781.

Cadalso y Vázquez, José de. *Suplemento al papel intitulado los eruditos a la violeta* [Supplement for the Paper Titled the Sciolists]. Madrid: Antonio de Sancha, 1772.

Calderón de la Barca, Pedro. *"La vida es un sueño" and "El alcalde de Zalamea"* [Life is a Dream and The Mayor of Zalamea]. Introduction by Sturgis E. Leavitt. New York: Dell, 1964.

Campbell, Gordon. "Milton and the Languages of the Renaissance." *SEDERI* 4 (1993): 11–21.

Campbell, Gordon. "Milton in Madras." *Milton Quarterly* 31, no. 2 (1997): 61–63.

Campbell, Gordon, and Thomas N. Corns. *John Milton: Life, Work, and Thought*. Oxford: Oxford University Press, 2008.

Cañizares-Esguerra, Jorge. *Puritan Conquistadores: Iberianizing the Atlantic, 1550–1700*. Stanford, CA: Stanford University Press, 2006.

Cannon, Calvin. "The Miltonic Rhythm of Unamuno's 'El Cristo de Velázquez.'" *Hispania* 44, no. 1 (1961): 95–98.

Cánovas del Castillo, Antonio. *Autores dramáticos contemporáneos y joyas del teatro española del siglo XIX* [Contemporary Dramatic Authors and Jewels of the Nineteenth-Century Spanish Theater]. Madrid: Fortanet, 1882.

Carr, Raymond. *Spain, 1808–1939*. Oxford: Clarendon, 1966.

Castillo y Soriana, José del. *Núñez de Arce: Apuntes para su biografía* [Notes for His Biography]. 2nd edition. Madrid: Hijos de M. G. Hernández, 1907.

Cavallo, Guglielmo, and Roger Chartier. Introduction to *A History of Reading in the West*, edited by Guglielmo Cavallo and Roger Chartier. Translated by Lydia G. Cochrane. Revised edition. Amherst: University of Massachusetts Press, 2003.

Cervantes Saavedra, Miguel de. *Don Quixote*. Translated by John Phillips. London: Thomas Hodgkin, 1687.

Cervantes Saavedra, Miguel de. *Don Quixote*. Vol. 1. Edited by Diego Clemencín. Madrid: La Viuda de Hernando, 1847.

Cervantes Saavedra, Miguel de. *Don Quixote*. Edited by Diana de Armas Wilson. Translated by Burton Raffel. New York: Norton, 1995.

Cervantes Saavedra, Miguel de. *El ingenioso hidalgo Don Quixote de la Mancha por Miguel de Cervantes Saavedra*. 4 vols. Edited by Real Academia Española. Madrid: Don Joaquin Ibarra Impresor de Céamara de S.M. y de la Real Academia, 1780.

The Character of the Rump. London, 1660.

Chartier, Roger. *El mundo como representación: Estudios sobre historia cultural* [The World as Representation: Studies on Cultural History]. Barcelona: Gedisa, 1992.
Chateaubriand. *Ensayo sobre la literatura inglesa, traducida por* [Essay on English Literature, translated by] *D. Francisco Madina-Veytia*. Madrid: Gaspar y Roig, 1857.
Cisneros, Sandra. *A House of My Own*. New York: Knopf, 2015.
Cisneros, Sandra. *The House on Mango Street*. Houston, TX: Arte Publico Press, 1984.
Colley, Linda. *Britons: Forging the Nation, 1707–1837*. Bath: Bath Press, 1992.
Collins-Baker, C. H. "Some Illustrations of Milton's *Paradise Lost* (1688–1850)." *Library* 5, no. 1 (1948): 1–21.
Conklin, George Newton. *Biblical Criticism and Heresy in Milton*. New York: King's Crown Press, Columbia University, 1949.
Consuelo de Inquisición (Spain). *Indice general de los libros prohibidos y mandados expurgar* [General Index of Books Prohibited and Ordered to Be Expurgated]. Madrid: Jose Felix Palacios, 1844.
Corns, Thomas N. "Milton and the Limitations of Englishness." In *Early Modern Nationalism and Milton's England*, edited by David Loewenstein and Paul Stevens. Toronto: University of Toronto Press, 2008.
Crowe, Martha J. "Cataloging Icelandic Materials." *Cataloging & Classification Quarterly* 17, nos. 1–2 (1993): 29–46.
Cruz, Anne J. *Material and Symbolic Circulation between Spain and England, 1554–1604*. Aldershot: Ashgate, 2008.
Damrosch, David. *What Is World Literature?* Princeton, NJ: Princeton University Press, 2003.
Darbishire, Helen, ed. *The Early Lives of Milton*. London: Constable, 1932.
Defourneaux, Marcelin. *Inquisición y censura de los libros en España del siglo XVIII* [Inquisition and Censorship of Books in Eighteenth-Century Spain]. Madrid: Taurus, 1973.
DeGuzmán, María. *Spain's Long Shadow: The Black Legend, Off-Whiteness, and Anglo-American Empire*. Minneapolis: University of Minnesota Press, 2005.
De Man, Paul. *Blindness and Insight: Essays in the Rhetoric of Contemporary Criticism*. 2nd edition. Minneapolis: University of Minnesota Press, 2005.
Dimock, Wai Chee. "Editor's Column: Infrastructure Art." In "Literature of the World," special issue, *PMLA* 132, no. 1 (2017): 9–15.
Dobranski, Stephen B. *Milton, Authorship, and the Book Trade*. Cambridge, UK: Cambridge University Press, 1999.
Dobson, Michael, and Stanley Wells, eds. *The Oxford Companion to Shakespeare*. Oxford: Oxford University Press, 2001.
Doré, Gustave. *Doré's Illustrations for "Paradise Lost."* 1993. New York: Dover, 2000.
Doré, Gustavo. *Ilustraciones: El Paraíso perdido*. Madrid: A. L. Mateos, 1992.
Dowling, Paul M. "Milton's Use (or Abuse) of History in *Areopagitica*." *Cithara* 23, no. 1 (1983): 28–37.
Dryden, John. "Ovid and the Art of Translation: Preface to the 'Translation from Ovid's Epistles' (1680)." In *Essays and Belles Lettres: Dryden's Dramatic Poesy and*

Other Essays. Introduction by William Henry Hudson. 1912. New York: E. P. Dutton, 1921.

Duran, Angelica, ed. *A Concise Companion to Milton.* Revised edition. Malden, MA: Wiley-Blackwell, 2010.

Duran, Angelica. "*El Paraíso Perdido* and Milton's Reception in Spain." In "Milton in Europe," edited by Joseph Shub, special issue, *European Legacy* 17, no. 3 (2012): 333–48.

Duran, Angelica. "English Bible Translators on the Spanish Inquisition's Index of Prohibited Books." In *The King James Bible across Borders and Centuries,* edited by Angelica Duran. Pittsburgh, PA: Duquesne University Press, 2014.

Duran, Angelica. "John Milton and Disability Studies in Literature Courses." *Journal of Literary & Cultural Disability Studies* 6, no. 3 (2012): 327–39.

Duran, Angelica. "Mexican Miltons." In *Making Milton,* edited by John Garrison, Marissa Nicosia, and Emma Depledge. Oxford: Oxford University Press, 2020.

Duran, Angelica. "Milton among Hispanics: Jorge Luis Borges and Milton's 'Condemnation of Rhyme.'" *Prose Studies* 28, no. 2 (2006): 234–44.

Duran, Angelica. "Not *Either/Or* but Rather *Both/And*: Both Material *and* Electronic Archival Research in *Both* English *and* Comparative Literature Graduate Courses." In *Teaching Early Modern Literature from the Archives,* edited by Heidi Brayman Hackel and Ian Frederick Moulton. New York: MLA Press, 2015.

Duran, Angelica, Islam Issa, and Jonathan R. Olson, eds. *Milton in Translation.* Oxford: Oxford University Press, 2017.

Duval, Alexandre. *Shakespeare enamorado: Comedia en un acto* [Shakespeare in Love: Comedy in One Act]. Translated by Ventura de la Vega. 1831. Madrid: Imprenta de Repullés, 1842.

Echevarría, Francisco Pérez, and Arturo Gil de Santivañes. *El Paraíso de Milton, drama en tres actos y en verso* [Milton's Paradise, A Drama in Three Acts and in Verse]. Madrid: José Rodríguez, 1878.

Edmond, Mary. *Rare Sir William Davenant: Poet Laureate, Playwright, Civil War General, Restoration Theatre Manager.* New York: St. Martin's Press, 1987.

Escóiquiz, Juan. *México conquistada. Poema heroyco* [The Conquest of Mexico. Heroic Poem]. 3 vols. Madrid: Imprenta Real, 1798.

Fallon, Robert. *Milton in Government.* University Park: Pennsylvania State University Press, 1993.

Fallon, Stephen M. *Milton's Peculiar Grace: Self-Representation and Authority.* Ithaca, NY: Cornell University Press, 2007.

Felperin, Howard. *Shakespearean Representation: Mimesis and Modernity in Elizabethan Tragedy.* Princeton, NJ: Princeton University Press, 1977.

Ferguson, John de Lancey. *American Literature in Spain.* New York: Columbia University Press, 1916.

Field, Albert, ed. *The Official Catalog of the Graphic Works of Salvador Dalí.* Astoria, NY: Salvador Dalí Archives, 1996.

Fletcher, Harris Francis. *The Intellectual Development of John Milton.* 2 vols. Urbana: University of Illinois Press, 1956–.

Flood, John. "Marian Controversies and Milton's Virgin Mary." In *Milton and Catholicism*, edited by Ronald Corthell and Thomas N. Corns. Notre Dame, IN: University of Notre Dame Press, 2017.
Flynn, Gerald. *Manuel Tamayo y Baús*. New York: Twayne, 1973.
Forsyth, Neil. *John Milton: A Biography*. Oxford: Lion Hudson, 2008.
Forsyth, Neil. "Sublime Conversations." *Times Literary Supplement* (December 2008): 14–18.
Flotats, Rosa. "Translating Milton into Catalan." *Milton Quarterly* 36, no. 2 (2002): 106–22.
French, J. M. *Life Records of John Milton*. 5 vols. New Brunswick, NJ: Rutgers University Press, 1949–58.
Friederich, Werner. *Dante's Fame Abroad, 1350–1850: The Influence of Dante Alighieri on the Poets and Scholars of Spain, France, England, Germany, Switzerland, and the United States*. Chapel Hill: University of North Carolina Press, 1950.
Friedman, Thomas L. *The World Is Flat: A Brief History of the Twenty-first Century*. New York: Picador, 2007.
Fuchs, Barbara. *Mimesis and Empire: The New World, Islam, and European Identities*. Cambridge, UK: Cambridge University Press, 2001.
Fuchs, Barbara. *The Poetics of Piracy: Emulating Spain in English Literature*. Philadelphia: University of Pennsylvania Press, 2013.
Furman, Wendy. "'Consider First, That Great / Or Bright Infers Not Excellence': Mapping the Feminine in Mary Groom's Cosmos." *Milton Studies* 28 (1992): 121–62.
Furman, Wendy, and Virginia Tufte. "'With Other Eyes': Legacy and Innovation in Four Artists' Re-visions of the Dinner Party in *Paradise Lost*." *Milton Studies* 35 (1997): 121–62.
Furman-Adams, Wendy. "The Fate of Place in *Paradise Lost*: Three Artists Reading Milton." In *To Repair the Ruins: Reading Milton*, edited by Mary C. Fenton and Louis Schwartz. Pittsburgh, PA: Duquesne University Press, 2012.
Furman-Adams, Wendy, and Virginia James Tufte. "The Choreography of Passion: Henry Fuseli's Milton Gallery, 1799/1988." In *Reassembling Truth: Twenty-First Century Milton*, edited by Charles W. Durham and Kristin A. Pruitt. Selinsgrove, PA: Susquehanna University Press, 2002.
Furman-Adams, Wendy, and Virginia Tufte. "Illustrations." In *The Milton Encyclopedia*, edited by Thomas C. Corns. New Haven, CT: Yale University Press, 2012.
García Blanco, Manuel. "Poetas Ingleses en la obra de Unamuno: II" [English Poets in the Works of Unamuno: II]. *Bulletin of Hispanic Studies* 36, no. 3 (1959): 146–65.
Gardner, Helen Louise. "Milton's First Illustrator." In *Essays and Studies 1956 Jubilee Volume*. London: John Murray, 1956.
Gardner-Flint, Judith. "The King's Book: The Puzzle of *Eikon Basilike*." *University of Rochester Library Bulletin* 34 (1981). https://rbscp.lib.rochester.edu/3561.
Gayangos de Riaño, Emilia. "Mr. Lowell and His Spanish Friends." *Century Magazine* 60 (1900): 292–93.
Genette, Gérard, ed. *Paratexts: Thresholds of Interpretation*. Translated by Jane E. Lewis. Cambridge, UK: Cambridge University Press, 1997.

Genette, Gérard, and Marie Maclean. "Introduction to the Paratext." *New Literary History* 22, no. 2 (1991): 261–72.

Gies, David T. *The Theatre in Nineteenth-Century Spain*. Cambridge, UK: Cambridge University Press, 1994.

Gigante, Denise. "Milton's Aesthetics of Eating." *Diacritics* 30, no. 2 (2000): 88–112.

Giner de los Ríos, Hermenegildo. *Historia abreviada de la literatura nacional y extranjera* [Abbreviated History of National and Foreign Literature]. Madrid: V. Suárez, 1902.

Giner de los Ríos, Hermenegildo. *Manual de literatura nacional y estranjera, antigua y moderna* [Manual of Literature, National and Foreign, Ancient and Modern]. 3 vols. Madrid: Victoriano Suárez, 1899.

Giner de los Ríos, Hermengildo. *Milton: Cuadro dramático en un acto y en verso* [A Dramatic Scene in One Act and in Verse]. Madrid: Aurelio J. Alaria, 1879.

Giner de los Ríos, Hermenegildo. *Milton: A Dramatic Scene in One Act and in Verse*. Translated by Angelica Duran and M. Cadwallader with Tim Bolton. *Milton Quarterly* 51, no. 4 (2017): 222–93.

Giner de los Ríos, Hermenegildo. *Teoría de la literatura y de las artes* [Theory of Literature and the Arts]. Barcelona: Sucesores de Manuel Soler, 1905.

Godwin, William. *Lives of Edward and John Philips, Nephews and Pupils of Milton*. London: Longman, Hurst, Rees, Orme, and Brown, 1815.

González de Amezúa, Agustín. *Fases y caracteres de la influencia del Dante en España* [Phases and Characteristics of Dante's Influence in Spain]. Madrid: Editorial Reus, 1922.

González Fernández de Sevilla, José Manuel. *Shakespeare en España: Crítica, traducciones y representaciones* [Shakespeare in Spain: Criticism, Translations and Representations]. Alicante: Universidad de Alicante, 1993.

González Herrán, José Manuel. "*Un Drama Nuevo* [A New Drama] en San Petersburgo, en 1885." *Romance Quarterly* 38, no. 1 (2014): 75–83.

González Valdés, Pedro, and Pedro de Novo y Colson. *Autores dramáticos contemporáneos y joyas del teatro español del siglo XIX* [Contemporary Dramatic Authors and Jewels of Nineteenth-Century Spanish Theater]. 2 vols. Madrid: Fortantet, 1881–82.

Gray, Erik. *Milton and the Victorians*. Ithaca, NY: Cornell University Press, 2009.

Greene, Roland. *Unrequited Conquests, Love and Empire in the Colonial Americas*. Chicago: University of Chicago Press, 1999.

Greenslet, Ferris. *James Russell Lowell: His Life and Work*. Boston: Houghton Mifflin, 1905.

Greer, Margaret R. "Thine and Mine: The Spanish 'Golden Age' and Early Modern Studies." *PMLA* 126, no. 1 (2011): 217–24.

Griffin, Eric J. *English Renaissance Drama and the Specter of Spain: Ethnopoetics and Empire*. Philadelphia: University of Pennsylvania Press, 2009.

Hadfield, Andrew. "Milton and Catholicism." In *Milton and Toleration*, edited by Sharon Achinstein and Elizabeth Sauer. Oxford: Oxford University Press, 2007.

Hale, John. *Milton as Multilingual: The Impact of Multilingualism on Style*. Cambridge, UK: Cambridge University Press, 1997.

Hale, John. "Milton's Greek Epigram." *Milton Quarterly* 16, no. 1 (1982): 8–9.
Hale, John. *Milton's Languages: The Impact of Multilingualism on Style.* Cambridge, UK: Cambridge University Press, 1997.
Halpern, Faye, and Peter J. Rabinowitz. "Introduction to 'Reading over Time.'" *PMLA* 133, no. 3 (2018): 631–32.
Harkness, Bruce. "The Precedence of the 1676 Editions of Milton's *Literae Pseudo-Senatus Anglicani.*" *Studies in Bibliography* 7 (1955): 181–84.
Harris, Jonathan. *Globalization and Contemporary Art.* Malden, MA: Wiley-Blackwell, 2010.
Hart, James Moran. "James Russell Lowell." *PMLA* 7, no. 2 (1892): 25–81.
Hartwell, Kathleen Ellen. *Lactantius and Milton.* Cambridge, MA: Harvard University Press, 1929.
Harvard University. "Official: From the Record of the Corporation." *Harvard University Bulletin* 4, no. 4 (1886): 202–5.
Hasting, Walter Scott. *The Drama of Honoré de Balzac.* Baltimore, MD: George Banta, 1917.
Helgerson, Richard. *Forms of Nationhood: The Elizabethan Writings of England.* Chicago: University of Chicago Press, 1992.
Hirsch, E. D. *Validity in Interpretation.* New Haven, CT: Yale University Press, 1967.
Hobson, Theo. *Milton's Vision: The Birth of Christian Liberty.* New York: Continuum, 2008.
Hoenselaars, A. J. *Images of Englishmen and Foreigners in the Drama of Shakespeare and His Contemporaries: A Study of Stage Characters and National Identity in English Renaissance Drama.* Madison, NJ: Fairleigh Dickinson University Press, 1992.
Holmes, James S. *Translated! Papers on Literature Translation and Translation Studies.* Amsterdam: Rodopi, 1988.
Horsfall, Nicholas. "The Origins of the Illustrated Book." *Aegyptus* 63, nos. 1–2 (1983): 199–216.
Hugo, Victor. *Oliver Cromwell.* Translated by I. G. Burnham. Philadelphia: Rittenhouse Press, 1896.
Huntley, Frank J. "A Justification of Milton's 'Paradise of Fools' (P.L. III, 431–99)." *English Literary History* 21, no. 2 (1954): 107–13.
Index Librorum prohibitorum, ac expurgandorum novissimus. Pro universis Hispaniarum regnis serenissimi Ferdinand VI. Regis Catholici, Hac Ulimma edition. Madrid: Calcographia Emmanuelis Fernandez, 1747.
Index librorum prohibitorum Innoc XI.P.M. Prague: Josephum Shilhart, 1726.
Index librorum prohibitorum justa exemplar romanum. Mechlinæ [Belgium]: H. Dessain, 1878.
Index librorum prohibitorum Leonis XIII sum. Pont. Auctoritate. Rome: Typis Vaticanis, 1904.
Institución Libre de Enseñanza. "James Russell Lowell." *Boletín* 15, no. 349 (August 31, 1891): 241–44.
Issa, Islam. "Fragmentation, Censorship and an Islamic Journal: A History of the Translation of Milton into Arabic." *Milton Quarterly* 46, no. 4 (2012): 219–32.
Jastrow, Joseph. "The Mind's Eye." *Popular Science Monthly* 54 (1899): 299–312.

Jennett, Sean. Preface to William Shakespeare, *The Sonnets of William Shakespeare with Twenty-Eight Drawings by Gregorio Prieto*. Edited by Seán Jennett. Illustrated by Gregorio Prieto. London: Grey Walls Press, 1948.

Johnson, Samuel. "Life of Milton." In *Lives of the English Poets*. 3 vols. Edited by George B. Hill. Oxford: Clarendon, 1905.

Kamen, Henry. *The Spanish Inquisition: An Historical Evaluation*. London: Weidenfeld & Nicolson, 1997.

Keitt, Andrew. *Inventing the Sacred: Imposture, Inquisition, and the Boundaries of the Supernatural in Golden Age Spain*. Boston: Brill, 2005.

Kelley, Maurice. "First Editions of Milton's 'Literae.'" *Times Literary Supplement*, no. 3035 (April 29, 1960): 273.

Kidd, Colin. *British Identities before Nationalism: Ethnicity and Nationhood in the Atlantic World, 1600–1800*. Cambridge, UK: Cambridge University Press, 1999.

King, John N. "Milton's Paradise of Fools: Ecclesiastical Satire in *Paradise Lost*." In *Catholicism and Anti-Catholicism in Early Modern English Texts*, edited by Arthur F. Marotti. London: Macmillan, 1999.

King, John N. "Milton's Transubstantiation." *Milton Studies* 36 (1998): 41–58.

Klibbe, Lawrence H. "James Russell Lowell's Residence in Spain." *Hispania* 41, no. 2 (May 1958): 190–94.

Kovács, Anna Zsófia. "Milton Dictating to His Daughters: Varieties on a Theme from Füssli to Munkácsy." In *Milton through the Centuries*, edited by Gábor Ittzés and Miklós Péti. Budapest: Károli Gáspár University, 2012.

Lafarga, Francisco. "El siglo XVIII, de la Ilustración al Romanticismo" [The Eighteenth Century, from the Enlightenment to Romanticism]. In *Historia de la traducción en España* [History of Translation in Spain], edited by Francisco Lafarga and Luis Pegenaute. Salamanca: Editorial Ambos Mundos, 2004.

Lafarga, Francisco, and Luis Pegenaute. *La Historia de la traducción en España* [The History of Translation in Spain]. Salamanca: Editorial Ambos Mundos, 2004.

Lawes, Henry, and John Milton. *A Maske Presented at Ludlow Castle*. London: Humphrey Robinson, 1637.

Lea, Henry. *A History of the Inquisition of Spain*. 2 vols. New York: Macmillan, 1906–7.

Lee, Sidney, ed. *Dictionary of National Biography*. Vol. 37. New York: Macmillan, 1894.

Legrand, Pierre. "Issues of Translatability of Law." In *Nations, Language, and the Ethics of Translation*, edited by Sandra Bermann and Michael Wood. Princeton, NJ: Princeton University Press, 2005.

Leonard, John. *Faithful Labourers: A Reception History of* Paradise Lost, *1667–1970*. 2 vols. Oxford: Oxford University Press, 2012.

Leonard, John. *The Value of Milton*. Cambridge, UK: Cambridge University Press, 2016.

Lessing, Gotthold Ephraim. *Laocoön: An Essay on the Limits of Painting and Poetry*. Translated by Edward Allen McCormick. Baltimore, MD: Johns Hopkins University Press, 1984.

Lewalski, Barbara. *The Life of John Milton: A Critical Biography*. Malden, MA: Blackwell, 2000.

Lieb, Michael. *Theological Milton: Deity, Discourse and Heresy in the Miltonic Canon.* Pittsburgh, PA: Duquesne University Press, 2006.

Loewenstein, David, and Paul Stevens, eds. *Early Modern Nationalism and Milton's England.* Toronto: University of Toronto Press, 2008.

Lope de Vega, Félix. *Arte nuevo de hacer comedias en este tiempo* [The New Art of Making Dramas at This Time (1609)]. Madrid: Viuda de A. Martin, 1621.

López Ruiz, José. *Historia del Teatro Apolo y de La Verbena de la Paloma* [History of the Apollo Theater and the Fair of the Dove]. Madrid: Editorial El Avapies, 1994.

Lorca, Federico García. *Selected Verse: Revised Bilingual Edition.* Edited by Christopher Maurer. Translated by Catherine Brown, Cola Franzen, Angela, Jaffray, Galway Kinnell, Will Kirkland, Christopher Maurer, Jerome Rothenberg, Greg Simon, Alan S. Trueblood, and Steven F. White. New York: Farrar, Straus and Giroux, 2004.

Lowell, James Russell. *A Fable for Critics.* Boston: Ticknor and Fields, 1864.

Lowell, James Russell. *Impressions of Spain.* London: G. P. Putnam's Sons, 1900.

Lowell, James Russell. *Latest Literary Essays and Addresses of James Russell Lowell.* London: Macmillan, 1891.

Lowell, James Russell. *More New Letters of James Russell Lowell.* Edited by Louse J. Budd. Durham, NC: Duke University Library, 1953.

Lowell, James Russell. *New Letters of James Russell Lowell.* Edited by M. A. De Wolfe Howe. New York: Harper, 1932.

Lowell, James Russell. *The Works of James Russell Lowell.* 16 vols. Boston: Houghton, Mifflin, 1892.

Lynch, Kathleen M. *Jacob Tonson: Kit-Cat Publisher.* Knoxville: University of Tennessee Press, 1971.

Mabbett, T. O. "Item 58." *Explicator* 8 (1950): 59.

MacLennan, Kerry. "John Milton's Contract for *Paradise Lost*: A Commercial Reading." *Milton Quarterly* 44, no. 4 (2010): 221–30.

Malan, Dan. *Gustave Doré, Adrift on Dreams of Splendor: A Comprehensive Biography and Bibliography.* St. Louis, MO: Malan Classical Enterprises, 1995.

Maltby, William S. *The Black Legend in England: The Development of Anti-Spanish Sentiment, 1558–1660.* Durham, NC: Duke University Press, 1971.

Mancing, Howard. *Don Quixote: A Reference Guide.* Westport, CT: Greenwood Press, 2006.

Marcus, Leah. "The Earl of Bridgewater's Legal Life: Notes toward a Political Reading of *Comus*." *Milton Quarterly* 21, no. 4 (1987): 13–23.

Marcus, Leah. "Justice for Margery Evans: A 'Local' Reading of *Comus*." In *Milton and the Idea of Woman*, edited by Julia M. Walker. Urbana: University of Illinois Press, 1988.

Martindale, Charles. *John Milton and the Transformation of the Ancient Epic.* Totowa, NJ: Barnes & Noble, 1986.

Martínez Arancón, Ana, ed. *Marcial—Quevedo.* Madrid: Editorial Nacional, 1975.

Martínez y Güertero, Luis Alfonso Roman [Larmig]. "Querellas del vate ciego" [The

Blind Poet's Complaints]. In *Album poético español: con composiciones inéditas de los señores* [Spanish Anthology of Poetry: With Unedited Compositions by Mssrs.] *Marqués de Molins, Hartzenbusch, Campoamor, Palacio, Calcano, Arnao, Grilo, Aguilera, Nuñez de Arce, Echevarría, Larmig, Alarcon, Trueba, Hurtado y Duque de Rivas.* Madrid: A. De Cárlos, 1874.

Martz, Louis. *Poet of Exile: A Study of Milton's Poetry.* New Haven, CT: Yale University Press, 1980.

Masson, David. *The Life of Milton.* New York: Peter Smith, 1896.

Mathews, M. M. *A Survey of English Dictionaries.* Oxford: Oxford University Press, 1933.

McCarthy, Eugene B. "Defoe, Milton, and Heresy." *Milton Quarterly* 3, no. 4 (1969): 71–73.

McDermott, James. *England and the Spanish Armada: The Necessary Quarrel.* New Haven, CT: Yale University Press, 2005.

McDowell, Nicholas. *The English Radical Imagination: Culture, Religion, and Revolution, 1630–1660.* Oxford: Clarendon, 2004.

McGlinchee, Clare. *James Russell Lowell.* New York: Twayne, 1967.

Miller, Leo. "The Italian Imprimaturs in Milton's 'Areopagitica.'" *Papers of the Bibliographical Society of America* 65, no. 4 (1971): 345–55.

Milton, John. *Areopagitica.* Translated by José Carner. Mexico City: Fondo de Cultura Económica, 1941.

Milton, John. *Areopagitica; A Speech of Mr. John Milton.* London, 1644.

Milton, John. *The Complete Poems.* Edited by John Leonard. New York: Penguin, 1998.

Milton, John. *Complete Poems and Major Prose.* Edited by Merritt Y. Hughes. New York: Odyssey Press, 1957.

Milton, John. *The Complete Poetry and Essential Prose of John Milton.* Edited by William Kerrigan, John Rumrich, and Stephen M. Fallon. New York: Random House, 2007.

Milton, John. *The Complete Prose Works of John Milton.* 8 vols. Edited by Don Wolfe. New Haven, CT: Yale University Press, 1953–82.

Milton, John. *The Complete Works of John Milton. Vol. 6: Vernacular Regicide and Republican Writings.* Edited by N. H. Keeble and Nicholas McDowell. Oxford: Oxford University Press, 2008.

Milton, John. *De educación.* Translated by Natalia Cossio. Madrid: Ediciones de la lectura, 1916.

Milton, John. *Del Paradiso perduto, poema Inglese di Giovanni Milton.* Translated by Paolo Rolli. London: Presso Carlo Bennet, 1736.

Milton, John F. [sic]. *El Paraíso perdido.* Translated by Manuel Álvarez de Toledo Morenés. Cádiz: Universidad de Cádiz, 1988.

Milton, John. *El Paraíso perdido.* Translated by Bel Atreides. Amazon Digital Services LLC: MJOLNIR Publishing Hall, 2017. Amazon.com.

Milton, John. *El Paraíso perdido: Edición bilingüe.* Translated by Bel Atreides. Madrid: Galaxia Gutenberg, 2005.

Milton, John. *El Paraíso perdido*. Translated by Enrique López Castellón. Madrid: Abada Editores, 2005.
Milton, John. *El Paraíso perdido*. Translated by Juan Escóiquiz. 1812. Barcelona: Administracion, Nueva San Francisco, 1883.
Milton, John. *El Paraíso perdido*. Translated by Antonio Fuster. Barcelona: Editorial Iberia, 1953.
Milton, John. *El Paraíso perdido*. 2 vols. Translated by Benito Ramón de Hermida Maldonado. Madrid: Ibarra, 1814.
Milton, John. *El Paraíso perdido*. Translated by Juan Matéos. Barcelona: Ibérica, 1914.
Milton, John. *El Paraíso perdido*. Translated by Esteban Pujals. Madrid: Cátedra, 1986.
Milton, John. *El Paraíso perdido*. Translated by [Cayetano Rosell]. Barcelona: Montaner y Simon, 1873.
Milton, John. *El Paraíso perdido*. 2nd edition. Translated by Rafael Rutiaga. Illustrated by Gustave Doré. Mexico City: Editorial Tomo, 2007.
Milton, John. *El Paraíso perdido*. 10th edition. Translated by [Dionisio Sanjuán]. 1868. Prologue by Joaquín Antonio Peñalosa. Mexico City: Editorial Porrua, 2011.
Milton, John. *El Paraíso perdido de John Milton, con notas de Addisson, Saint-Maur y otros*. Translated by Dionisio Sanjuán. Barcelona: La Ilustración, 1868.
Milton, John. *El Paraíso perdido: Edición bilingüe*. Translated by Enrique López Castellón. Madrid: Abada Editores, 2005.
Milton, John. *El Paraíso recobrado*. In *El Paraíso perdido*. Translated by Enrique Leopoldo de Verneuill. Barcelona: Montaner y Simón, 1873–74.
Milton, John. *Il Paradiso perduto poema inglese de Giovanni Milton*. Translated by Paolo Rolli. Paris: Giannalberto Tumermani Stamp, 1742.
[Milton, John.] *A Manifesto of the Lord Protector of the Commonwealth of England*. In *The Prose Works of John Milton*. Vol. 2. Philadelphia: Herman Hooker, 1845.
Milton, John. *Milton's Paradise Lost, by Richard Bentley, D.D.* London: Jacob Tonson, 1732.
[Milton, John.] *Miltons Republican Letters or A Collections a Such as Were Written by Command of the Late Commonwealth of England; from the year 1648. To the Year 1659. Originally writ by the Learned John Milton, Secretary to Those Times, and Now Translated into English by a Wel-wisher of Englands Honour*. Amsterdam[?], 1682.
Milton, John. *Paradis perdu*. 3 vols. Translated by Jacques Delille. Paris: Giguet et Michaud, 1805.
Milton, John. *Paradis perdu*. 3. vols. Translated by Nicolas Dupré de Saint-Maur. La Haye: Isaac vander Kloot, 1730.
Milton, John. *Paradis perdu: Quatrième chant*. Translated by Pierre Messian. Illustrated by Salvador Dalí. Paris: Les Bibliophiles de l'Automobile-club de France, 1974.
Milton, John. *Paradise Lost*. London: Cassell, Petter, Galpin, 1866.
Milton, John. *Paradise Lost*. London: Cassell, 1880–85.
Milton, John. *Paradise Lost*. Edited by Henry C. Walsh. Illustrated by Gustave Doré. Philadelphia: Henry Altemus, 1880–85.

Milton, John. *Paradise Lost.* Edited by David Masson. Illustrated by William Blake. Liverpool: Lyceum, 1906.
Milton, John. *Paradise Lost.* Vol. 2. Edited by A. W. Verity. Cambridge, UK: Cambridge University Press, 1929.
Milton, John. *Paradise Lost.* Edited by Philip Hofer and John Tracy Winterich. Illustrated by William Blake. New York: Heritage Press, 1940.
Milton, John. *Paradise Lost.* Edited by Alastair Fowler. New York: Longman, 1971.
Milton, John. *Paradise Lost.* 2nd edition. Edited by Alastair Fowler. New York: Longman, 1998.
Milton, John. *Paradise Lost.* Edited by Gordon Teskey. New York: Norton, 2005.
Milton, John. *Paradise Lost: Books III–IV.* Edited by Lois Potter and John Broadbent. Cambridge, UK: Cambridge University Press, 1976.
Milton, John. *Paradise Lost: Books V–VI.* Edited by Robert Hodge and Isabel G. MacCaffrey. Cambridge, UK: Cambridge University Press, 1975.
Milton, John. *Poems, &c.* [. . .] *Mr. John Milton.* London: Thomas Dring, 1673.
Milton, John. *Poems of Mr. John Milton both English and Latin.* London: Humphrey Moseley, 1645.
Milton, John. *The Riverside Milton.* Edited by Roy Flannagan. New York: Houghton Mifflin, 1998.
Milton, John. *Sonetos; Sansón Agonista.* Translated by A. Saravia Santender. Barcelona: Bosch, 1977.
Milton, John, and William Blake. *Thirteen Watercolor Drawings by William Blake Illustrating* Paradise Lost *by John Milton.* Edited by Robert N. Essick and John T. Shawcross. San Francisco: Arion Press, 2004.
Mitchell, David T., and Sharon L. Snyder, eds. *Narrative Prosthesis: Disability and the Dependencies of Discourse.* Ann Arbor: University of Michigan Press, 2000.
Mugglestone, Lynda. *Lost for Words: The Hidden History of the Oxford English Dictionary.* New Haven, CT: Yale University Press, 2005.
Murgia, Mario. "Milton in Revolutionary Hispanoamerica." In *Milton Studies 58, Special Issue: Milton in the Americas,* edited by Elizabeth Sauer and Angelica Duran. Pittsburgh, PA: Duquesne University Press, 2017.
Nardo, Anna K. *George Eliot's Dialogue with John Milton.* Columbia: University of Missouri Press, 2003.
Nardo, Anna K. "John Phillips's Translation of *Don Quixote* and 'the Humour of Our Modern Language.'" *Restoration* 36, no. 1 (2012): 1–22.
Nardo, Anna K. *Oculto a los ojos mortales* [Hidden from Mortal Eyes]. Valencia: JPM Ediciones, 2014.
Norbrook, David. *Poetry and Politics in the English Renaissance.* Oxford: Oxford University Press, 2002.
Obach, Robert. *The Catholic Church on Marital Intercourse: From St. Paul to Pope John Paul II.* Lanham, MD: Lexington, 2009.
Oliveras, Jordi, Eduard Fornes, and Salvador Dalí. *Dalí and His Books.* Barcelona: Editorial Mediterrània S.A., 1987 [Catalán orig. 1982].

Osuna, Rafael. *Polifemo y el tema de la abundancia natural en Lope de Vega y su tiempo* [Polyphemus and the Theme of Natural Abundance in Lope de Vega and His Times]. Kassel: Edition Reichenberger, 1996.
Pancrazio, James J. "El triste viejo de García Márquez: Sexo y soledad del narcisismo" [García Márquez's Sad Old Man: Narcissism's Sex and Solitude]. *Cuadernos de Literatura* [Literature Notebooks] (Bogotá) 10, no. 20 (2006): 44–52.
Par, Anfòs. *Representaciones Shakespearianas en España* [Shakespearean Representations in Spain]. Madrid: Librería General de Vicotiano Suárez, 1936.
Pardo Bazán, Emilia. "Milton." In *Los poetas épicos Cristianos: Obras completas de* [The Christian Epic Poets: Complete Works by] *Emilia Pardo Bazán*. Vol. 12. Madrid: Administración, [c. 1880].
Parker, William Riley. *Milton: A Biography*. 2 vols. 2nd edition. Oxford: Clarendon Press, 1996.
Parker, William Riley. *Milton's Contemporary Reputation*. 1940. New York: Haskell House, 1979.
Parkinson Zamora, Lois. "Eccentric Periodization: Comparative Perspectives on the Enlightenment and the Baroque." *PMLA* 128, no. 3 (2013): 690–97.
Pask, Kevin. *The Emergence of the English Author: Scripting the Life of the Poet in Early Modern England*. Cambridge, UK: Cambridge University Press, 2005.
Paulson, Ronald. *Don Quixote in England: The Aesthetics of Laughter*. Baltimore, MD: Johns Hopkins University Press, 1998.
Peers, E. Allison. "The Influence of Young and Gray in Spain." *Modern Language Review* 21, no. 4 (1926): 404–18.
Peers, E. Allison. "Milton in Spain." *Studies in Philology* 23, no. 2 (1926): 169–83.
Pegenaute, Luis. "La recepción de Milton en la España ilustrada: Visiones de *El Paraíso perdido*" [Milton's Reception in Enlightenment Spain: Visions of *Paradise Lost*]. In *La traducción en España, 1750–1830: Lengua, literatura, cultura* [Translation in Spain, 1750–1830: Language, Literature, Culture], edited by Francisco Lafarga. Lleida: Universidad de Lleida, 1999.
Peratoner, Amancio. *El ceno de las mujeres* [Women's Breasts]. Barcelona: Felipe N. Curriols, 1893.
Peréz, Joseph. *The Spanish Inquisition: A History*. New Haven, CT: Yale University Press, 2005.
Pointon, Marcia R. *Milton and English Art*. Manchester, UK: Manchester University Press, 1970.
Prieto, Gregorio. *García Lorca as a Painter*. London: De La More Press, 1946.
Prieto, Gregorio. *Lorca y la Generación del 27*. Madrid: Editorial Biblioteca Nueva, 1977.
Prieto, Gregorio, and Biblioteca Nacional. *Milton y Gregorio Prieto: Biblioteca Nacional, exposición en el III centenario de la muerte de John Milton, 15 de febrero a 17 de marzo de 1974* [Milton and Gregorio Prieto: National Library Exposition in the Tricentenary of the Death of John Milton, 15 February to 17 March 1974]. Madrid: Biblioteca Nacional, 1974.
Prieto, Gregorio, and Federico García Lorca. *Lorca en color*. Madrid: Editora Nacional, 1969.

Prieto, Gregorio, and John Milton. *Milton | El Paraíso perdido: Dibujos de Gregorio Prieto para el Paraíso perdido de Milton* [*Paradise Lost*: Drawings by Gregorio Prieto for Milton's *Paradise Lost*]. Introduction by Vicente Aleixandre. Madrid: Arte y Bibliofilia, 1972.

Prieto, Gregorio, and William Shakespeare. *Shakespeares Sonnets: 17 Drawings by Gregorio Prieto*. London: Alex, Reid & Lefevre, 1943.

Prieto, Gregorio, and William Shakespeare. *The Sonnets of William Shakespeare: With Twenty-eight Drawings by Gregorio Prieto*. London: Grey Walls Press, 1948.

Puchner, Martin. *The Written World: The Power of Stories to Shape People, History, Civilization*. New York: Penguin, 2017.

Pujals, Esteban. "Estructura y concepto de 'El Paraíso perdido' de Milton" [The Structure and Concept of Milton's *Paradise Lost*]. *Atlántida* 5, no. 27 (1967): 209–19.

Puttenham, George. *The Art of English Poesy by George Puttenham: Critical Edition*. Edited by Frank Whigham and Wayne A. Rebhorn. Ithaca, NY: Cornell University Press, 2007.

Rapple, Brendan. "James Russell Lowell and England." *Contemporary Review* 277, no. 1614 (2000): 40–44.

Ravenhall, Mary D. "Francis Atterbury and the First Illustrated Edition of *Paradise Lost*." *Milton Quarterly* 16, no. 2 (1982): 29–36.

Ravenhall, Mary D. "Sources and Meaning in Dr. Aldrich's 1688 Illustrations of *Paradise Lost*." *English Language Notes* 19, no. 3 (1982): 208–18.

Rawlings, Helen. *The Spanish Inquisition*. Malden, MA: Blackwell, 2006.

Redman, Harry, Jr. *Major French Milton Critics of the Nineteenth Century*. Pittsburgh, PA: Duquesne University Press, 1994.

Reinos, J. Felix Jose, and Alberti Lista. *La inocencia perdida* [Innocence Lost]. Madrid: Imprenta Real, 1804.

Revard, Stella. *Milton and the Tangles of Neaera's Hair: The Making of the 1645 Poems*. Columbia: University of Missouri Press, 1997.

Richardson, Gary A. *American Drama from the Colonial Period through World War I: A Critical History*. New York: Twayne, 1993.

Richardson, Joanna. *Gustave Doré: A Biography*. London: Cassell, 1980.

Robertson, John George. *Milton's Fame on the Continent*. London: British Academy, 1970.

Robertson, Randy. *Censorship and Conflict in Seventeenth-Century England: The Subtle Art of Division*. University Park: Pennsylvania State University Press, 2009.

Romero, Antonio Nadal. *Síntesis de historia de la literatura universal: Curso Unico* [Synthesis of the History of Universal Literature: Single Course]. Xalapa, Mexico: Editoria Xalapeña 1961.

Rubín de Cevallos, Agustín. *Indice ultimo de los libros prohibidos y mandados expurgar* [Most Recent Index of Books Prohibited and Ordered to Be Expurgated]. Madrid: Don Antonio de Sancha, 1790.

Russell, P. E. "English Seventeenth-Century Interpretations of Spanish Literature." *Atlante* 1, no. 2 (1953): 65–77.

Sagrada Biblia [Holy Bible]. Edited by Juan Staubinger. Chicago: La Prensa Católica, 1958.
Sakai, Naoki. "Translation and the Figure of Border: Toward the Apprehension of Translation in a Social Action." In *Profession 2010*, edited by Rosemary Feal. New York: Modern Language Association of America, 2010.
Sarmiento y Valladeres, Diego, and Vidal Marín. *Novissimus librorum prohibitorum et expurgandorum*. 2 vols. Madrid: Ex Typographia Musicae, 1707.
Schwartz, Louis. "Review of *The Tyranny of Heaven: Milton's Rejection of God as King—Michael Bryson*." *Milton Quarterly* 40, no. 3 (2006): 239–45.
Schwartz, Regina. "Real Hunger: Milton's Version of the Eucharist." *Religion and Literature* 31, no. 3 (1999): 1–17.
Scudder, Horace Elisha. *James Russell Lowell: A Biography*. Boston: Houghton Mifflin, 1901.
Shakespeare, William. *Romeo and Juliet*. In *The Riverside Shakespeare*, edited by G. Blakemore Evans. Boston: Houghton Mifflin, 1974.
Sharpe, Kevin. *The Personal Rule of Charles I*. New Haven, CT: Yale University Press, 1992.
Sharpe, Kevin. "'So Hard a Text'? Images of Charles I, 1612–1700." *Historical Journal* 43, no. 2 (2000): 383–405.
Shawcross, John T. *The Arms of the Family: The Significance of John Milton's Relatives and Associates*. Lexington: University of Kentucky Press, 2004.
Shawcross, John T. "John Milton and His Spanish and Portuguese Presence." *Milton Quarterly* 32, no. 2 (1998): 41–52.
Shawcross, John T. *John Milton: The Self and the World*. Lexington: University of Kentucky Press, 1993.
Sidney, Philip. *A Defence of Poetry*. Edited by Jan Van Dorsten. Oxford: Oxford University Press, 1986.
Sims, James H. "Christened Classicism in *Paradise Lost* and *The Lusiad*." *Comparative Literature* 24, no. 4 (Autumn 1974): 338–56.
Sirluck, Ernest. "Milton's Critical Use of Historical Sources: An Illustration." *Modern Philology* 50, no. 4 (1953): 226–31.
Skerpan-Wheeler, Elizabeth. "Authorship and Authority: John Milton, William Marshall, and the Two Frontispieces of *Poems 1645*." *Milton Quarterly* 33, no. 4 (1999): 105–14.
Smith, Nigel. *Is Milton Better than Shakespeare?* Cambridge, MA: Harvard University Press, 2008.
Smith, Nigel. "Milton and the European Contexts of Toleration." In *Milton and Toleration*, edited by Sharon Achinstein and Elizabeth Sauer. Oxford: Oxford University Press, 2007.
Spenser, Edmund. *The Faerie Queene*. Edited by A. C. Hamilton. New York: Longman, 2001.
Spivak, Gayatri Chakravorty. "Postcolonial Theory and Literature." In *New Dictionary of the History of Ideas*, vol. 5, edited by Maryanne Cline Horowitz. Detroit: Charles Scribner's Sons, 2005. *Gale Virtual Reference Library*, accessed July 1, 2016.

Starn, Randolph. "The 2006 Josephine Waters Bennett Lecture: A Postmodern Renaissance?" *Renaissance Quarterly* 60, no. 1 (2007): 1–24.
Steiner, George. *After Babel: Aspects of Language and Translation*. Oxford: Oxford University Press, 1975.
Stoll, Abraham. *Milton and Monotheism*. Pittsburgh, PA: Duquesne University Press, 2009.
Strunk, William, Jr., and E. B. White. *The Elements of Style*. 1959. 4th edition. New York: Longman, 2000.
Sullivan, Ernest W., II, "Illustration as Interpretation." In *Milton's Legacy in the Arts*, edited by Albert C. Labriola and Edward Sichi Jr. University Park: Pennsylvania State University Press, 1988.
Sumillera, Rocío G. "Manuel Tamayo y Baus's *Un Drama Nuevo* (1867) and the Reception of Hamlet [sic] in 19th-Century Spain." *Elope* 10, no. 1 (2013): 71–80.
Symmons, Charles. *The Life of John Milton*. 2nd edition. London: T. Bensley, 1810.
Tamayo y Baus, Manuel. *Un drama nuevo* [A New Drama]. In *La locura de amor* [The Madness of Love]: *Un drama nuevo*. 3rd edition. Edited and prologue by Alfonso M. Escudero. Madrid: Espasa-Calpe, 1970.
Tamayo y Baus, Manuel. *Un drama nuevo* [A New Drama]. Edited by Amancio Labandeira. Madrid: Taurus, 1982.
Thomas, Henry. *Shakespeare in Spain*. London: British Academy, 1949.
Thorpe, James E. *Milton Criticism*. New York: Rinehart, 1950.
Tosca, Hugo. "El tema de la ceguera en la literatura religiosa de Lope" [The Theme of Blindness in the Religious Literature of Lope de Vega]. *Revista de literatura* 66 (2004): 389–407.
Tournu, Christophe. *Milton in France*. New York: Peter Lang, 2008.
Treadwell, James. "Blake, John Martin, and the Illustration of *Paradise Lost*." *Word & Image* 9, no. 4 (1993): 363–82.
Unamuno, Miguel de. *The Life of Don Quixote and Sancho According to Miguel de Cervantes Saavedra*. Translated by Homer P. Earle. New York: Knopf, 1927.
Unamuno, Miguel de. *Del sentimiento trágico de la vida en los hombres y en los pueblos* [The Tragic Sense of Life of Humans and in Villages]. Madrid: Espasa-Calpe, 1976.
Unamuno, Miguel de. *The Tragic Sense of Life*. Translated by J. E. Crawford Flitch. New York: Dover, 1954.
Universidad Complutense de Madrid. *Veinticuatro diarios* [Twenty-four Dailies]. In *Madrid, 1830–1900: Artículos y noticias de escritores españoles del siglo XIX* [Articles and News about Spanish Writers of the Nineteenth Century]. 4 vols. Madrid: Instituto de Miguel de Cervantes, 1968–.
Vallve, Manuel. *El Paraíso perdido*. Mexico City: Biblioteca Juvenal Porrúa, 1992.
Varo, Marcus Terentius. *On the Latin Language*. Cambridge, MA: President and Fellows of Harvard College, 2018. Loeb Classics.com, accessed October 2018.
Vílchez Díaz, Alfredo. *Autores y anónimos españoles en los índices inquisitoriales* [Spanish Authors and Anonymous Spaniards in the Inquisitorial Indexes]. Madrid: Universidad Complutense, 1986.

Virgil. *Aeneid I–VI*. Translated and with an introduction by R. Deryck Williams. London: Macmillan Educational, 1972.
von Maltzahn, Nicholas. "Acts of Kind Service: Milton and the Patriot Literature of Empire." In *Milton and the Imperial Vision*, edited by Balachandra Rajan and Elizabeth Sauer. Pittsburgh, PA: Duquesne University Press, 1999.
von Maltzahn, Nicholas. "Milton and the Restoration *Literae*." In *Milton in the Long Restoration*, edited by Blair Hoxby and Ann Coiro. Oxford: Oxford University Press, 2016.
von Maltzahn, Nicholas. "Samuel Butler's Milton." *Studies in Philology* 92, no. 4 (1995): 482–95.
Walker, Joseph. *Historia de la Inquisición Española* [History of the Spanish Inquisition]. Madrid: Edimat, 2001.
Warnke, Frank J. *European Metaphysical Poetry*. New Haven, CT: Yale University Press, 1961.
Waterhouse, Ellis K. *Painting in Britain, 1530–1790*. London: Penguin Books, 1953.
Watt, Stephen, and Gary A. Richardson. *American Drama: Colonial to Contemporary*. Fort Worth, TX: Harcourt Brace College Publishers, 1995.
Weinfield, Henry. *The Blank-Verse Tradition from Milton to Stevens: Freethinking and the Crisis of Modernity*. Cambridge, UK: Cambridge University Press, 2012.
Wells, Claude E. "Milton's 'Vulgar Readers' and 'The Verse.'" *Milton Quarterly* 9, no. 3 (1975): 67–70.
Williams, Raymond. "The Analysis of Culture." In *Culture, Ideology and Social Process*, edited by Tony Bennett, Graham Martin, Colin Mercer, and Jane Woolacott. London: Open University, 1981.
Williams, Raymond. *Marxism and Literature*. Oxford: Oxford University Press, 1977.
Wittreich, Joseph, Jr. "Illustrators." In *A Milton Encyclopedia*, vol. 4., edited by William B. Hunter Jr. et al. Lewisburg, PA: Bucknell University Press, 1978.
Wittreich, Joseph, Jr. "Milton's 'First' Illustrator." *Seventeenth Century News* 32 (1974): 70–71.
Wittreich, Joseph Anthony, Jr. *The Romantics on Milton: Formal Essays and Critical Asides*. Cleveland, OH: Press of Case Western Reserve University, 1970.
Wordsworth, William. *The Sonnets of William Wordsworth Collected in One Volume*. London: Edward Moxon, 1838.

Index

Italicized page numbers refer to figures.

"Adán" (Lorca), 143, 199n62
Addison, Joseph, 4, 70, 72-73
Aeneid, The (Virgil), 50-51
After Babel (Steiner), 12
Aldrich, Henry, 113
Aleixandre, Vicente, 16, 125-27, 133, 135, 137, 138-39, 199n56
Álvarez de Toledo, Manuel, 49-54, 58, 60, 64, 67, 71-73, 81
American Literature in Spain (de Lancey Ferguson), 7, 202n22
Anxiety of Influence (Bloom), 8
Areopagitica (Milton), 13-14, 18-25, 28-29, 31-33, 43-44, 156, 159, 178n18, 181n91, 182n1, 202n26
Ariosto, Ludovico, 50
Art of English Poesy (Puttenham), 53
Atreides, Bel, 50-51, 53-54, 57-60, 62-65, 82
Atterbury, Francis, 115
Augustine, 30, 77

Bacon, Francis, 80
Balzac, Honoré de, 84
Benítez, Rubén, 4, 6, 24, 36-38, 50-51
Bentley, Richard, 64, 69, 134
Berman, Antoine, 47
Bernini, Gian Lorenzo, 115
Bible, 43, 74; precedence of the, 78-79; reading of the, 77, 157
Blake, William, 15, 112, 116, 127-28, 131, 134, 141, 152, 159, 198n42

Blanchot, Maurice, 103
blank verse, 53-54, *104*, 184n31, 194n74. *See also* poetry
"Blind Poet's Complaint, The" (Martínez y Güertero), 40, 44
Bloom, Harold, 8
Bonaparte, Joseph, 36
Bonaparte, Napoleon, 36
Braga, Francisco, 84
Braider, Christopher, 7
Brown, Thomas, 29
Bryson, Michael, 62
Butler, Samuel, 178n26
Byron, George Gordon, 5

Cadalso y Vázquez, José de, 36-38, 40-43, 47
Camões, Luís de, 103
Cañizares-Esguerra, Jorge, 10
Caracciolo-Trejo, Enrique, 159
Carmelites, 63-64. *See also* Roman Catholicism
Carner, Josep de, 156
Carr, Raymond, 23
Castellón, Enrique López, 53, 56, 58, 65, 67-68, 71, 72, 76, 78, 80-82
Catholic Counter-Reformation, 65. *See also* Roman Catholicism
Cavallo, Guglielmo, 112
censorship: ancient, 19; history of English book, 19, 45; in Roman Catholicism, 21-22; of self, 60. *See also* heresy; publishing

INDEX

Cervantes Saavedra, Miguel de, 1–4, 8, 29, 38–39, 80, 155, 196n17
Character of the Rump (Butler?), 24
Charles I, King, 24, 40, 72, 111, 112
Charles II, King, 24, 72, 90
Chartier, Roger, 112
Christian Epic Poets, The (Pardo Bazán), 41, 88, 112, 124. *See also poetas épicos Cristianos, Los*
Christianity: ecumenism, 62; persecution of, 22; Trinitarian doctrine of, 38, 50. *See also* religion
Clark, Jaime, 47
Clement XI, Pope, 26
Collins-Baker, C. H., 115
Conklin, George N., 30
Conn, George, 21
Contreras, Antonia, 93, 176n45
Corns, Thomas, 27
Council of Trent, 19–20, 25, 74. *See also* Roman Catholicism
Counter-Reformation, 65. *See also* Roman Catholicism
Cromwell (Balzac), 84
Cromwell, Oliver, 10, 34, 41, 150

Dalí, Salvador, 125–26
Daly, Augustin, 102
Dante, 41–42, 74, 76, 102, 182n5, 192n46
décima, 10, 94, 99, 106–7, 135, 144, 156, 200n64. *See also* poetry
De doctrina Christiana (Milton), 30, 80
Defence of Poesy, A (Sidney), 3
Delille, Jacques, 3, 60, 70, 78
Del sentimiento trágico de la vida (Unamuno), 150. *See also Tragic Sense of Life, The*
Dialogo (Galileo), 20–21
Díaz, Alfredo Vílchez, 25, 34
DiCesare, Mario, 5
Dictionary of National Biography, 27
divina comedia, La (Dante and Rosell), 51
Divine Comedy, The (Dante), 42, 51, 76, 155, 192n46
divorce, 9–10, 35
Djilas, Milovan, 71

Dobranski, Stephen, 45
Dolle, William, 139
Dominicans, 23, 63–64, 80. *See also* Roman Catholicism
Donne, John, 47
Don Quixote/Don Quijote (Cervantes), 1–2, 4, 8, 16, 26, 80, 150; editions of, 38–39; translations of, 4, 149
Doré, Gustave, 4, 7, 15–16, 112–13, 118, 120, 120-28, 130–31, 139, 141, 147, 151, 155, 160, 169–72
"Dos Normas" (Lorca), 143-46, 200n63
Du Bartas, Guillaume de Saluste, 2–3
Du Bocage, Anne-Marie, 38
Duns Scotus, John, 77
DuRocher, Richard, 5

Echegary, José, 93
Eikonoklastes (Milton), 24, 90, 111–12, 178n27
Emerson, Ralph Waldo, 95, 193n53
England, 2–3, 8, 12, 41; bureaucracy of, 23; cultural status of, 27–28; literature of, 4; politics of, 33–34; Restoration, 24, 87-89, 156; Spanish culture in, 2–4
English Renaissance Drama and the Specter of Spain (Griffin), 6
eruditos a la violeta, Los (Cadalso y Vázquez). *See also Sciolists, The*
Escóiquiz, Juan, 9, 34, 47–51, 53, 57–64, 70, 72–73, 151, 156, 167
Evans, J. Martin, 10

Faerie Queene, The (Spenser), 50
Fallon, Stephen, 5
Felperin, Howard, 4
Ferdinand VII, King, 35, 156
Ferguson, John de Lancey, 7
Fernández de Moratín, Leandro, 47
Flannagan, Roy, 10
Florence, 20–21. *See also* Italy
Forms of Nationhood (Helgerson), 6
Forsyth, Neil, 31–32
Foucault, Michel, 29
Fowler, Alastair, 63, 80
France, 2–3, 62; Spanish culture in, 3–4
Franciscans, 63. *See also* Roman Catholicism

Franco Bahamonde, Francisco, 156
Fuchs, Barbara, 155
Furman/Furman-Adams, Wendy, 112, 116, 198n42
Fuster, Antonio, 58, 64, 167

Galaxia Gutenberg Press, 82. *See also* publishing
Galileo, 20–21, 23, 26, 160
Gardner, Helen, 115
gender: grammatical, 53, 56–59, 68; roles of, 57–59. *See also* sexuality
Genette, Gérard, 111, 147
Georgii Conaei De Duplici Statu Religionis Apud Scotos Libro Duo (Conn), 21
Germany, 4, 95
Gibson, Ian, 139
Gies, David T., 6, 85, 94, 101, 192n38, 193n60, 193n68
Gil de Santivañes, Arturo, 20, 27, 84, 88
Giner de los Ríos, Hermenegildo, 15, 84–96, 101–4, 106–9, 156, 160–61, 194n79, 200n64
Girard, René, 8
González Herrán, José Manuel, 102
Granados Maldonado, Francisco, 71
Gray, Thomas, 47
Greenblatt, Stephen, 15
Greene, Roland, 9
Greer, Margaret R., 155
Gregory the Great, Pope, 30
Griffin, Eric, 4, 6–7, 9

Hale, John, 157, 178n34
Helgerson, Richard, 6
Henry VIII, King, 25
heresy: authors in, 26, 40-41, 44; concepts of, 23–24, 29–33. *See also* censorship
Hermida Maldonado, Benito Ramón de, 34, 49–54, 56, 61, 63–65, 70–71, 76, 78–79, 81, 167
Hojeda, Fray Diego de, 42
Holbein, Hans, 15
Holmes, James S., 14, 47–48
Homer, 1, 36, 39, 42, 104, 194n80
Howells, William Dean, 94, 102, 193n68

Hugo, Victor, 84
Huntley, Frank, 64

Index librorum prohibitorum, 3, 10, 13-14, 17-20, 18, 22-36, 40, 45, 47, 69, 112
Is Milton Better than Shakespeare? (Smith), 8
Issa, Islam, 6
Italy, 20, 45

Jastrow, Joseph, 12
Jesuits, 21. *See also* Roman Catholicism
John Milton among the Polygamophiles (Miller), 5
Johnson, Samuel, 10, 53, 61, 72
Jovellanos, Gaspar Melchor de, 23
Julius Caesar (Shakespeare), 80
Jungmann, Josef, 71

Kadotettu paratiisi (Jylhä), 119, 197n33
Kafka, Franz, 103
Kamen, Henry, 20, 25, 36
Keats, John, 139
King, John, 64, 66
Kipling, Rudyard, 115
Kyd, Thomas, 7

La Christiada (Hojeda), 42
Lafarga, Francisco, 47
Lamartine, Alphonse de, 40
language: English, 48–49, 53–54, 56–58; plurality of, 8; Romance, 53, 56; Spanish, 13, 48–49, 57–58
Larmig. *See* Martínez y Güertero, Luis Alfonso Roman
Lea, Henry, 26
Lens, Bernard, 113
Leonard, John, 22, 67, 78, 80
Levinas, Emmanuel, 8
Lewis, C. S., 72
Literae pseudo-senatus (Milton?), 33–35
literature: comparative, 7–8; English, 16, 75; French, 3; genres of, 8; Greek, 22; Latin, 3; Spanish, 75; study of, 1; in translation, 9; world, 2, 16, 39, 42, 70, 80, 83. *See also* poetry

INDEX

London, 40–41, 88–89, 105, 118, 134, 151. *See also* England
Longfellow, Henry Wadsworth, 95
Lorca, Federico García, 16, 125–27, 139, 142–47
Lorca en color (Lorca), 139, *140*, 141, 145
Lowell, James Russell, 15, 156, 160
Lycidas (Milton), 16

Macaulay, Thomas, 41–43
Maclean, Marie, 111
Macpherson y Hemas, Guillermo, 47
Manifiesto del Protector de Inglaterra...causa contra España (Milton?), 27
Marín Index (1707), 18, 26–28, 30–31, 33, 163–65
Marín, Vidal, 28–29
Mariology, 75-77, 116
Marlowe, Christopher, 7, 24
Marshall, William, 111
Martial, 1, 3, 36
Martin, Catherine, 5
Martin, John, 15
Martínez y Güertero, Luis Alfonso Roman, 40–41, 44, 61
Martz, Louis, 156
Marvell, Andrew, 53, 180n70, 181n70
Mask Presented at Ludlow-Castle, A (Milton), 15, 25, 85, 91-93, 108, 156
Matéos, Juan, 51, 70, 72, 81
McDowell, Nicholas, 33
Medina, John Baptiste de, 15, 113-15, *117*, *118*, 125, 147
Menéndez y Pelayo, Marcelino, 47
Merello, Rafael Alberti, 125
México conquistada (Escóiquiz), 51, 156
Miller, Leo, 5, 20-21
Milton: A Dramatic Scene in One Act and in Verse (Giner de los Ríos), 10, 15, 84-86, 89-94, 98-101, 103-8, 125, 154-55, 161
Milton among the Philosophers (Fallon), 5
Milton among the Romans (DuRocher), 5
Milton and English Art (Pointon), 113
Milton: Cómedia en un acto (Braga), 84
Milton: Cuadro dramático en un acto y en verso

(Giner de los Ríos), 10, 84. *See also Milton: A Dramatic Scene in One Act and in Verse* (Giner de los Ríos)
Milton | El Paraíso perdido (Prieto), 10, 11, *12*, 16, 125-44, *126*, 129, *132*, *136*, 143, 147-48, 161
Milton in France (Tournu), 5
Milton in Italy (DiCesare), 5
Milton in the Arab-Muslim World (Issa), 6
Milton in Translation (Duran, Issa, and Olson), 6, 158
Milton, John: advocacy of divorce of, 9–10; birth of, 1 education of, 2; era of, 41; fame of, 4; as heretic, 17–45, 61; poetics of, 49, 54, 58; on the Spanish Catholic Indexes, 24–36; and the Spanish Catholic Inquisition, 18–24; Spanish interest in, 5, 12–14, 17; translations of, 6, 13, 46-83; works circulating under the name of, 3, 26–27; young, 20. *See also Areopagitica; Eikonoklastes; Lycidas; Paradise Lost; Paradise Regained; Pro populo Anglicano defensio; Samson Agonistes*
Milton's Imperial Epic (Evans), 10
Milton's Italy (Martin), 5–6
Milton y Gregorio Prieto (Milton and Prieto), 137, 139, 152
Mohl, Ruth, 20
More, Thomas, 3
Munkácsy, Mihály, 151, *155*

Nardo, Anna K., 46, 81–82
New Drama, A (Tamayo y Baús), 101–2, 201n13
Newton, Sir Isaac, 29
"Night Thoughts" (Young), 71, 156
Norbrook, David, 45

Oculto a los ojos mortales (Nardo), 81–82
Of Education (Milton), 157
Of Reformation (Milton), 30
Oliver Cromwell (Hugo), 84
Olson, Jonathan R., 6
Origen, 77
Orlando Furioso (Ariosto), 50
Ovid, 80

Palacios Index (1844), *18*, 27, 31, 33–36
Pamela (Richardson), 71
papacy, 21. *See also* Roman Catholicism
Paradise Lost (Milton), 1–2, 13, 21, 28, 34–38, 42–43, 53–60, 63–69, 73–78, 81, *158*, *159*; Anglophone editions of, 15, 80, 113–16, 118–19, *118*, 127–28, 131, 134; French translations of, 14, 46, 60; Italian translations of, 14, 31; poetics of, 54, 58; prose translations of, 54–55; readers of, 12, 41; Spanish editions of, 80, 83, 112; Spanish illustrations of, 66, 110–48; Spanish translations of, 3–4, 7, 10, 13–16, 34–35, 46–84, 167–68; translations of, 7, 9, 36, 63
Paradise Regained (Milton), 28, 39–40, 43, 66–67, 158
Paradiso perduto, Il (Rolli), 34–35
Paradis perdu, Le (Delille), 78
Paradis perdu, Le (François-René), 159
Paradis terrestre (Du Bocage), 38
Paraíso de Milton, El (Pérez Echevarría and Gil de Santivañes), 84
Paraíso perdido, El (Álvarez de Toledo), 67, 71–72, 78, 81, 184n35
Paraíso perdido, El (Atreides), 66–67, 71–73, 76, 78, 81–82
Paraíso perdido, El (Castellón), 68, 71–72, 76, 78–79, 81–82
Paraíso perdido, El (Escóiquiz), 7, 34–35, 51, 55–57, 63–66, 68–69, 71–72, 74–78, 120, 124, 158–60, 169–72
Paraíso perdido, El (Fuster), 72, 78, 81, 183n16
Paraíso perdido, El (Hermida Maldonado), 34, 52, 55, 61, 67, 71, 74, 76, 78–79, 81
Paraíso perdido, El (Matéos), 70, 72, 81
Paraíso perdido, El (Pujals), 55, 78, 81–82
Paraíso perdido, El (Rosell), 51–52, 54–55, 64–68, 71–72, 78, 120, 124, 169–72, 183n12, 186n92, 187n112, 192n46, 202n1
Paraíso perdido, El (Sanjuán), 58, 64–67, 71–72, 74, 167
Paratexts (Genette), 147
Pardo Bazán, Emilia, 40–44, 88, 112, 124
Paris, 21, 24, 70, 118. *See also* France
Parkinson Zamora, Lois, 6

Paul IV, Pope, 25
Paulson, Ronald, 4
Peers, E. Allison, 47
Pegenaute, Luis, 5
Peñalosa, Joaquin Antonio, 71
Pérez Echevarría, Francisco, 20, 27, 84, 88
Petrarch, 102
Philip II, King, 3, 25
Phillips, John, 1–3, 149, 155
Picasso, Pablo, 125
poetas épicos Cristianos, Los (Pardo Bazán), 41, 88, 112. *See also Christian Epic Poets, The*
poetry: English heroic, 53; epic, 1, 9, 14, 32, 39, 42, 44, 48, 51, 53, 61, 69; Latin, 1, 51; Marian devotional, 77; Spanish, 10, 54. *See also décima*; literature; *quintilla*
Pointon, Marcia, 113, 115
Pope, Alexander, 5
Porrúa Press, 71. *See also* publishing
Presencia de Milton en la literatura española (Benítez), 6
Prieto, Gregorio, 9–10, 16, *126*; portrait of John Milton by, *152*; sketches by, *11*, 16, *125*, *132*, *136*, *142*, *144*, *145*, *147*, *151*, *160*
Pro populo Anglicano defensio (Milton), 17, 24–25, 33–35
publishing: delays of Spanish translations of Milton's works in, 17; of works from Catholic countries, 20, 71. *See also* censorship; Porrúa Press; Simmons, Samuel
Pujals, Esteban, 52–53, 55–56, 58
Puritan Conquistadors (Cañizares-Esguerra), 10
Puttenham, George, 53

"Querellas del vate ciego" (Martínez y Güertero), 40. *See also* "Blind Poet's Complaint, The"
quintilla, 104–7, 194n76. *See also* poetry

Ravenhall, Mary, 115
Real Academia Española, 38–40, 42–43, 101. *See also* Royal Spanish Academy
Redman Jr., Henry, 24, 191n24
Reformation, 22, 30, 42, 65, 177n7

religion: conflict in, 13; divisiveness in, 52; freedom of, 22; matters of, 59–69; sensibilities of, 69; tolerance in, 56. *See also* Christianity; Roman Catholicism
Renaissance Self-Fashioning (Greenblatt), 15
Richardson, Joanna, 141
Richardson, Samuel, 71
Robertson, John George, 4–5
Robertson, Randy, 21
Rolli, Paolo, 17, 31, 35
Roman Catholic Indexes, 25–26, 33, 181n70. *See also* Roman Catholic Inquisition
Roman Catholic Inquisition, 18–20, 23, 26, 35, 45. *See also* Spanish Catholic Indexes
Roman Catholicism: authorities of, 20, 157; doctrines of, 60, 63, 74, 77; in England, 21–22; Marian devotion in, 75–77; plurality of, 19–20. *See also* Council of Trent; Jesuits; papacy; religion; Spanish Catholic Inquisition
Romantics, 32
Rosell, Cayetano, 48–52, 59
Royal Spanish Academy, 38–40, 93, 101. *See also* Real Academia Española
Rubens, Peter Paul, 115
Rubín Index (1790), 18, 27, 31–34, 36

Said, Edward, 192n48
Saiki, Naoki, 69
Saint-Maur, Nicolas-François Dupré de, 71, 183n22
Samson Agonistes (Milton), 28, 158
Sanjuán, Dionisio, 58–59, 62, 64, 65, 66-67, 71-72, 74, 80, 81, 89, 189n138
Saumaise, Claude/Salmasius, 17, 24
Saussure, Ferdinand de, 8
Sciolists, The (Cadalso y Vázquez), 36–37
Scotland, 114
Scott, Walter, 5
sexuality: angelic, 74; divinely sanctioned, 74; marital, 52, 74, 137; postlapsarian, 52; prelapsarian, 74. *See also* gender
Shakespeare, William, 4, 6–8, 28, 36-37, 40, 46-47, 86, 91, 96, 101-2, 104, 106, 139, 154, 174n10, 187n110, 193n52, 201n13, 202n13; Spanish translations of, 154

Shawcross, John, 6, 89, 198n42, 198n46
Shelley, Percy Bysshe, 139
Shelton, Thomas, 2
Sidney, Sir Philip, 3, 29
Siglo de Oro, 6
Simmons, Samuel, 53. *See also* publishing
Sirluck, Ernest, 19, 21
Sixtus IV, Pope, 25
Skerpan-Wheeler, Elizabeth, 111–12
Smith, Nigel, 8
Spain, 8, 12, 25, 32, 41; American territories of, 10, 13; cultural isolation of, 151; dangers for, 26; early modern, 77; intellectuals of, 5; literary discussion in, 4–5, 12; literary self-definition of, 3; perceptions of, 9; politics of, 47; polity of, 35; restoration of the monarchy of, 15
Spanish Catholic Indexes, 3, 10, 13, 17, 18, 19, 44, 69; Milton on the, 24–36, 44. *See also* Spanish Catholic Inquisition
Spanish Catholic Inquisition, 3, 13–14, 17–45, 69, 160; Milton on the, 18–24, 46–47; reading Milton in the wake of the, 36–44. *See also* Roman Catholic Inquisition
Spanish theater: Golden Age of, 15, 94-95, 101, 106; Silver Age of, 15, 85. *See also* theater
Spectator, The (Addison), 4
Spenser, Edmund, 50, 102
Spivak, Gayatri Chakravorty, 192n48
Steiner, George, 12–13

Taine, Hippolyte, 42
Tamayo y Baús, Manuel, 101–2
Taming of the Shrew (Shakespeare), 28
Tasso, Torquato, 102
Teresa of Avila, Saint, 79–80
Tetrachordon (Milton), 35
theater: English, 15, 54; Spanish, 13, 15, 17, 84–109. *See also* Spanish theater
Theodotus, 77
Thomson, James, 5
Tonson, Jacob, 113, 116–19, 127–28, 131, 134
Tosca, Hugo, 99
Tournu, Christophe, 5, 38
Towards a Translation Criticism (Berman), 47

Tragic Sense of Life, The (Unamuno), 160. See
  also *Del sentimiento trágico de la vida*
Treadwell, James, 126
Treatise of Civil Power (Milton), 80
Tufte, Virginia, 116
Tyranny of Heaven, The (Bryson), 62

Unamuno, Miguel de, 4, 149–50, 154, 160
United States, 15, 98
Utopia (More), 3

Valdés Index (1559), 25, 27
Van Dyck, Anthony, 115

Varro, 68
Vaughan, Robert, 71
Verity, A. W., 64
Vico, Antonio, 93, 101
Virgil, 39, 42, 50
Voltaire, 4, 62, 70, 72

Whitman, Walt, 139
Wittreich, Joseph, 112, 115, 197n40
Wordsworth, William, 102–3

Yorick's Love (Howells), 102
Young, Edward, 5, 47, 71, 156

www.ingramcontent.com/pod-product-compliance
Lightning Source LLC
Chambersburg PA
CBHW021352300426
44114CB00012B/1198